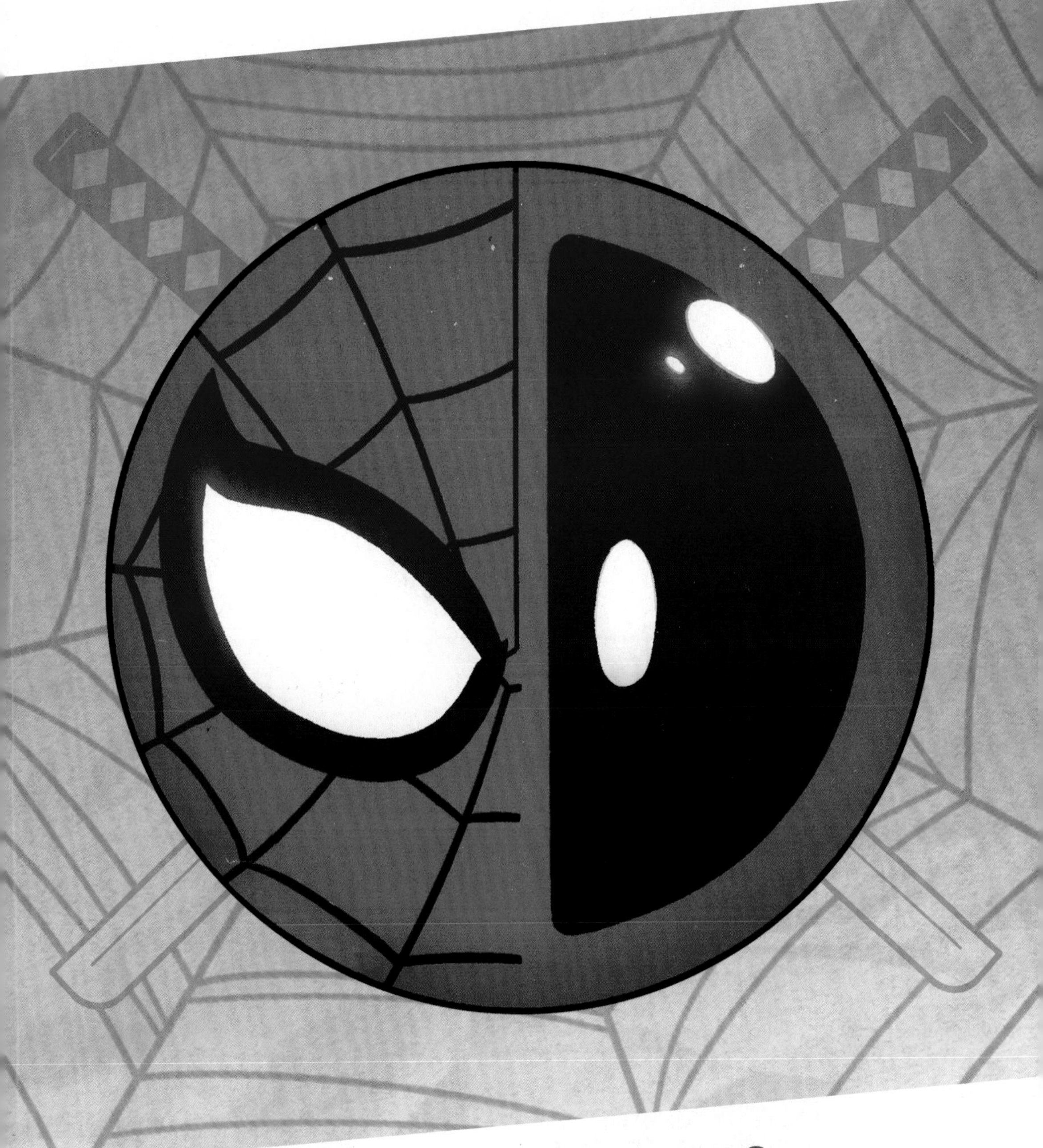

SERIOUS BUSINESS

Collection Editor JENNIFER GRÜNWALD
Assistant Editor CAITLIN O'CONNELL
Associate Managing Editor KATERI WOODY
Editor, Special Projects MARK D. BEAZLEY
VP Production & Special Projects JEFF YOUNGQUIST
SVP Print, Sales & Marketing DAVID GABRIEL
Book Designer ADAM DEL RE

Editor In Chief C.B. CEBULSKI
Chief Creative Officer JOE QUESADA
President DAN BUCKLEY
Executive Producer ALAN FINE

MARVEL COMICS
BEGRUDGINGLY PRESENTS...

PETER PARKER WAS BITTEN BY AN IRRADIATED SPIDER, GRANTING HIM AMAZING ABILITIES, INCLUDING THE PROPORTIONAL SPEED, STRENGTH AND AGILITY OF A SPIDER, AS WELL AS ADHESIVE FINGERTIPS AND TOES. AFTER LEARNING THAT WITH GREAT POWER, THERE MUST ALSO COME GREAT RESPONSIBILITY, HE BECAME THE WORLD'S GREATEST SUPER HERO! HE'S...

THE WORLD'S GREATEST SUPER HERO!
The AMAZING SPIDER-MAN

AVENGER...ASSASSIN...SUPERSTAR! WADE WILSON WAS CHOSEN FOR A TOP-SECRET GOVERNMENT PROGRAM THAT GAVE HIM A HEALING FACTOR THAT ALLOWS HIM TO HEAL FROM ANY WOUND. DESPITE EARNING A SMALL FORTUNE AS A GUN FOR HIRE, WADE HAS BECOME THE WORLD'S MOST BELOVED HERO. AND IS THE STAR OF THE WORLD'S GREATEST COMICS MAGAZINE (NO MATTER WHAT THAT JERK IN THE WEBS MAY THINK). CALL HIM THE MERC WITH THE MOUTH...CALL HIM THE REGENERATIN' DEGENERATE...CALL HIM...

DEADPOOL

#19-20: "NO LAUGHING MATTER"

JOSHUA CORIN
Writer

WILL ROBSON
Penciler

WILL ROBSON & SCOTT HANNA
Inkers

JORDAN BOYD
Color Artist

#21: "ONE NIGHT IN MADRIPOOR MAKES SPIDER-MAN LOOK HUMBLE"
#22: "IT'S A MURDER, MURDER, MURDER, MURDER WORLD"

ELLIOTT KALAN
Writer

TODD NAUCK
Artist

RACHELLE ROSENBERG
Color Artist

WILL ROBSON with **RICHARD ISANOVE** (#18-19), **FRANK D'ARMATA** (#20) & **ANDREW CROSSLEY** (#22)
Cover Artists

VC's JOE SABINO
Letterer

ALLISON STOCK
Assistant Editor

DEVIN LEWIS
Editor

JORDAN D. WHITE
Supervising Editor

SPIDER-MAN created by **STAN LEE & STEVE DITKO**

DEADPOOL created by **ROB LIEFELD & FABIAN NICIEZA**

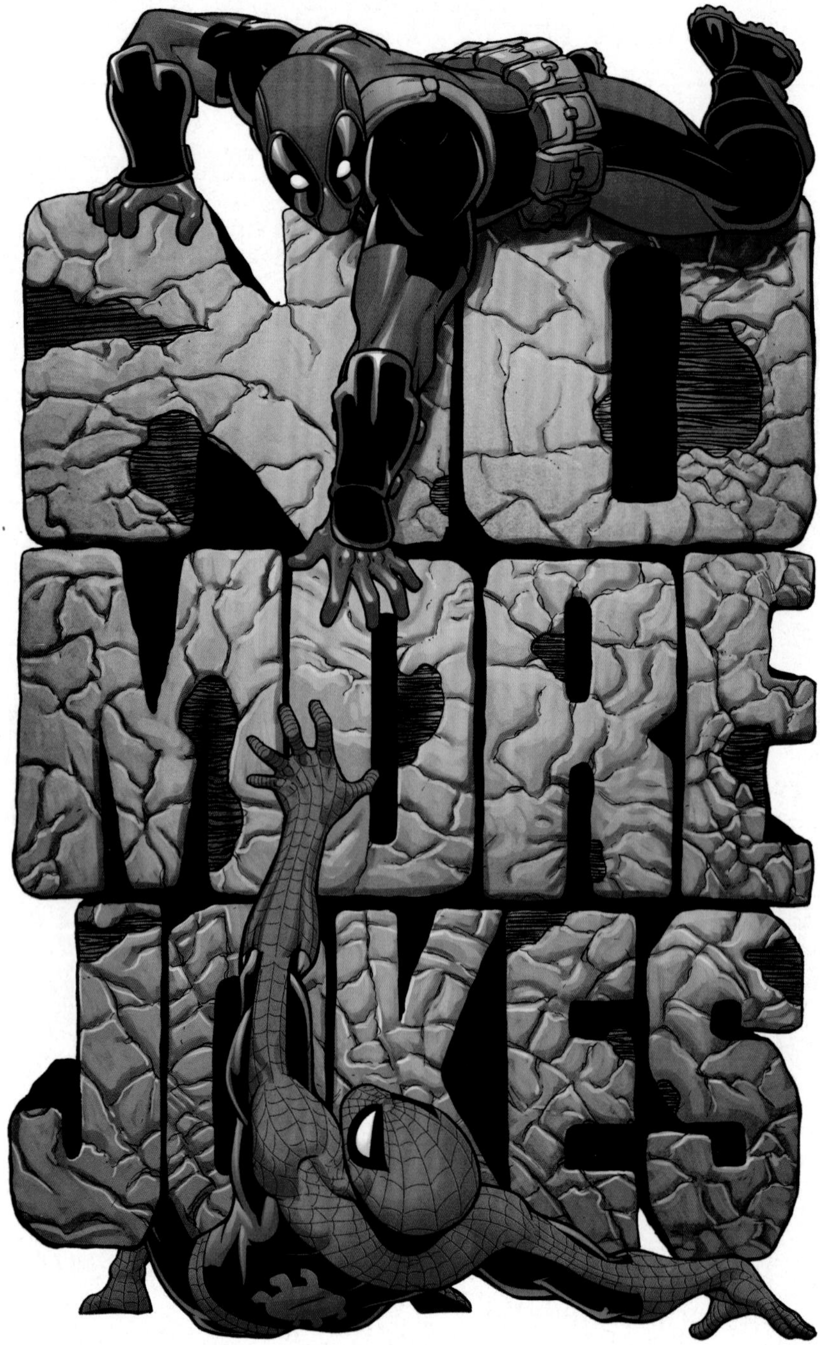
NO MORE JOKES

NO LAUGHING MATTER

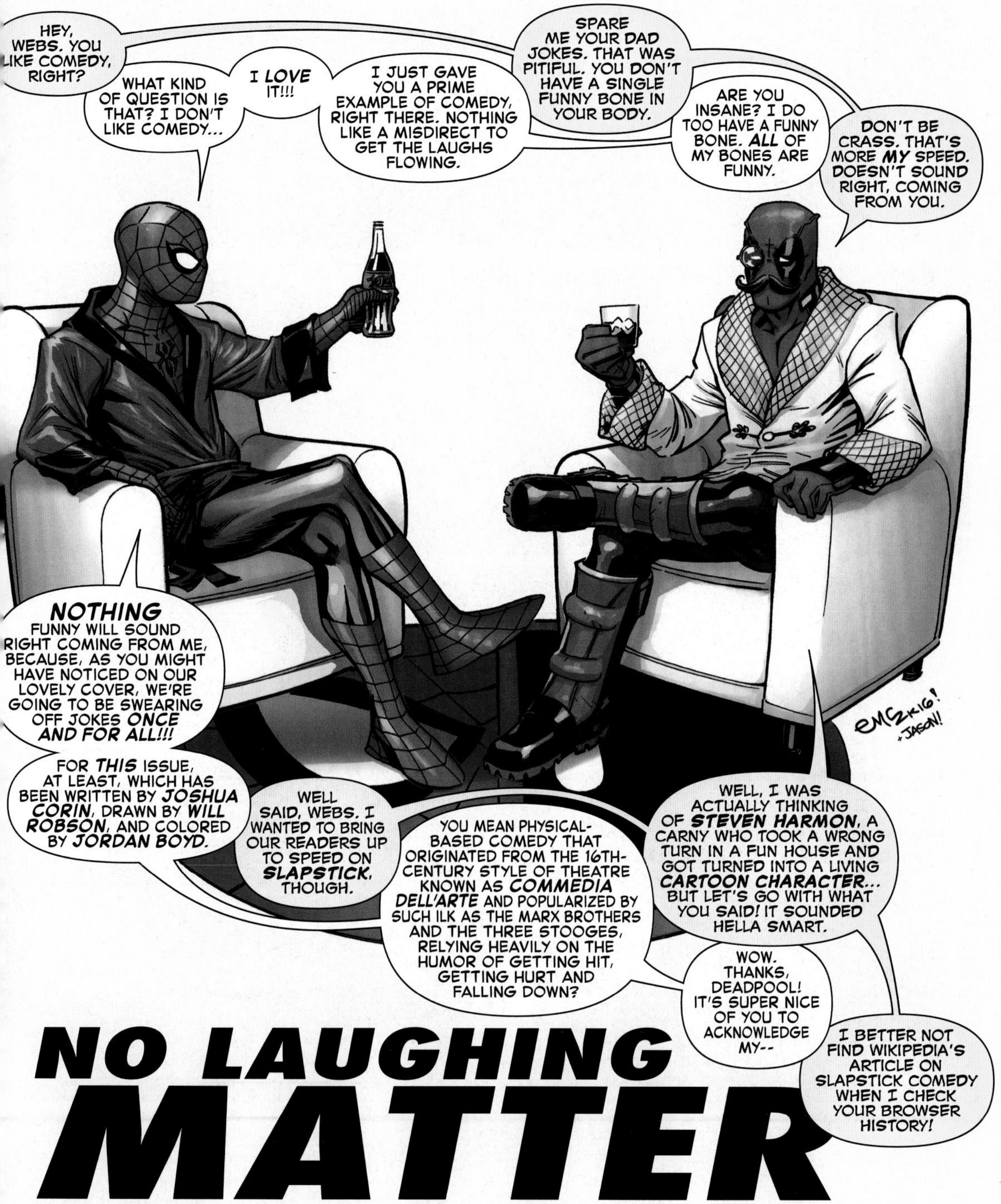

HEY, WEBS. YOU LIKE COMEDY, RIGHT?
WHAT KIND OF QUESTION IS THAT? I DON'T LIKE COMEDY...
I LOVE IT!!!
I JUST GAVE YOU A PRIME EXAMPLE OF COMEDY, RIGHT THERE. NOTHING LIKE A MISDIRECT TO GET THE LAUGHS FLOWING.
SPARE ME YOUR DAD JOKES. THAT WAS PITIFUL. YOU DON'T HAVE A SINGLE FUNNY BONE IN YOUR BODY.
ARE YOU INSANE? I DO TOO HAVE A FUNNY BONE. ALL OF MY BONES ARE FUNNY.
DON'T BE CRASS. THAT'S MORE MY SPEED. DOESN'T SOUND RIGHT, COMING FROM YOU.
NOTHING FUNNY WILL SOUND RIGHT COMING FROM ME, BECAUSE, AS YOU MIGHT HAVE NOTICED ON OUR LOVELY COVER, WE'RE GOING TO BE SWEARING OFF JOKES ONCE AND FOR ALL!!!
FOR THIS ISSUE, AT LEAST, WHICH HAS BEEN WRITTEN BY JOSHUA CORIN, DRAWN BY WILL ROBSON, AND COLORED BY JORDAN BOYD.
WELL SAID, WEBS. I WANTED TO BRING OUR READERS UP TO SPEED ON SLAPSTICK, THOUGH.
YOU MEAN PHYSICAL-BASED COMEDY THAT ORIGINATED FROM THE 16TH-CENTURY STYLE OF THEATRE KNOWN AS COMMEDIA DELL'ARTE AND POPULARIZED BY SUCH ILK AS THE MARX BROTHERS AND THE THREE STOOGES, RELYING HEAVILY ON THE HUMOR OF GETTING HIT, GETTING HURT AND FALLING DOWN?
WELL, I WAS ACTUALLY THINKING OF STEVEN HARMON, A CARNY WHO TOOK A WRONG TURN IN A FUN HOUSE AND GOT TURNED INTO A LIVING CARTOON CHARACTER... BUT LET'S GO WITH WHAT YOU SAID! IT SOUNDED HELLA SMART.
WOW. THANKS, DEADPOOL! IT'S SUPER NICE OF YOU TO ACKNOWLEDGE MY--
I BETTER NOT FIND WIKIPEDIA'S ARTICLE ON SLAPSTICK COMEDY WHEN I CHECK YOUR BROWSER HISTORY!

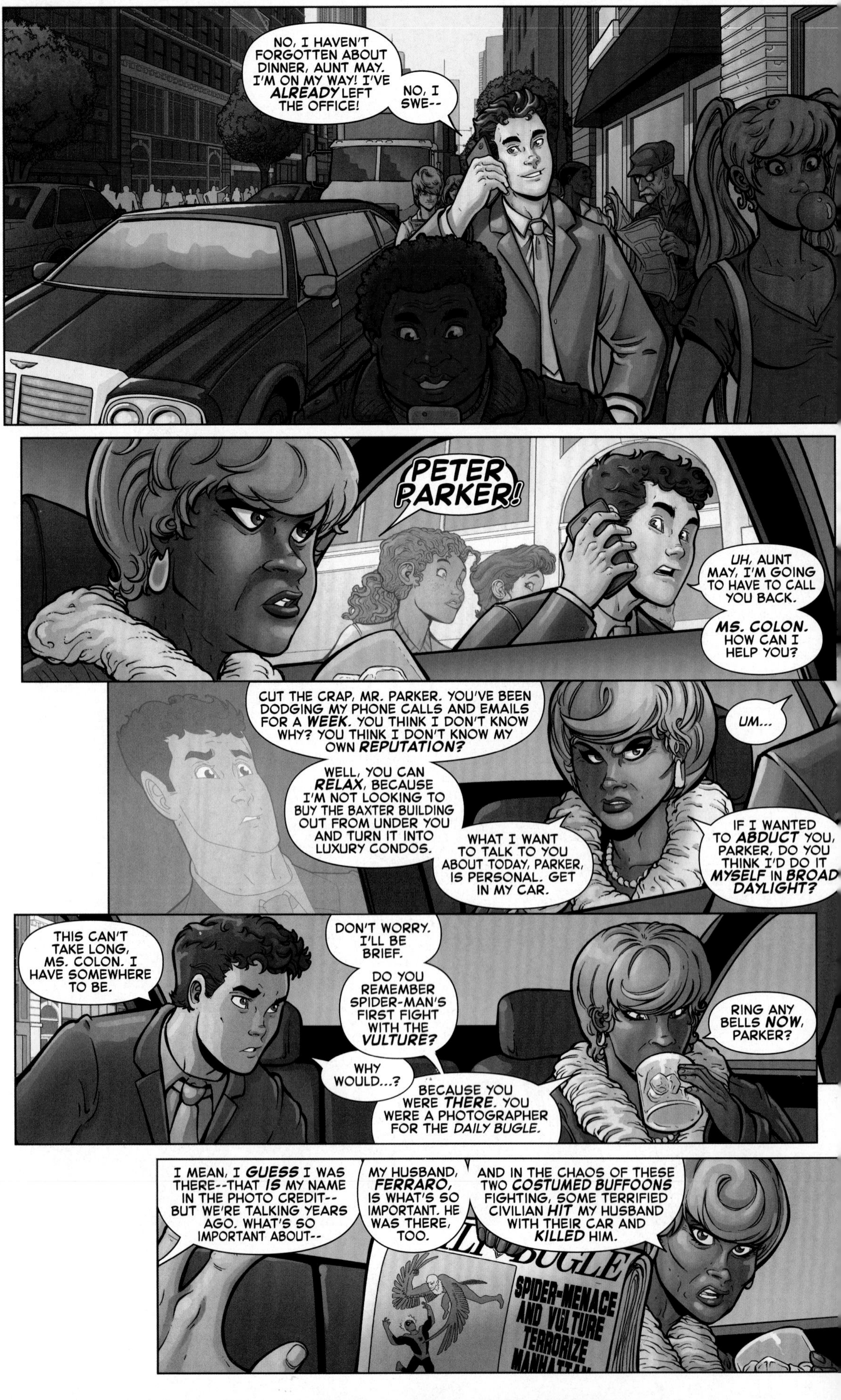

NO, I HAVEN'T FORGOTTEN ABOUT DINNER, AUNT MAY. I'M ON MY WAY! I'VE ALREADY LEFT THE OFFICE!
NO, I SWE--
PETER PARKER!
UH, AUNT MAY, I'M GOING TO HAVE TO CALL YOU BACK.
MS. COLON. HOW CAN I HELP YOU?
CUT THE CRAP, MR. PARKER. YOU'VE BEEN DODGING MY PHONE CALLS AND EMAILS FOR A WEEK. YOU THINK I DON'T KNOW WHY? YOU THINK I DON'T KNOW MY OWN REPUTATION?
UM...
WELL, YOU CAN RELAX, BECAUSE I'M NOT LOOKING TO BUY THE BAXTER BUILDING OUT FROM UNDER YOU AND TURN IT INTO LUXURY CONDOS.
WHAT I WANT TO TALK TO YOU ABOUT TODAY, PARKER, IS PERSONAL. GET IN MY CAR.
IF I WANTED TO ABDUCT YOU, PARKER, DO YOU THINK I'D DO IT MYSELF IN BROAD DAYLIGHT?
THIS CAN'T TAKE LONG, MS. COLON. I HAVE SOMEWHERE TO BE.
DON'T WORRY. I'LL BE BRIEF.
DO YOU REMEMBER SPIDER-MAN'S FIRST FIGHT WITH THE VULTURE?
WHY WOULD...?
BECAUSE YOU WERE THERE. YOU WERE A PHOTOGRAPHER FOR THE DAILY BUGLE.
RING ANY BELLS NOW, PARKER?
I MEAN, I GUESS I WAS THERE--THAT IS MY NAME IN THE PHOTO CREDIT--BUT WE'RE TALKING YEARS AGO. WHAT'S SO IMPORTANT ABOUT--
MY HUSBAND, FERRARO, IS WHAT'S SO IMPORTANT. HE WAS THERE, TOO.
AND IN THE CHAOS OF THESE TWO COSTUMED BUFFOONS FIGHTING, SOME TERRIFIED CIVILIAN HIT MY HUSBAND WITH THEIR CAR AND KILLED HIM.
BUGLE
SPIDER-MENACE AND VULTURE TERRORIZE

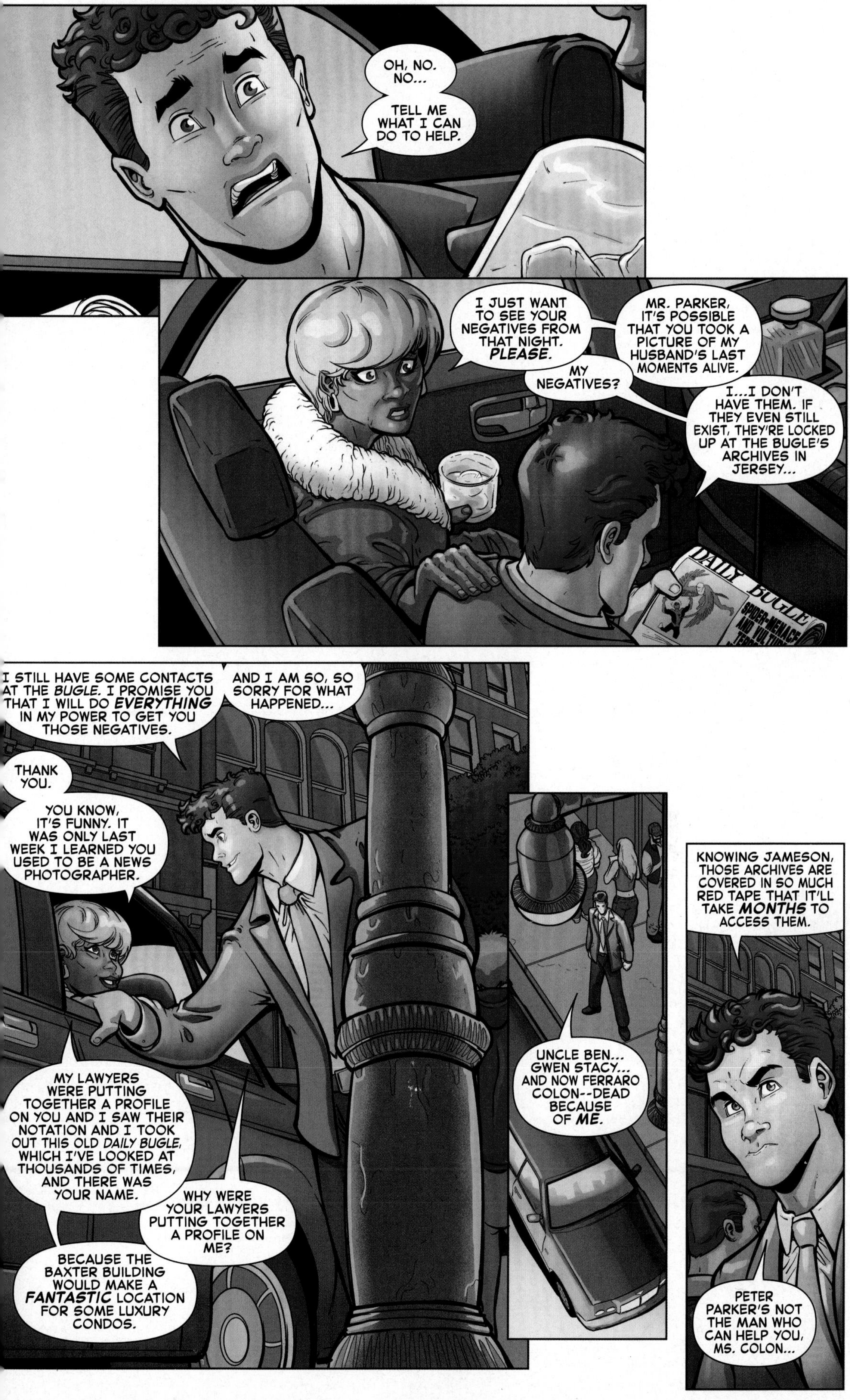
OH, NO. NO...
TELL ME WHAT I CAN DO TO HELP.
I JUST WANT TO SEE YOUR NEGATIVES FROM THAT NIGHT. PLEASE.
MR. PARKER, IT'S POSSIBLE THAT YOU TOOK A PICTURE OF MY HUSBAND'S LAST MOMENTS ALIVE.
MY NEGATIVES?
I...I DON'T HAVE THEM. IF THEY EVEN STILL EXIST, THEY'RE LOCKED UP AT THE BUGLE'S ARCHIVES IN JERSEY...
DAILY BUGLE
SPIDER-MENACE
I STILL HAVE SOME CONTACTS AT THE BUGLE. I PROMISE YOU THAT I WILL DO EVERYTHING IN MY POWER TO GET YOU THOSE NEGATIVES.
AND I AM SO, SO SORRY FOR WHAT HAPPENED...
THANK YOU.
YOU KNOW, IT'S FUNNY. IT WAS ONLY LAST WEEK I LEARNED YOU USED TO BE A NEWS PHOTOGRAPHER.
MY LAWYERS WERE PUTTING TOGETHER A PROFILE ON YOU AND I SAW THEIR NOTATION AND I TOOK OUT THIS OLD DAILY BUGLE, WHICH I'VE LOOKED AT THOUSANDS OF TIMES, AND THERE WAS YOUR NAME.
WHY WERE YOUR LAWYERS PUTTING TOGETHER A PROFILE ON ME?
BECAUSE THE BAXTER BUILDING WOULD MAKE A FANTASTIC LOCATION FOR SOME LUXURY CONDOS.
UNCLE BEN... GWEN STACY... AND NOW FERRARO COLON--DEAD BECAUSE OF ME.
KNOWING JAMESON, THOSE ARCHIVES ARE COVERED IN SO MUCH RED TAPE THAT IT'LL TAKE MONTHS TO ACCESS THEM.
PETER PARKER'S NOT THE MAN WHO CAN HELP YOU, MS. COLON...

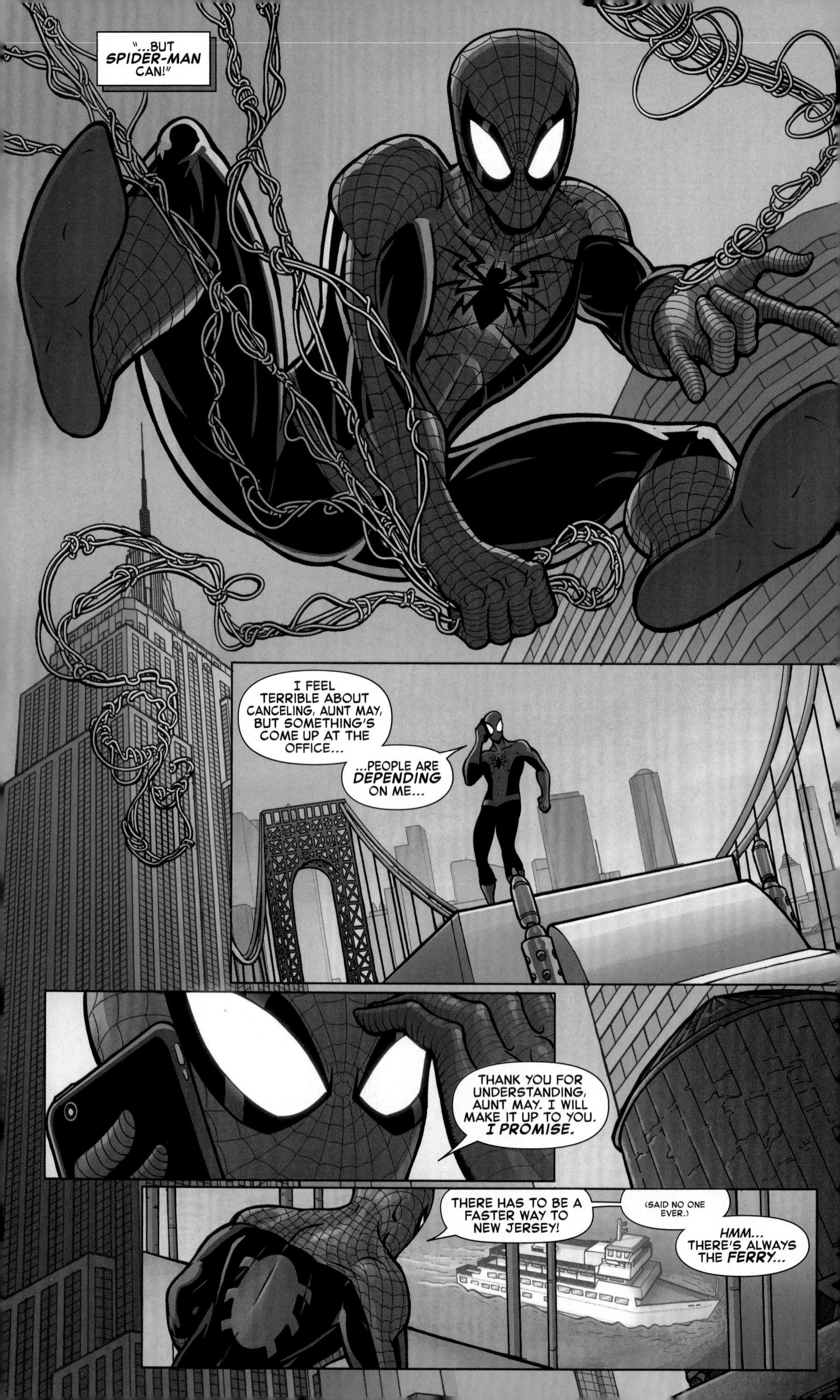
"...BUT SPIDER-MAN CAN!"
I FEEL TERRIBLE ABOUT CANCELING, AUNT MAY, BUT SOMETHING'S COME UP AT THE OFFICE...
...PEOPLE ARE DEPENDING ON ME...
THANK YOU FOR UNDERSTANDING, AUNT MAY. I WILL MAKE IT UP TO YOU. I PROMISE.
THERE HAS TO BE A FASTER WAY TO NEW JERSEY!
(SAID NO ONE EVER.)
HMM... THERE'S ALWAYS THE FERRY...

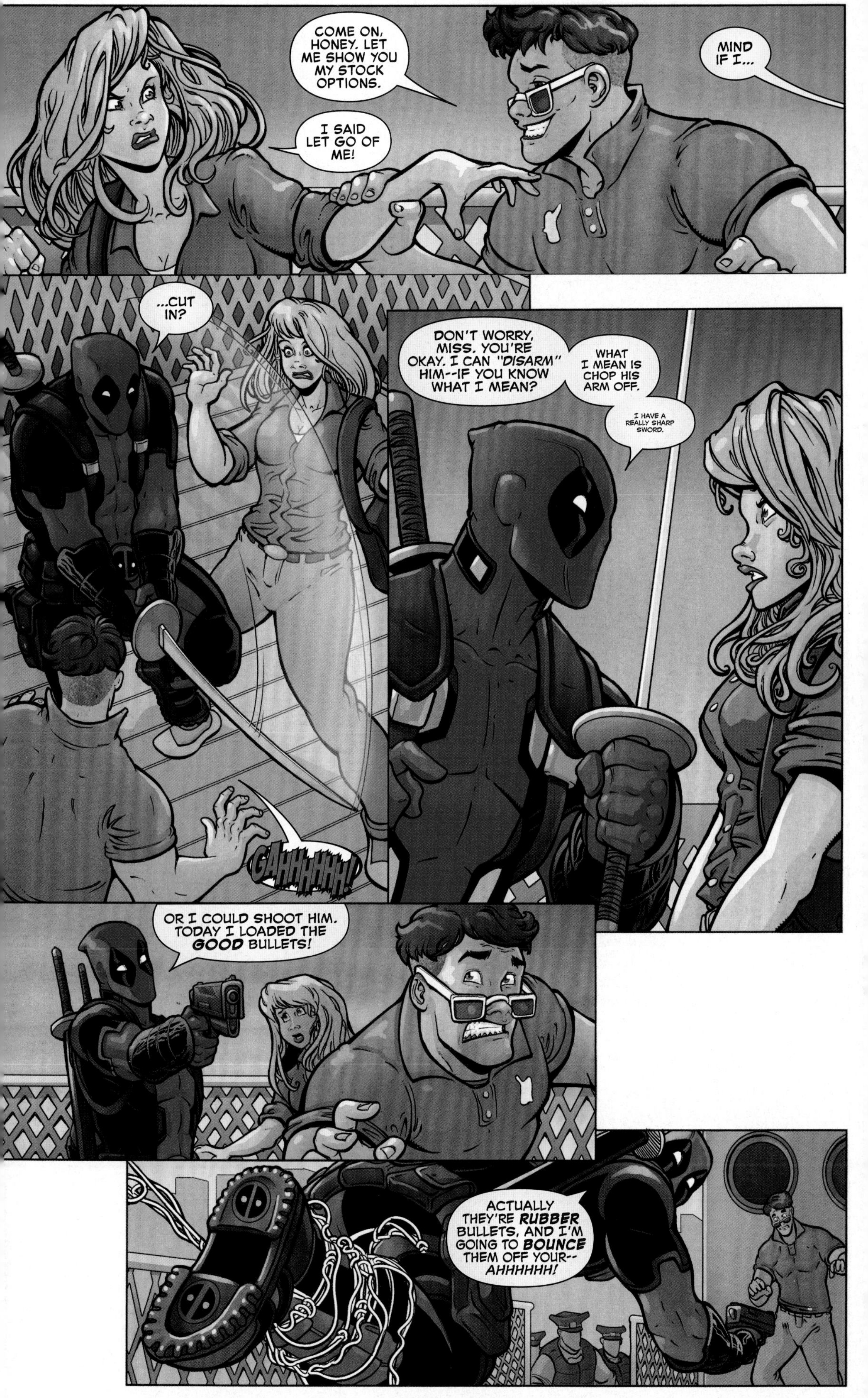
COME ON, HONEY. LET ME SHOW YOU MY STOCK OPTIONS.
I SAID LET GO OF ME!
MIND IF I...
...CUT IN?
GAHHHHHH!
DON'T WORRY, MISS. YOU'RE OKAY. I CAN "DISARM" HIM--IF YOU KNOW WHAT I MEAN?
WHAT I MEAN IS CHOP HIS ARM OFF.
I HAVE A REALLY SHARP SWORD.
OR I COULD SHOOT HIM. TODAY I LOADED THE GOOD BULLETS!
ACTUALLY THEY'RE RUBBER BULLETS, AND I'M GOING TO BOUNCE THEM OFF YOUR-- AHHHHHH!

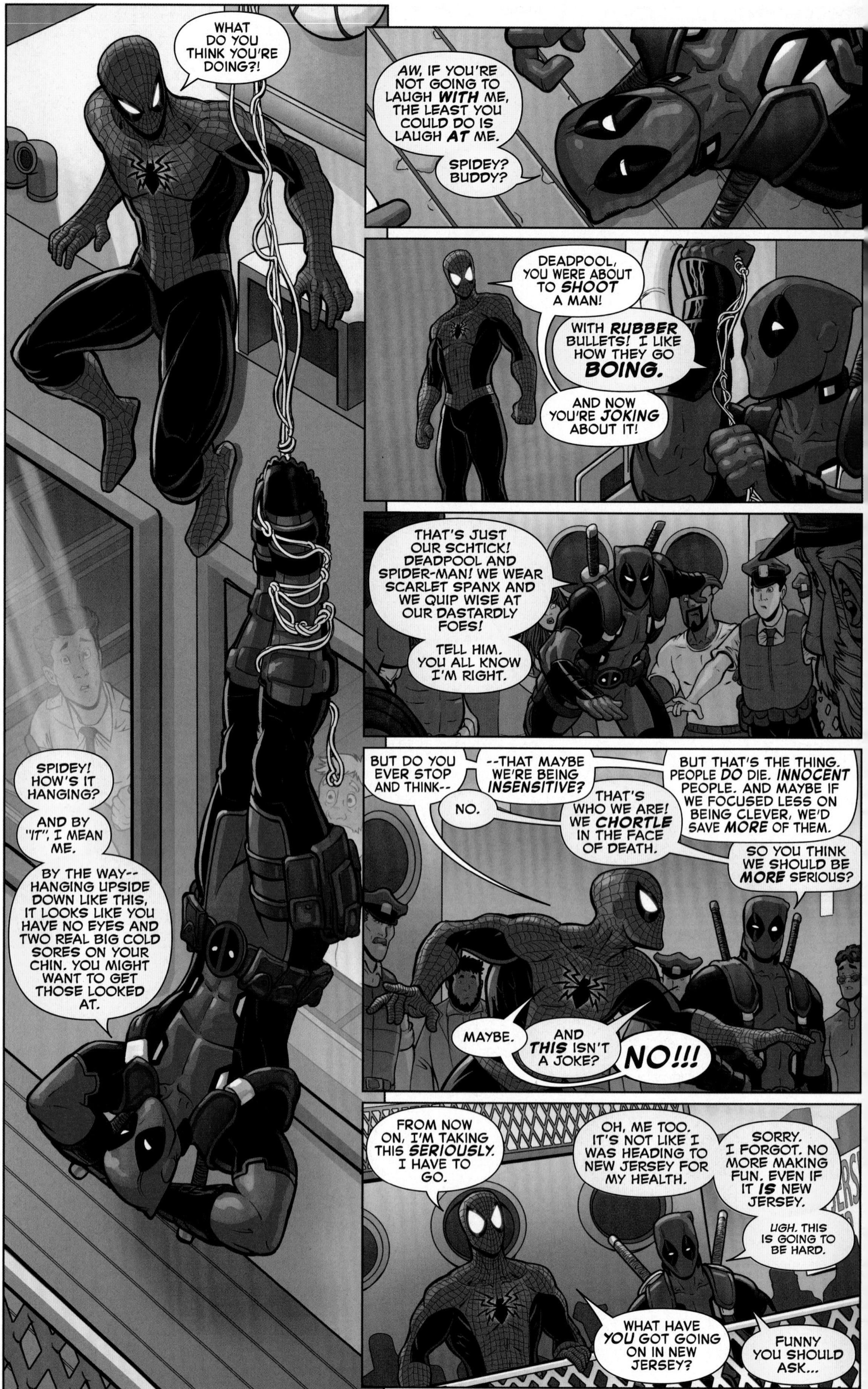
WHAT DO YOU THINK YOU'RE DOING?!
SPIDEY! HOW'S IT HANGING?
AND BY "IT", I MEAN ME.
BY THE WAY-- HANGING UPSIDE DOWN LIKE THIS, IT LOOKS LIKE YOU HAVE NO EYES AND TWO REAL BIG COLD SORES ON YOUR CHIN. YOU MIGHT WANT TO GET THOSE LOOKED AT.
AW, IF YOU'RE NOT GOING TO LAUGH WITH ME, THE LEAST YOU COULD DO IS LAUGH AT ME.
SPIDEY? BUDDY?
DEADPOOL, YOU WERE ABOUT TO SHOOT A MAN!
WITH RUBBER BULLETS! I LIKE HOW THEY GO BOING.
AND NOW YOU'RE JOKING ABOUT IT!
THAT'S JUST OUR SCHTICK! DEADPOOL AND SPIDER-MAN! WE WEAR SCARLET SPANX AND WE QUIP WISE AT OUR DASTARDLY FOES!
TELL HIM. YOU ALL KNOW I'M RIGHT.
BUT DO YOU EVER STOP AND THINK--
--THAT MAYBE WE'RE BEING INSENSITIVE?
NO.
THAT'S WHO WE ARE! WE CHORTLE IN THE FACE OF DEATH.
BUT THAT'S THE THING. PEOPLE DO DIE. INNOCENT PEOPLE. AND MAYBE IF WE FOCUSED LESS ON BEING CLEVER, WE'D SAVE MORE OF THEM.
SO YOU THINK WE SHOULD BE MORE SERIOUS?
MAYBE.
AND THIS ISN'T A JOKE?
NO!!!
FROM NOW ON, I'M TAKING THIS SERIOUSLY. I HAVE TO GO.
OH, ME TOO. IT'S NOT LIKE I WAS HEADING TO NEW JERSEY FOR MY HEALTH.
SORRY. I FORGOT. NO MORE MAKING FUN. EVEN IF IT IS NEW JERSEY.
UGH. THIS IS GOING TO BE HARD.
WHAT HAVE YOU GOT GOING ON IN NEW JERSEY?
FUNNY YOU SHOULD ASK...

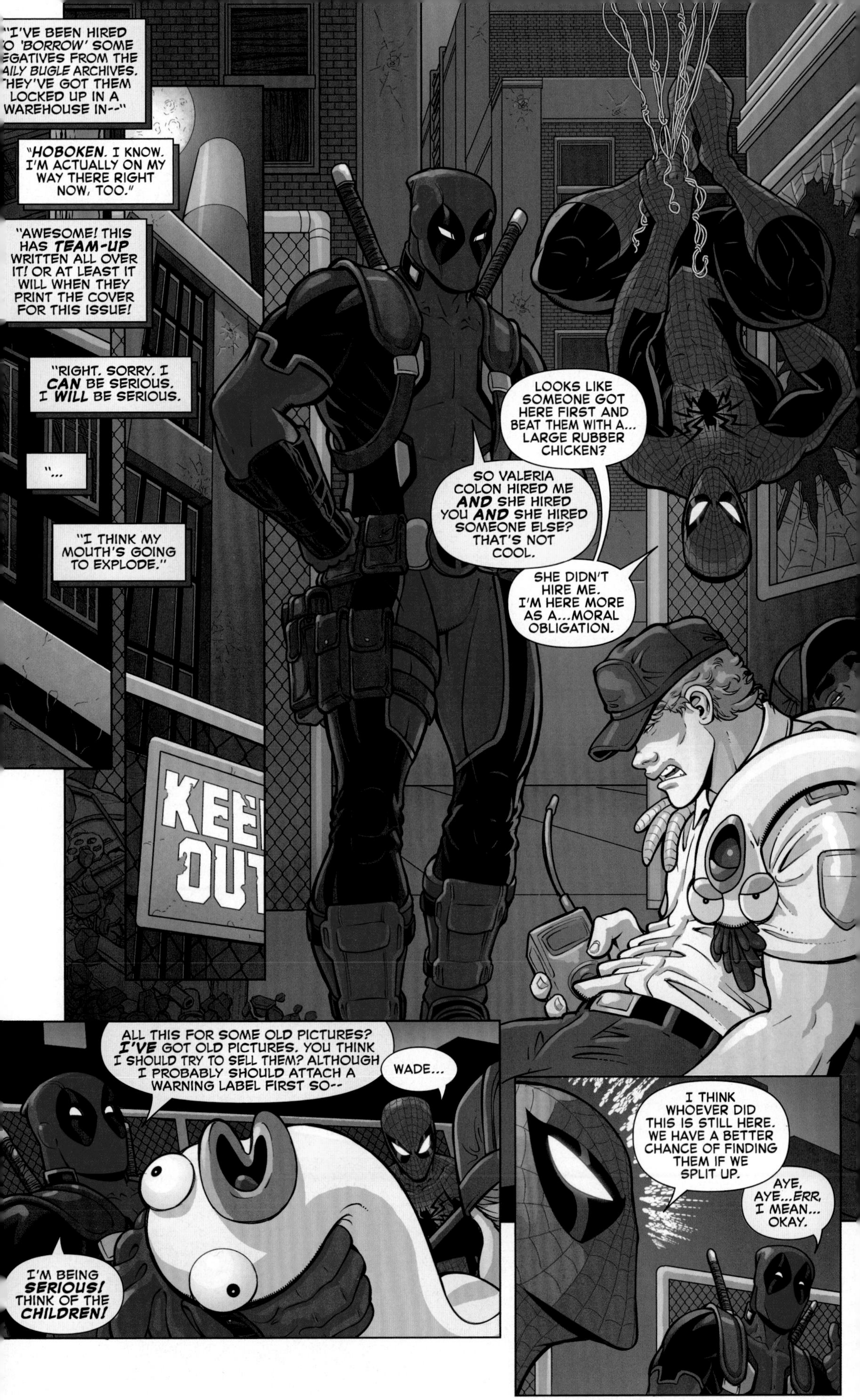
"I'VE BEEN HIRED
O 'BORROW' SOME
EGATIVES FROM THE
AILY BUGLE ARCHIVES.
HEY'VE GOT THEM
LOCKED UP IN A
WAREHOUSE IN--"
"HOBOKEN. I KNOW. I'M ACTUALLY ON MY WAY THERE RIGHT NOW, TOO."
"AWESOME! THIS HAS TEAM-UP WRITTEN ALL OVER IT! OR AT LEAST IT WILL WHEN THEY PRINT THE COVER FOR THIS ISSUE!
"RIGHT. SORRY. I CAN BE SERIOUS. I WILL BE SERIOUS.
"...
"I THINK MY MOUTH'S GOING TO EXPLODE."
LOOKS LIKE SOMEONE GOT HERE FIRST AND BEAT THEM WITH A... LARGE RUBBER CHICKEN?
SO VALERIA COLON HIRED ME AND SHE HIRED YOU AND SHE HIRED SOMEONE ELSE? THAT'S NOT COOL.
SHE DIDN'T HIRE ME. I'M HERE MORE AS A...MORAL OBLIGATION.
KEE
OUT
ALL THIS FOR SOME OLD PICTURES? I'VE GOT OLD PICTURES. YOU THINK I SHOULD TRY TO SELL THEM? ALTHOUGH I PROBABLY SHOULD ATTACH A WARNING LABEL FIRST SO--
WADE...
I'M BEING SERIOUS! THINK OF THE CHILDREN!
I THINK WHOEVER DID THIS IS STILL HERE. WE HAVE A BETTER CHANCE OF FINDING THEM IF WE SPLIT UP.
AYE, AYE...ERR, I MEAN... OKAY.

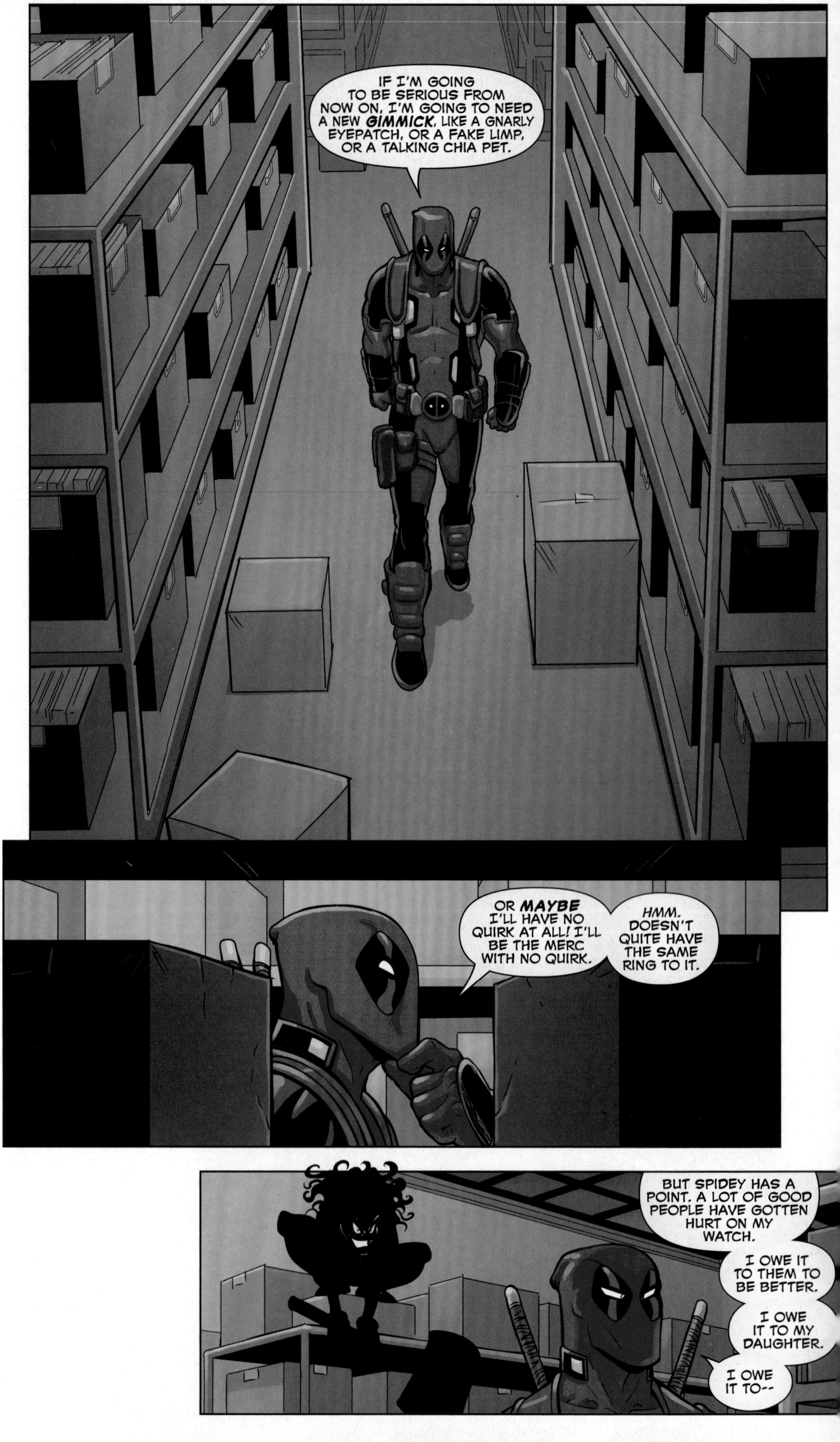
IF I'M GOING TO BE SERIOUS FROM NOW ON, I'M GOING TO NEED A NEW GIMMICK, LIKE A GNARLY EYEPATCH, OR A FAKE LIMP, OR A TALKING CHIA PET.
OR MAYBE I'LL HAVE NO QUIRK AT ALL! I'LL BE THE MERC WITH NO QUIRK.
HMM. DOESN'T QUITE HAVE THE SAME RING TO IT.
BUT SPIDEY HAS A POINT. A LOT OF GOOD PEOPLE HAVE GOTTEN HURT ON MY WATCH.
I OWE IT TO THEM TO BE BETTER.
I OWE IT TO MY DAUGHTER.
I OWE IT TO--

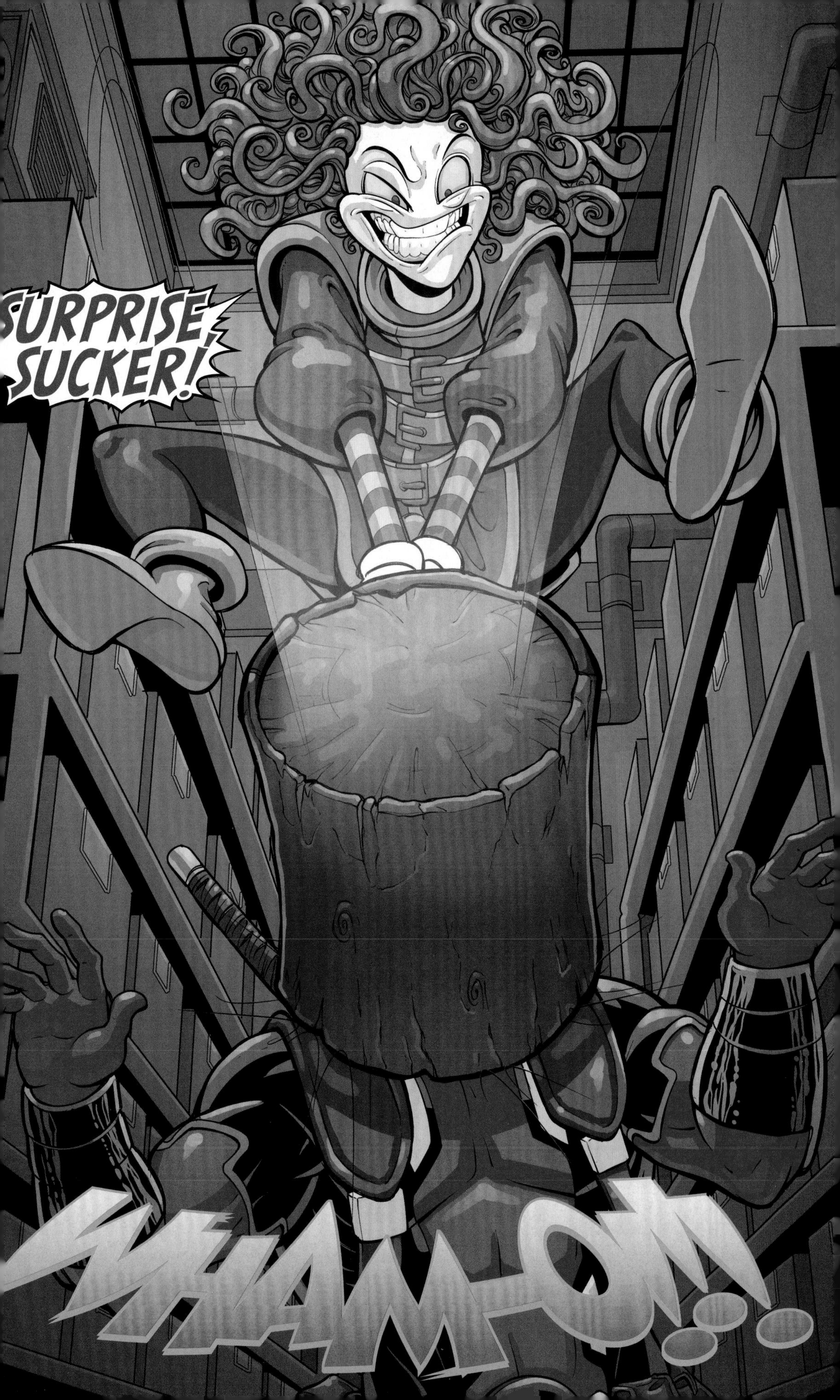
SURPRISE, SUCKER!
WHAM-OM...

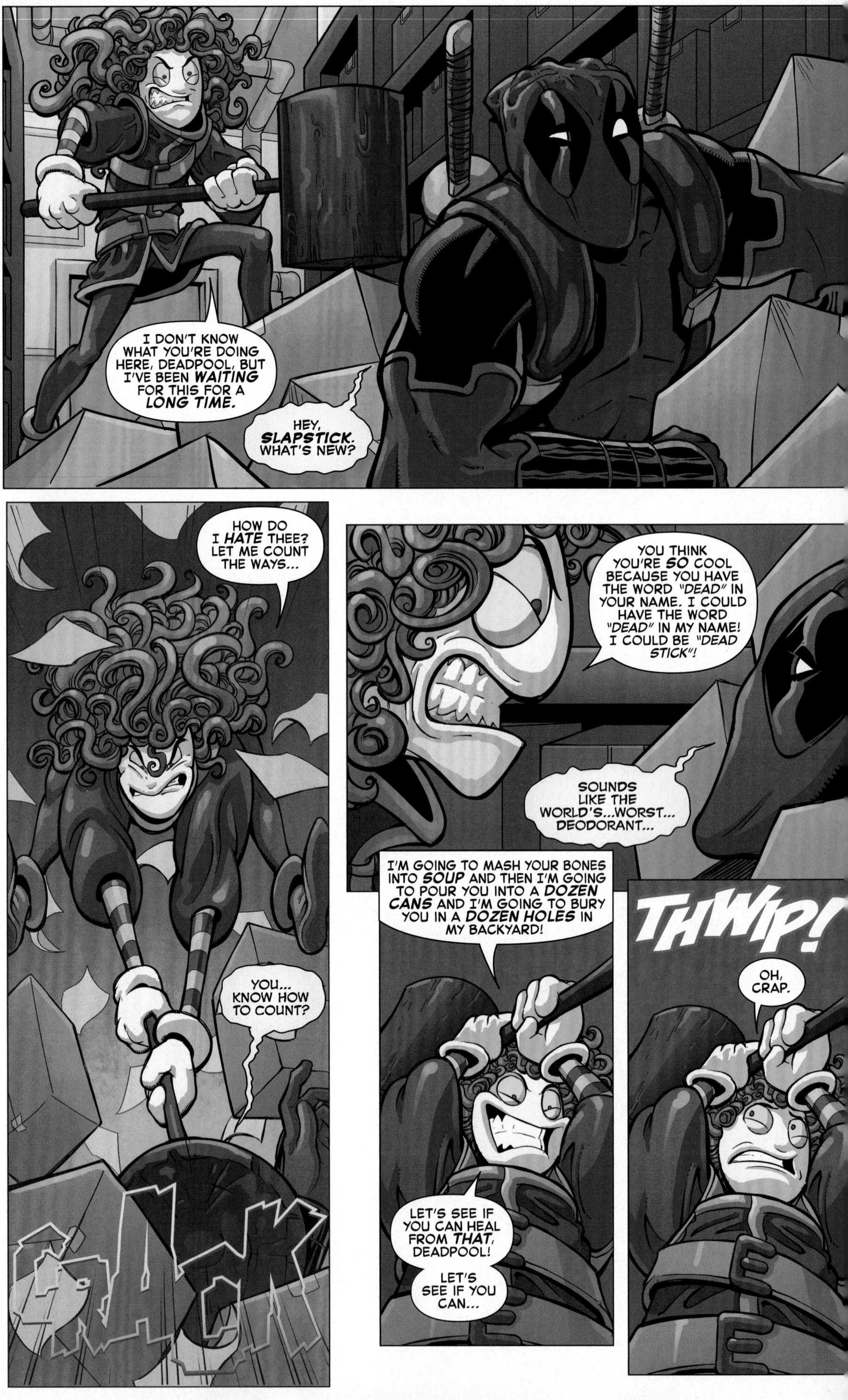
I DON'T KNOW WHAT YOU'RE DOING HERE, DEADPOOL, BUT I'VE BEEN WAITING FOR THIS FOR A LONG TIME.
HEY, SLAPSTICK. WHAT'S NEW?
HOW DO I HATE THEE? LET ME COUNT THE WAYS...
YOU... KNOW HOW TO COUNT?
YOU THINK YOU'RE SO COOL BECAUSE YOU HAVE THE WORD "DEAD" IN YOUR NAME. I COULD HAVE THE WORD "DEAD" IN MY NAME! I COULD BE "DEAD STICK"!
SOUNDS LIKE THE WORLD'S...WORST... DEODORANT...
I'M GOING TO MASH YOUR BONES INTO SOUP AND THEN I'M GOING TO POUR YOU INTO A DOZEN CANS AND I'M GOING TO BURY YOU IN A DOZEN HOLES IN MY BACKYARD!
LET'S SEE IF YOU CAN HEAL FROM THAT, DEADPOOL!
LET'S SEE IF YOU CAN...
THWIP!
OH, CRAP.

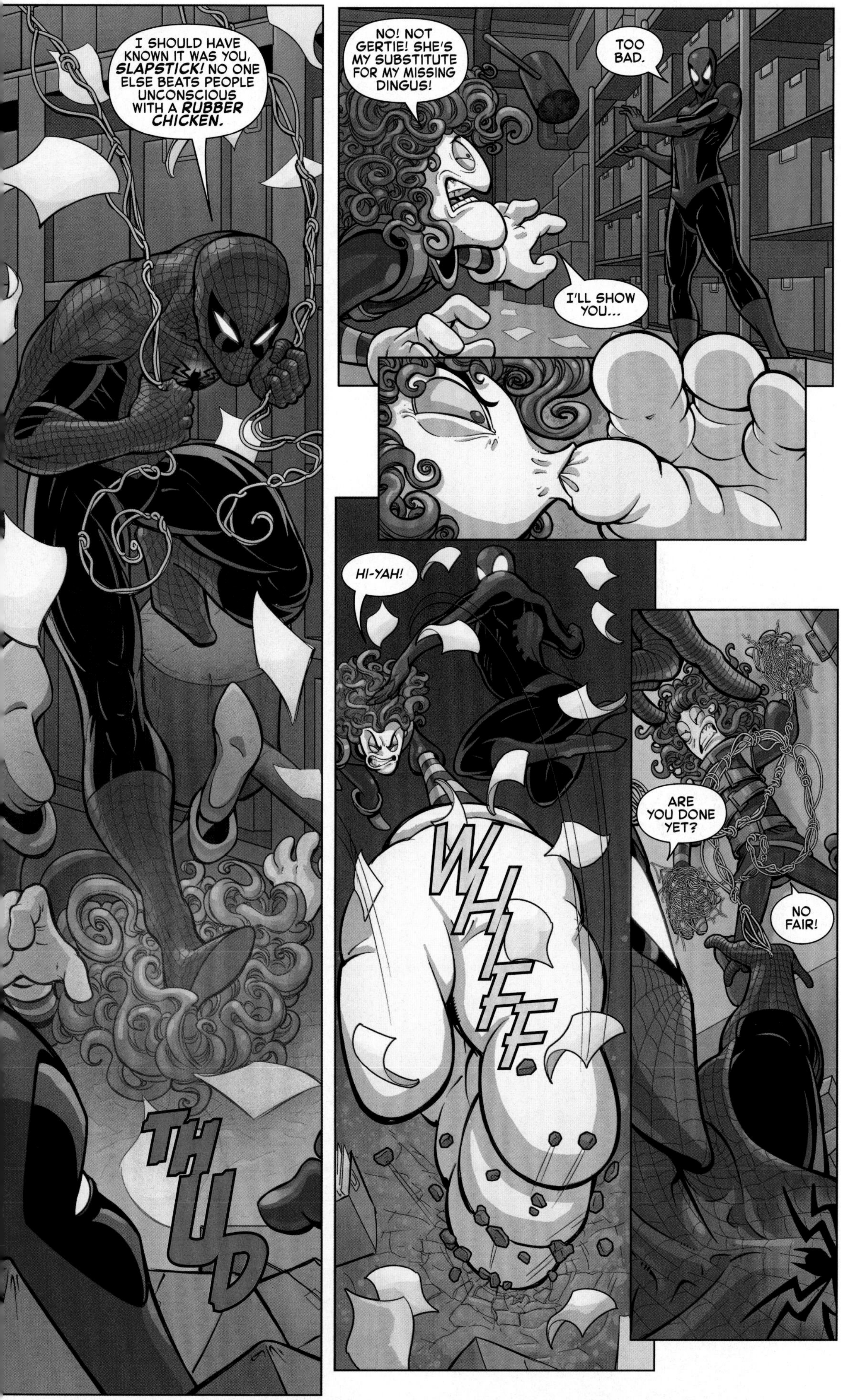
I SHOULD HAVE KNOWN IT WAS YOU, SLAPSTICK! NO ONE ELSE BEATS PEOPLE UNCONSCIOUS WITH A RUBBER CHICKEN.
THUD
NO! NOT GERTIE! SHE'S MY SUBSTITUTE FOR MY MISSING DINGUS!
TOO BAD.
I'LL SHOW YOU...
HI-YAH!
WHIFFF.
ARE YOU DONE YET?
NO FAIR!

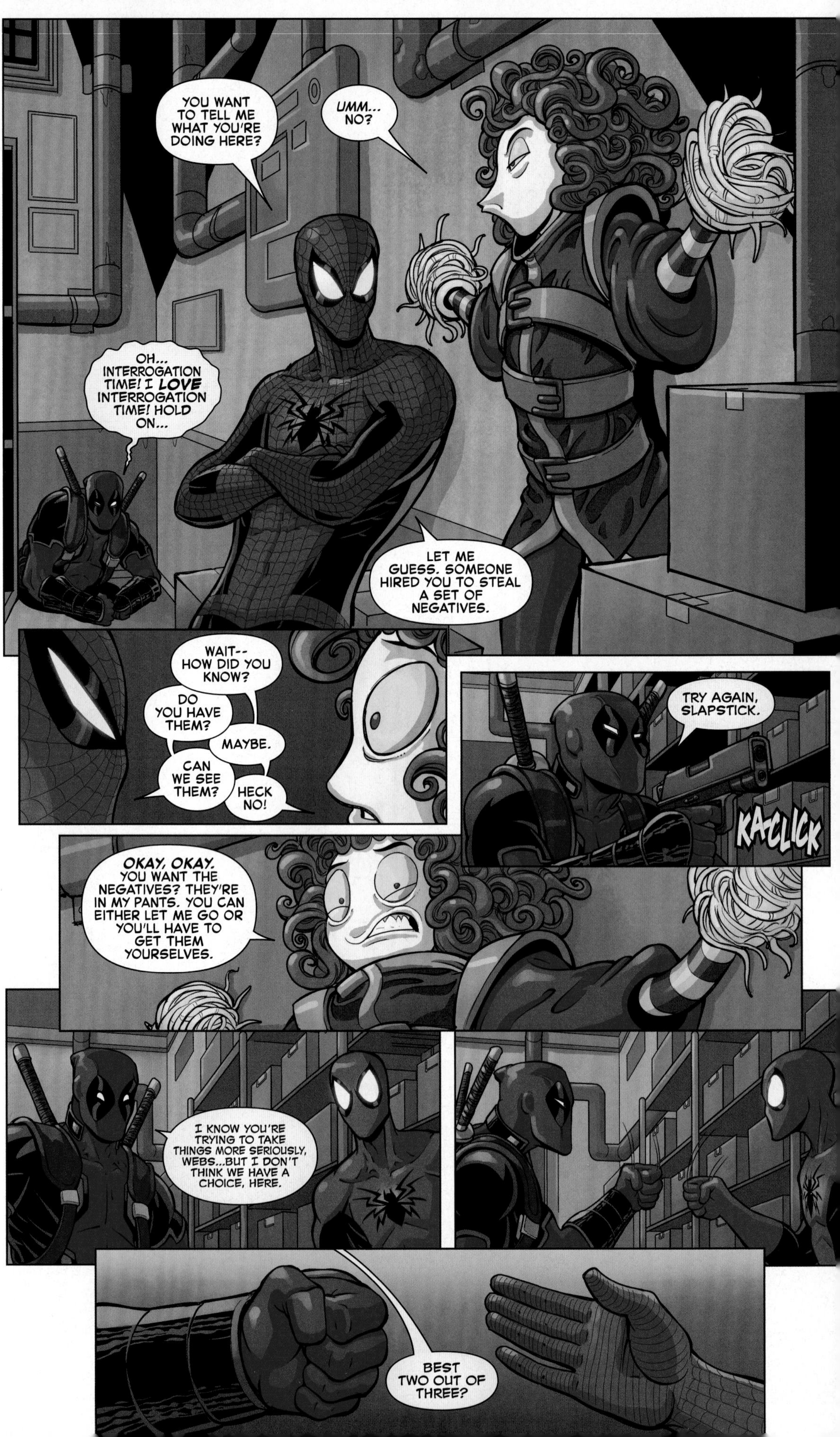
YOU WANT TO TELL ME WHAT YOU'RE DOING HERE?
UMM... NO?
OH... INTERROGATION TIME! I LOVE INTERROGATION TIME! HOLD ON...
LET ME GUESS. SOMEONE HIRED YOU TO STEAL A SET OF NEGATIVES.
WAIT-- HOW DID YOU KNOW?
DO YOU HAVE THEM?
MAYBE.
CAN WE SEE THEM?
HECK NO!
TRY AGAIN, SLAPSTICK.
KA-CLICK
OKAY, OKAY. YOU WANT THE NEGATIVES? THEY'RE IN MY PANTS. YOU CAN EITHER LET ME GO OR YOU'LL HAVE TO GET THEM YOURSELVES.
I KNOW YOU'RE TRYING TO TAKE THINGS MORE SERIOUSLY, WEBS...BUT I DON'T THINK WE HAVE A CHOICE, HERE.
BEST TWO OUT OF THREE?

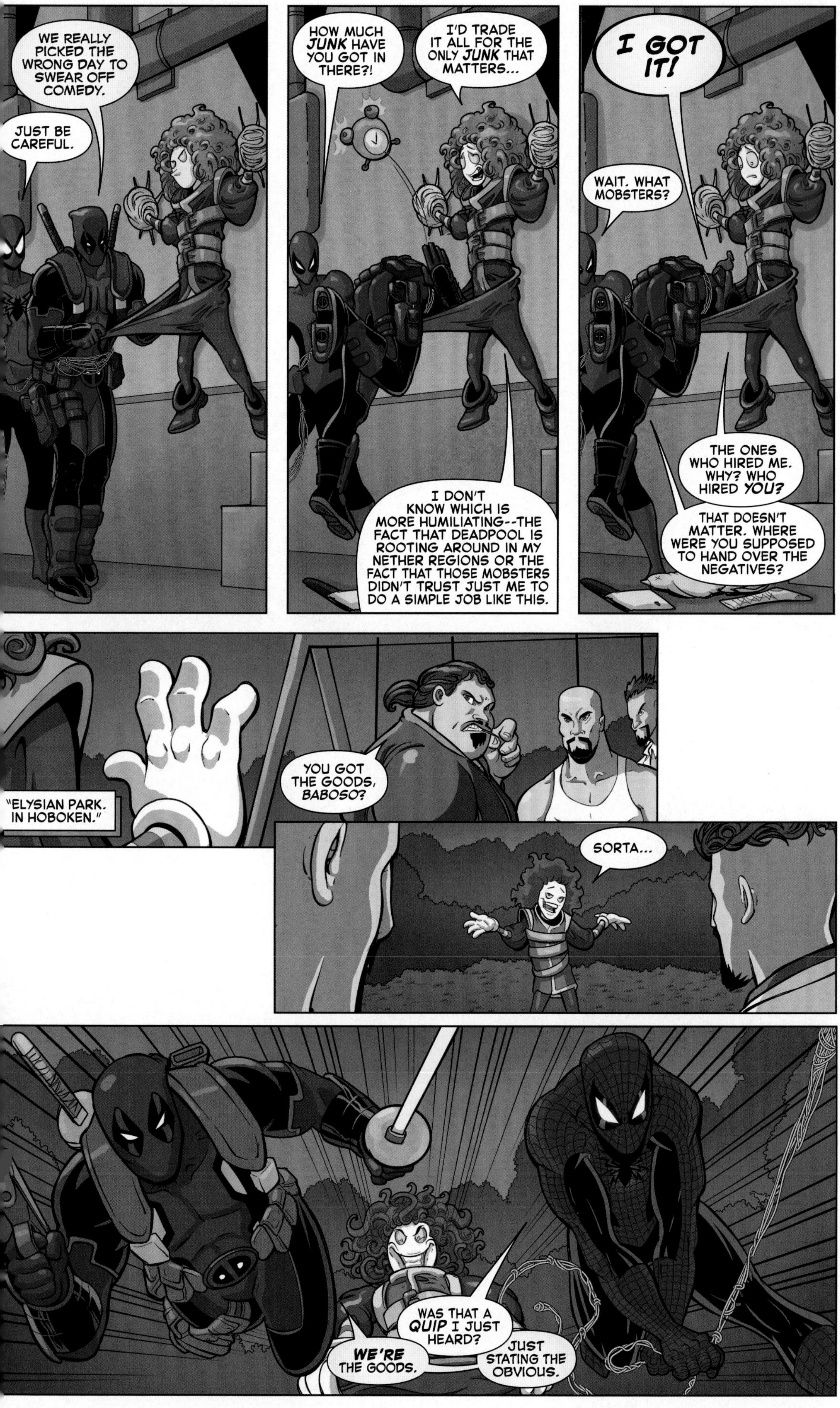
WE REALLY PICKED THE WRONG DAY TO SWEAR OFF COMEDY.
JUST BE CAREFUL.
HOW MUCH JUNK HAVE YOU GOT IN THERE?!
I'D TRADE IT ALL FOR THE ONLY JUNK THAT MATTERS...
I DON'T KNOW WHICH IS MORE HUMILIATING--THE FACT THAT DEADPOOL IS ROOTING AROUND IN MY NETHER REGIONS OR THE FACT THAT THOSE MOBSTERS DIDN'T TRUST JUST ME TO DO A SIMPLE JOB LIKE THIS.
I GOT IT!
WAIT. WHAT MOBSTERS?
THE ONES WHO HIRED ME. WHY? WHO HIRED YOU?
THAT DOESN'T MATTER. WHERE WERE YOU SUPPOSED TO HAND OVER THE NEGATIVES?
"ELYSIAN PARK. IN HOBOKEN."
YOU GOT THE GOODS, BABOSO?
SORTA...
WE'RE THE GOODS.
WAS THAT A QUIP I JUST HEARD?
JUST STATING THE OBVIOUS.

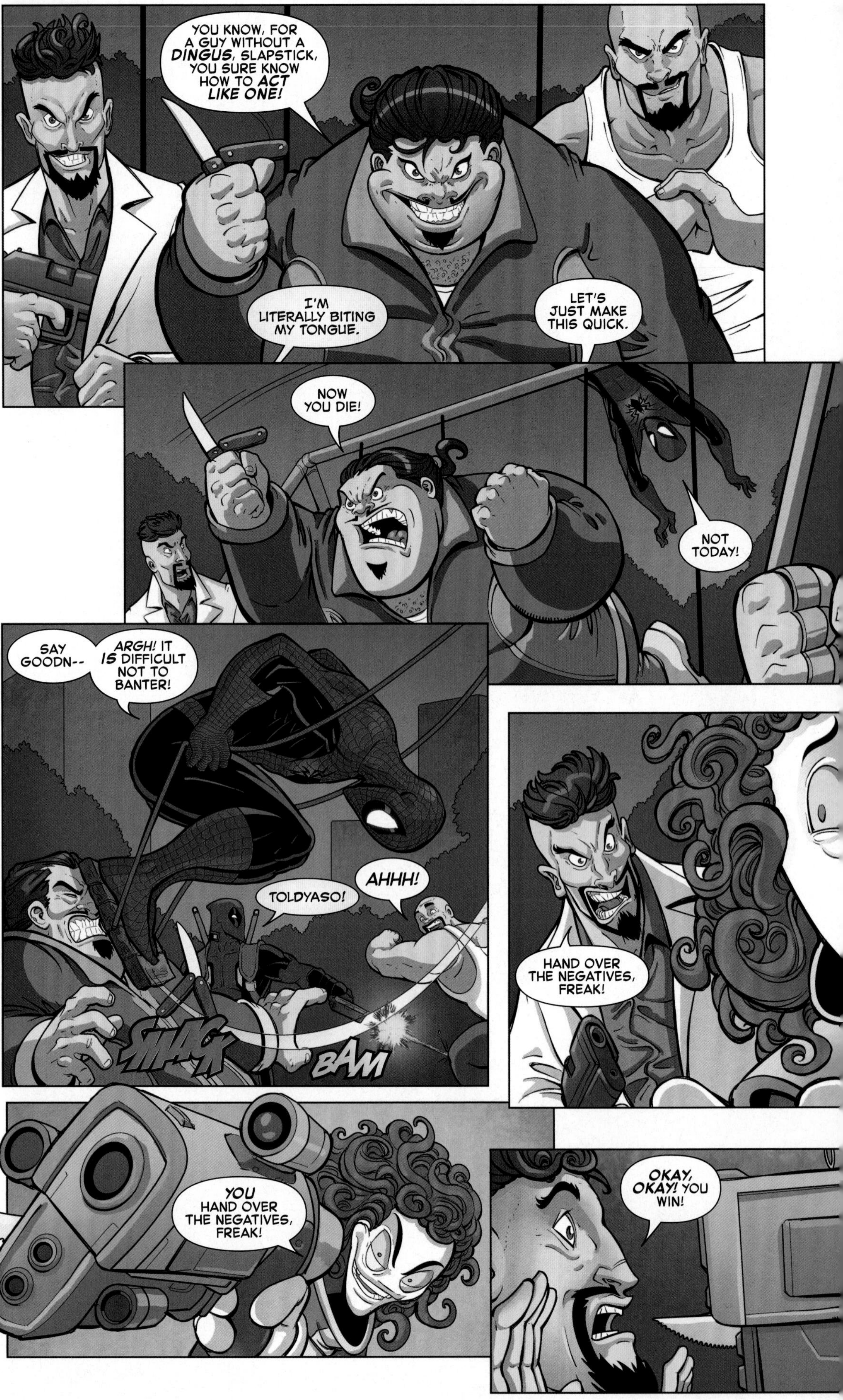
YOU KNOW, FOR A GUY WITHOUT A DINGUS, SLAPSTICK, YOU SURE KNOW HOW TO ACT LIKE ONE!
I'M LITERALLY BITING MY TONGUE.
LET'S JUST MAKE THIS QUICK.
NOW YOU DIE!
NOT TODAY!
SAY GOODN--
ARGH! IT IS DIFFICULT NOT TO BANTER!
TOLDYASO!
AHHH!
SHHAGK
BAM
HAND OVER THE NEGATIVES, FREAK!
YOU HAND OVER THE NEGATIVES, FREAK!
OKAY, OKAY! YOU WIN!

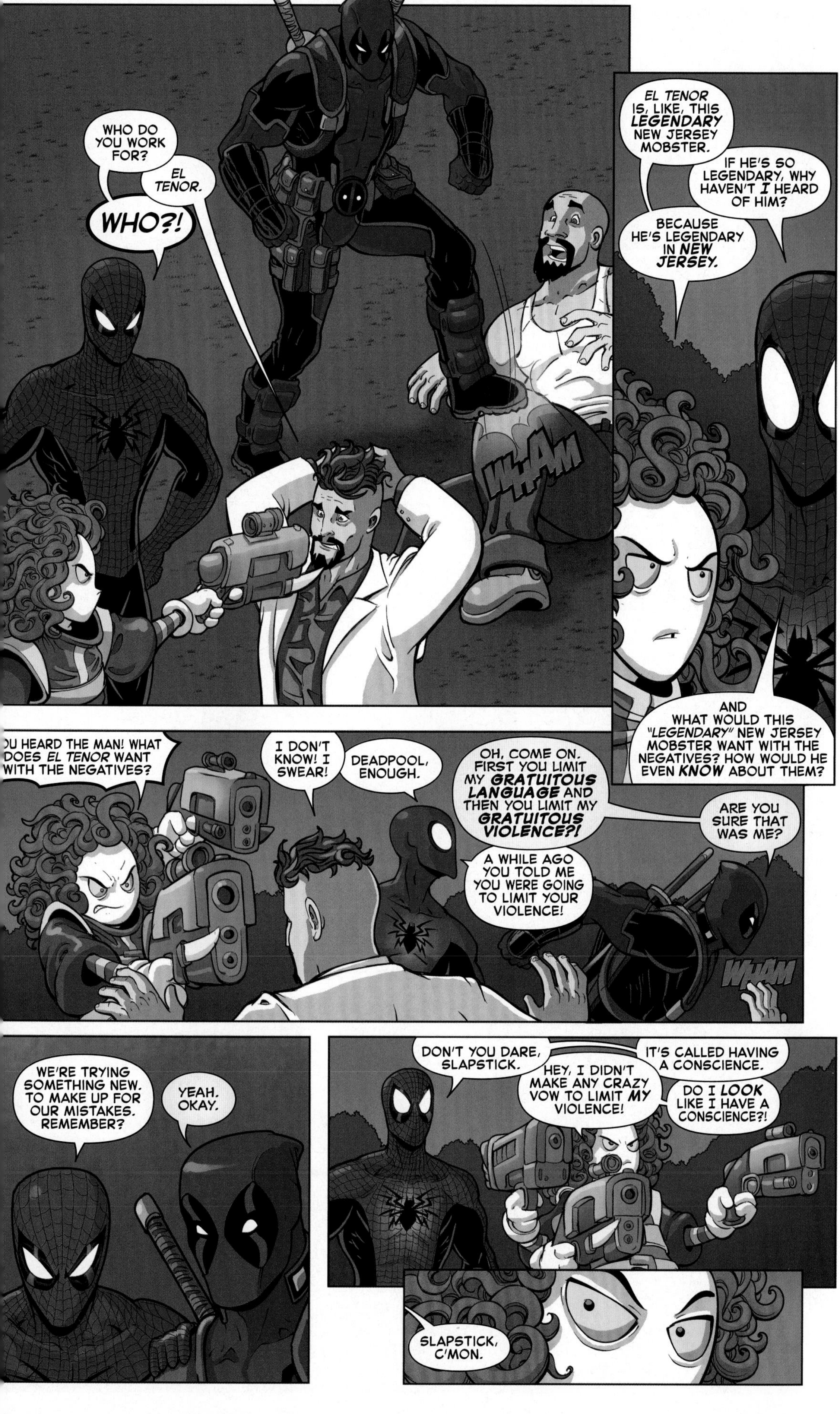

WHO DO YOU WORK FOR?
EL TENOR.
WHO?!
EL TENOR IS, LIKE, THIS LEGENDARY NEW JERSEY MOBSTER.
IF HE'S SO LEGENDARY, WHY HAVEN'T I HEARD OF HIM?
BECAUSE HE'S LEGENDARY IN NEW JERSEY.
AND WHAT WOULD THIS "LEGENDARY" NEW JERSEY MOBSTER WANT WITH THE NEGATIVES? HOW WOULD HE EVEN KNOW ABOUT THEM?
WHAM
OU HEARD THE MAN! WHAT DOES EL TENOR WANT WITH THE NEGATIVES?
I DON'T KNOW! I SWEAR!
DEADPOOL, ENOUGH.
OH, COME ON. FIRST YOU LIMIT MY GRATUITOUS LANGUAGE AND THEN YOU LIMIT MY GRATUITOUS VIOLENCE?!
A WHILE AGO YOU TOLD ME YOU WERE GOING TO LIMIT YOUR VIOLENCE!
ARE YOU SURE THAT WAS ME?
WHAM
WE'RE TRYING SOMETHING NEW. TO MAKE UP FOR OUR MISTAKES. REMEMBER?
YEAH. OKAY.
DON'T YOU DARE, SLAPSTICK.
HEY, I DIDN'T MAKE ANY CRAZY VOW TO LIMIT MY VIOLENCE!
IT'S CALLED HAVING A CONSCIENCE.
DO I LOOK LIKE I HAVE A CONSCIENCE?!
SLAPSTICK, C'MON.

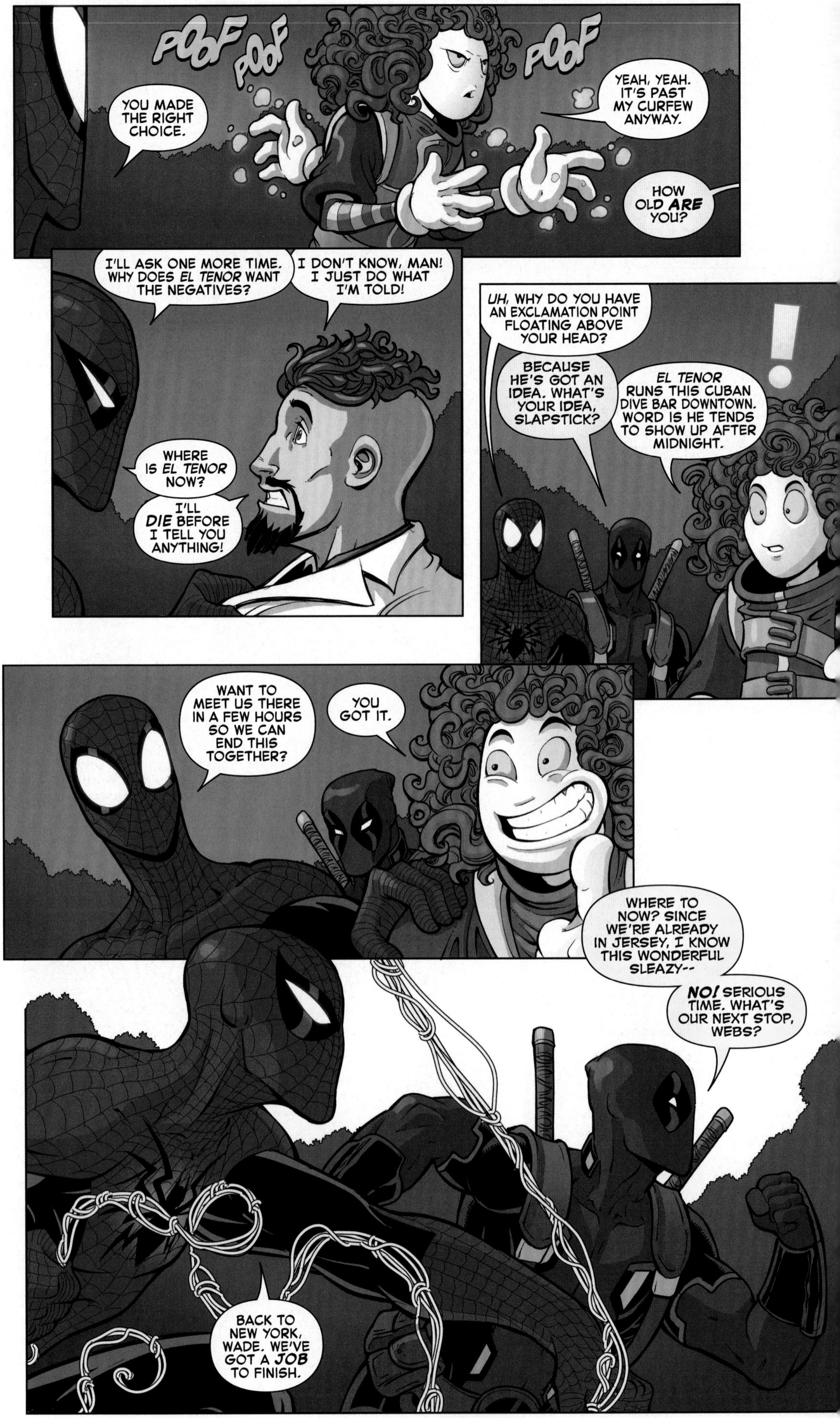
POOF POOF POOF
YOU MADE THE RIGHT CHOICE.
YEAH, YEAH. IT'S PAST MY CURFEW ANYWAY.
HOW OLD *ARE* YOU?
I'LL ASK ONE MORE TIME. WHY DOES *EL TENOR* WANT THE NEGATIVES?
I DON'T KNOW, MAN! I JUST DO WHAT I'M TOLD!
WHERE IS *EL TENOR* NOW?
I'LL *DIE* BEFORE I TELL YOU ANYTHING!
UH, WHY DO YOU HAVE AN EXCLAMATION POINT FLOATING ABOVE YOUR HEAD?
BECAUSE HE'S GOT AN IDEA. WHAT'S YOUR IDEA, SLAPSTICK?
EL TENOR RUNS THIS CUBAN DIVE BAR DOWNTOWN. WORD IS HE TENDS TO SHOW UP AFTER MIDNIGHT.
WANT TO MEET US THERE IN A FEW HOURS SO WE CAN END THIS TOGETHER?
YOU GOT IT.
WHERE TO NOW? SINCE WE'RE ALREADY IN JERSEY, I KNOW THIS WONDERFUL SLEAZY--
NO! SERIOUS TIME. WHAT'S OUR NEXT STOP, WEBS?
BACK TO NEW YORK, WADE. WE'VE GOT A *JOB* TO FINISH.

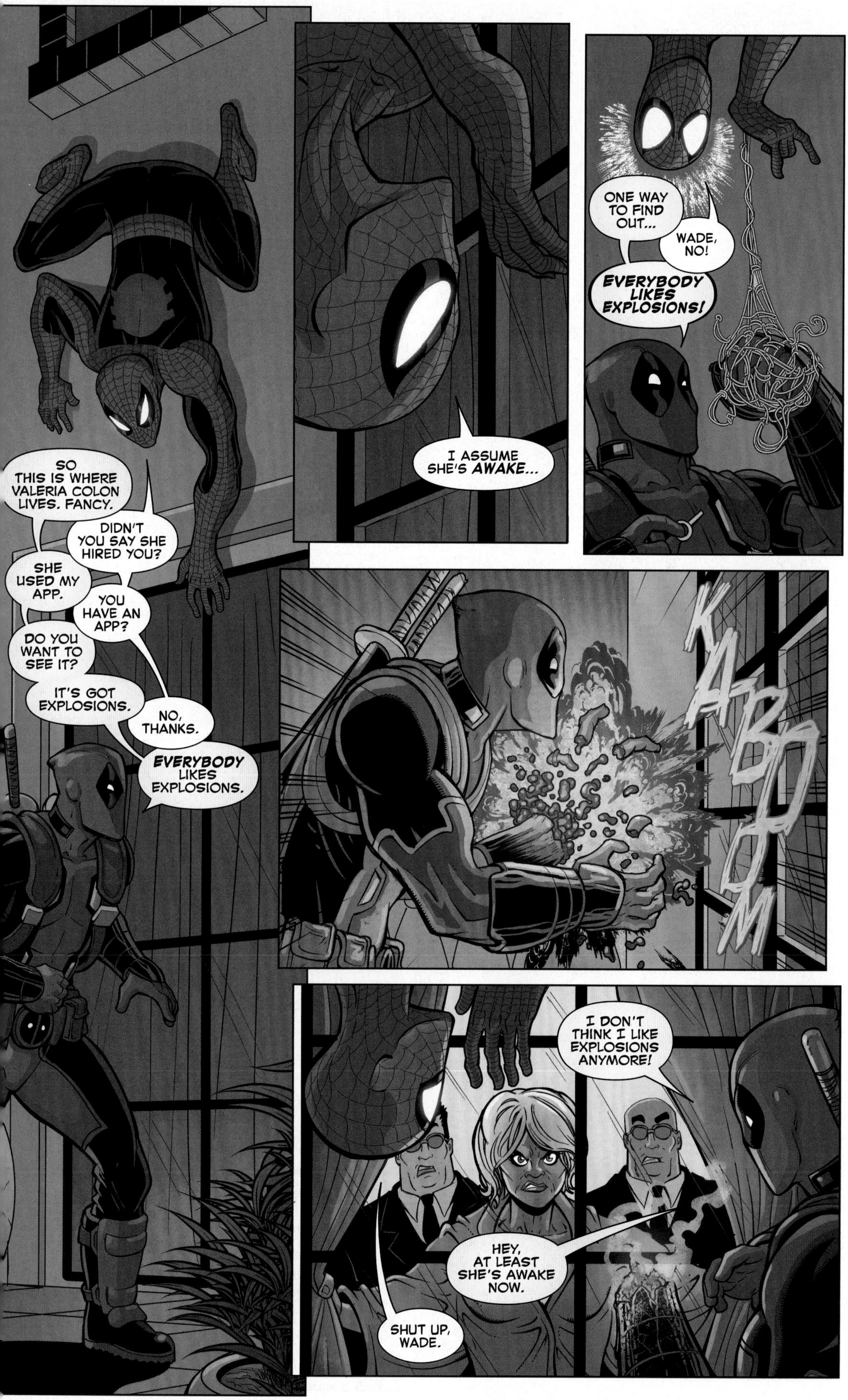
SO THIS IS WHERE VALERIA COLON LIVES. FANCY.
DIDN'T YOU SAY SHE HIRED YOU?
SHE USED MY APP.
YOU HAVE AN APP?
DO YOU WANT TO SEE IT?
IT'S GOT EXPLOSIONS.
NO, THANKS.
EVERYBODY LIKES EXPLOSIONS.
I ASSUME SHE'S AWAKE...
ONE WAY TO FIND OUT...
WADE, NO!
EVERYBODY LIKES EXPLOSIONS!
KA-BOOM
I DON'T THINK I LIKE EXPLOSIONS ANYMORE!
HEY, AT LEAST SHE'S AWAKE NOW.
SHUT UP, WADE.

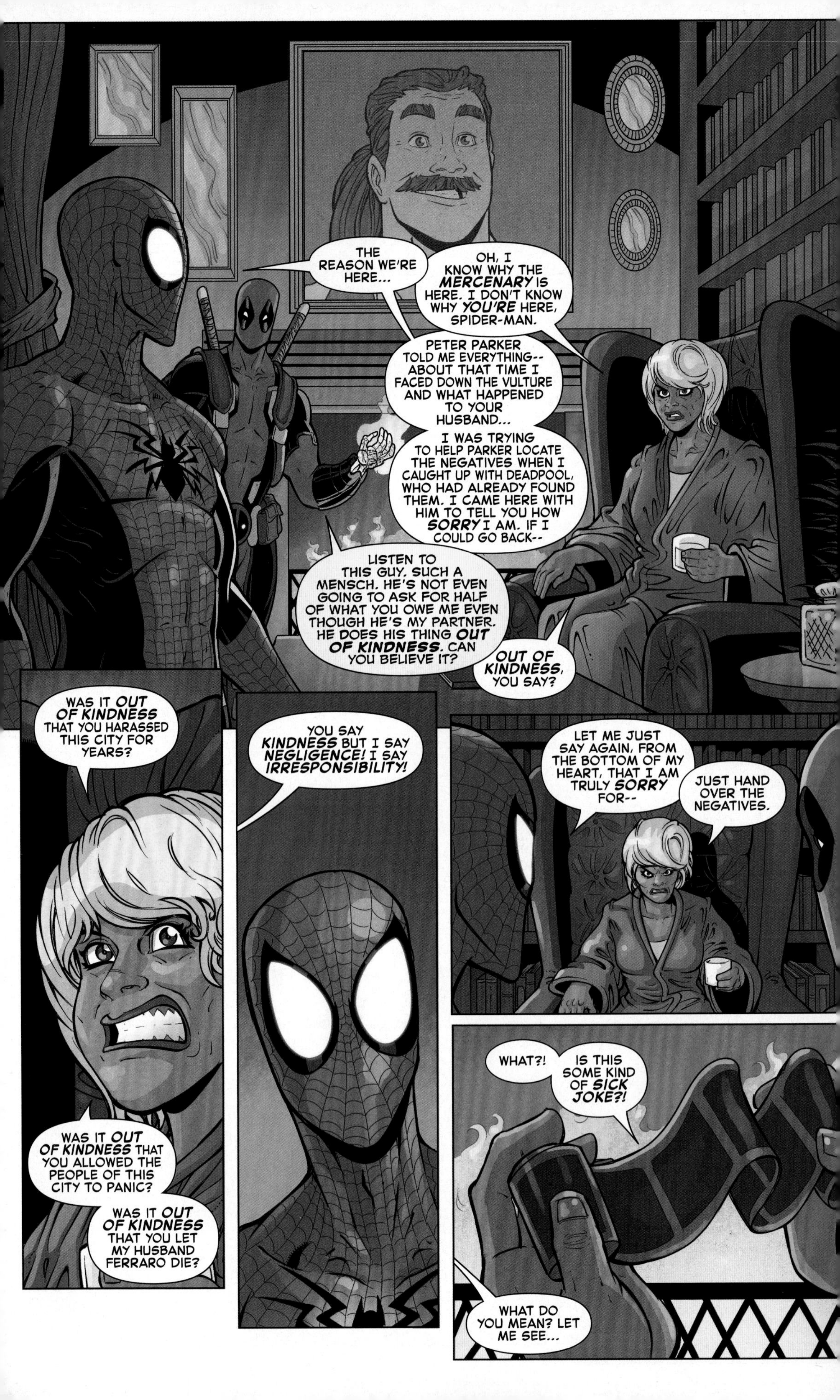

THE REASON WE'RE HERE...
OH, I KNOW WHY THE *MERCENARY* IS HERE. I DON'T KNOW WHY *YOU'RE* HERE, SPIDER-MAN.
PETER PARKER TOLD ME EVERYTHING-- ABOUT THAT TIME I FACED DOWN THE VULTURE AND WHAT HAPPENED TO YOUR HUSBAND...
I WAS TRYING TO HELP PARKER LOCATE THE NEGATIVES WHEN I CAUGHT UP WITH DEADPOOL, WHO HAD ALREADY FOUND THEM. I CAME HERE WITH HIM TO TELL YOU HOW *SORRY* I AM. IF I COULD GO BACK--
LISTEN TO THIS GUY. SUCH A MENSCH. HE'S NOT EVEN GOING TO ASK FOR HALF OF WHAT YOU OWE ME EVEN THOUGH HE'S MY PARTNER. HE DOES HIS THING *OUT OF KINDNESS*. CAN YOU BELIEVE IT?
OUT OF KINDNESS, YOU SAY?
WAS IT *OUT OF KINDNESS* THAT YOU HARASSED THIS CITY FOR YEARS?
WAS IT *OUT OF KINDNESS* THAT YOU ALLOWED THE PEOPLE OF THIS CITY TO PANIC?
WAS IT *OUT OF KINDNESS* THAT YOU LET MY HUSBAND FERRARO DIE?
YOU SAY *KINDNESS* BUT I SAY *NEGLIGENCE!* I SAY *IRRESPONSIBILITY!*
LET ME JUST SAY AGAIN, FROM THE BOTTOM OF MY HEART, THAT I AM TRULY *SORRY* FOR--
JUST HAND OVER THE NEGATIVES.
WHAT?!
IS THIS SOME KIND OF *SICK JOKE?!*
WHAT DO YOU MEAN? LET ME SEE...

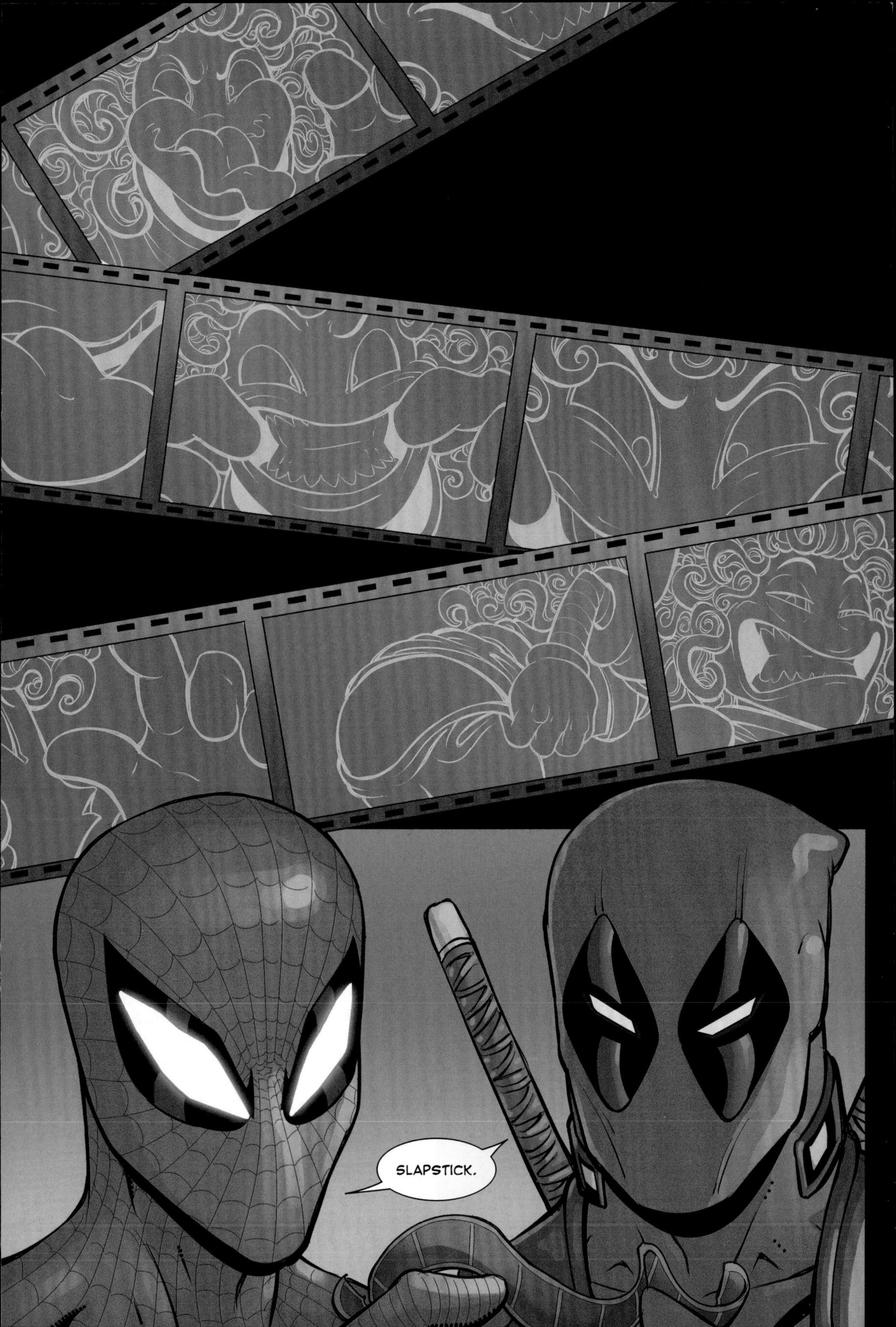
SLAPSTICK.

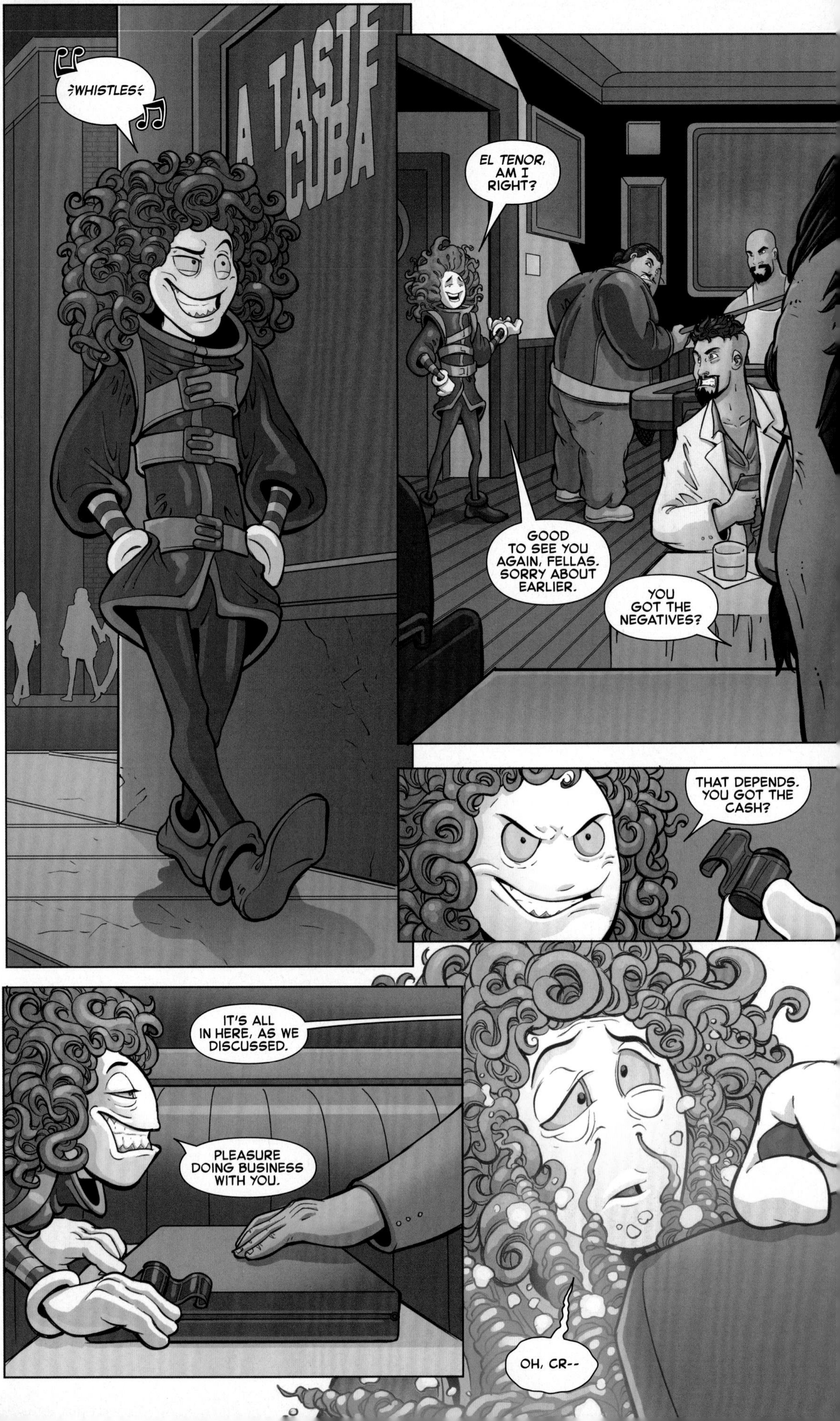

WHISTLES
A TASTE CUBA
EL TENOR, AM I RIGHT?
GOOD TO SEE YOU AGAIN, FELLAS. SORRY ABOUT EARLIER.
YOU GOT THE NEGATIVES?
THAT DEPENDS. YOU GOT THE CASH?
IT'S ALL IN HERE, AS WE DISCUSSED.
PLEASURE DOING BUSINESS WITH YOU.
OH, CR--

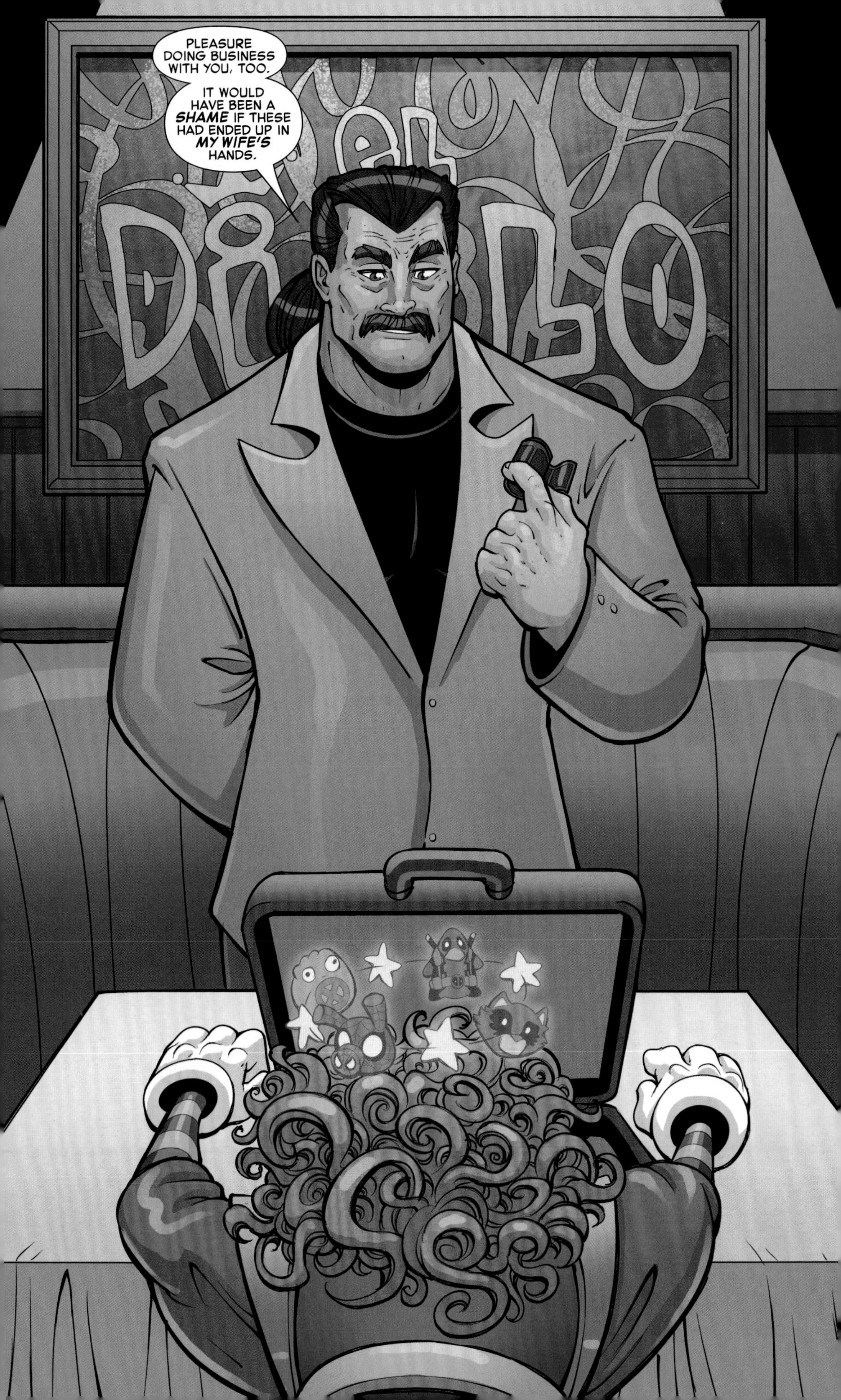
PLEASURE DOING BUSINESS WITH YOU, TOO.
IT WOULD HAVE BEEN A SHAME IF THESE HAD ENDED UP IN MY WIFE'S HANDS.

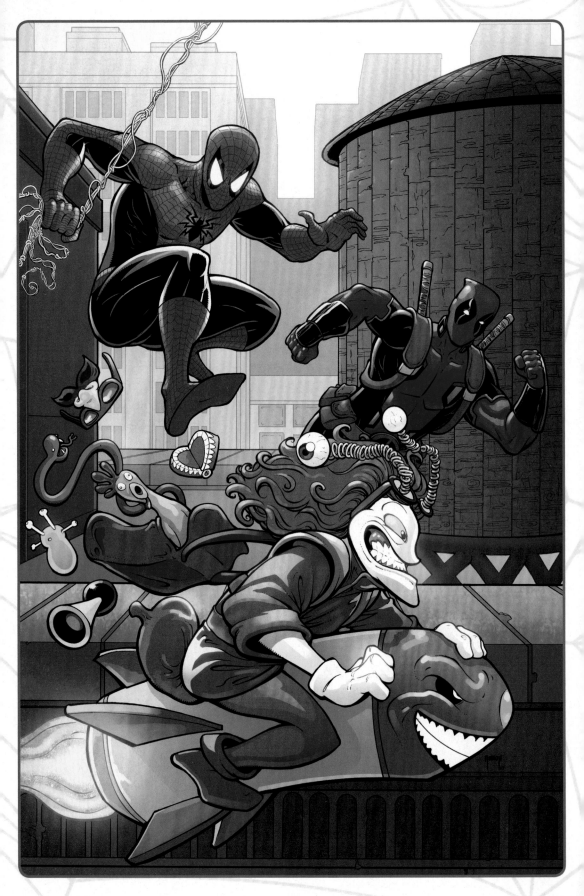

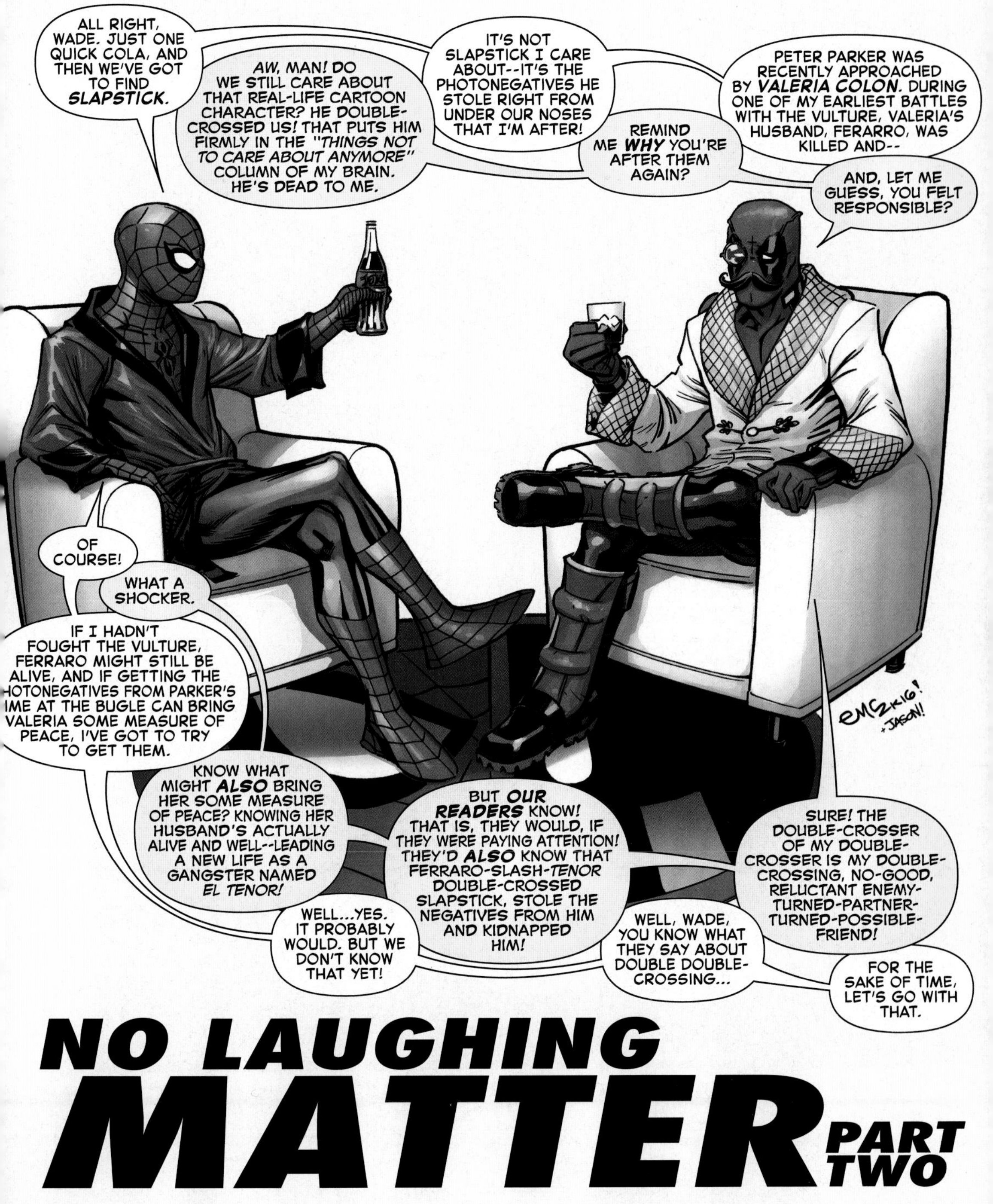
ALL RIGHT, WADE. JUST ONE QUICK COLA, AND THEN WE'VE GOT TO FIND SLAPSTICK.
AW, MAN! DO WE STILL CARE ABOUT THAT REAL-LIFE CARTOON CHARACTER? HE DOUBLE-CROSSED US! THAT PUTS HIM FIRMLY IN THE "THINGS NOT TO CARE ABOUT ANYMORE" COLUMN OF MY BRAIN. HE'S DEAD TO ME.
IT'S NOT SLAPSTICK I CARE ABOUT--IT'S THE PHOTONEGATIVES HE STOLE RIGHT FROM UNDER OUR NOSES THAT I'M AFTER!
REMIND ME WHY YOU'RE AFTER THEM AGAIN?
PETER PARKER WAS RECENTLY APPROACHED BY VALERIA COLON. DURING ONE OF MY EARLIEST BATTLES WITH THE VULTURE, VALERIA'S HUSBAND, FERARRO, WAS KILLED AND--
AND, LET ME GUESS, YOU FELT RESPONSIBLE?
OF COURSE!
WHAT A SHOCKER.
IF I HADN'T FOUGHT THE VULTURE, FERRARO MIGHT STILL BE ALIVE, AND IF GETTING THE HOTONEGATIVES FROM PARKER'S IME AT THE BUGLE CAN BRING VALERIA SOME MEASURE OF PEACE, I'VE GOT TO TRY TO GET THEM.
KNOW WHAT MIGHT ALSO BRING HER SOME MEASURE OF PEACE? KNOWING HER HUSBAND'S ACTUALLY ALIVE AND WELL--LEADING A NEW LIFE AS A GANGSTER NAMED EL TENOR!
WELL...YES. IT PROBABLY WOULD. BUT WE DON'T KNOW THAT YET!
BUT OUR READERS KNOW! THAT IS, THEY WOULD, IF THEY WERE PAYING ATTENTION! THEY'D ALSO KNOW THAT FERRARO-SLASH-TENOR DOUBLE-CROSSED SLAPSTICK, STOLE THE NEGATIVES FROM HIM AND KIDNAPPED HIM!
WELL, WADE, YOU KNOW WHAT THEY SAY ABOUT DOUBLE DOUBLE-CROSSING...
SURE! THE DOUBLE-CROSSER OF MY DOUBLE-CROSSER IS MY DOUBLE-CROSSING, NO-GOOD, RELUCTANT ENEMY-TURNED-PARTNER-TURNED-POSSIBLE-FRIEND!
FOR THE SAKE OF TIME, LET'S GO WITH THAT.

NO LAUGHING MATTER PART TWO

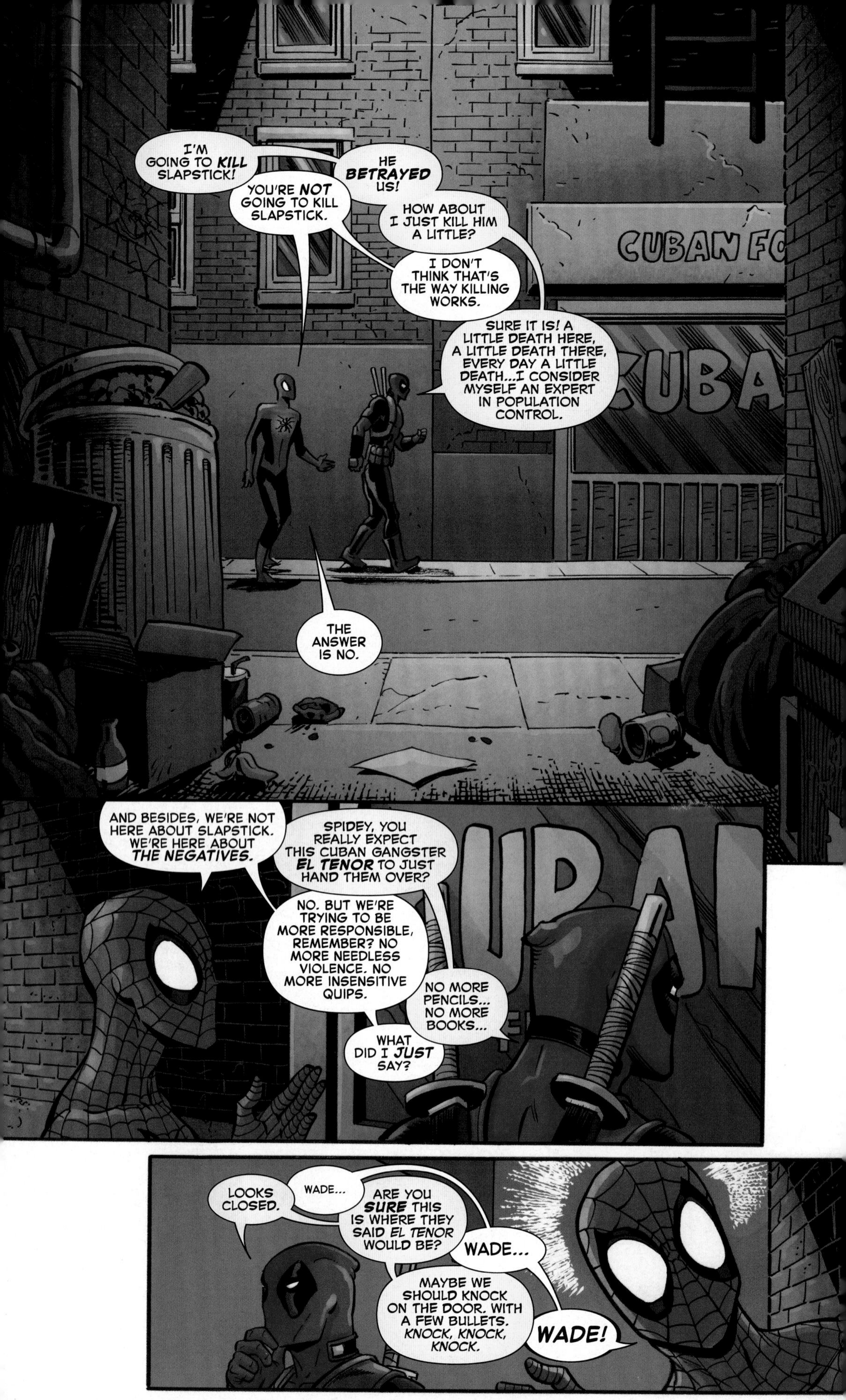
I'M GOING TO KILL SLAPSTICK!
HE BETRAYED US!
YOU'RE NOT GOING TO KILL SLAPSTICK.
HOW ABOUT I JUST KILL HIM A LITTLE?
I DON'T THINK THAT'S THE WAY KILLING WORKS.
SURE IT IS! A LITTLE DEATH HERE, A LITTLE DEATH THERE, EVERY DAY A LITTLE DEATH...I CONSIDER MYSELF AN EXPERT IN POPULATION CONTROL.
THE ANSWER IS NO.
CUBAN FO
CUBA
AND BESIDES, WE'RE NOT HERE ABOUT SLAPSTICK. WE'RE HERE ABOUT THE NEGATIVES.
SPIDEY, YOU REALLY EXPECT THIS CUBAN GANGSTER EL TENOR TO JUST HAND THEM OVER?
NO. BUT WE'RE TRYING TO BE MORE RESPONSIBLE, REMEMBER? NO MORE NEEDLESS VIOLENCE. NO MORE INSENSITIVE QUIPS.
NO MORE PENCILS... NO MORE BOOKS...
WHAT DID I JUST SAY?
LOOKS CLOSED.
WADE...
ARE YOU SURE THIS IS WHERE THEY SAID EL TENOR WOULD BE?
WADE...
MAYBE WE SHOULD KNOCK ON THE DOOR. WITH A FEW BULLETS. KNOCK, KNOCK, KNOCK.
WADE!

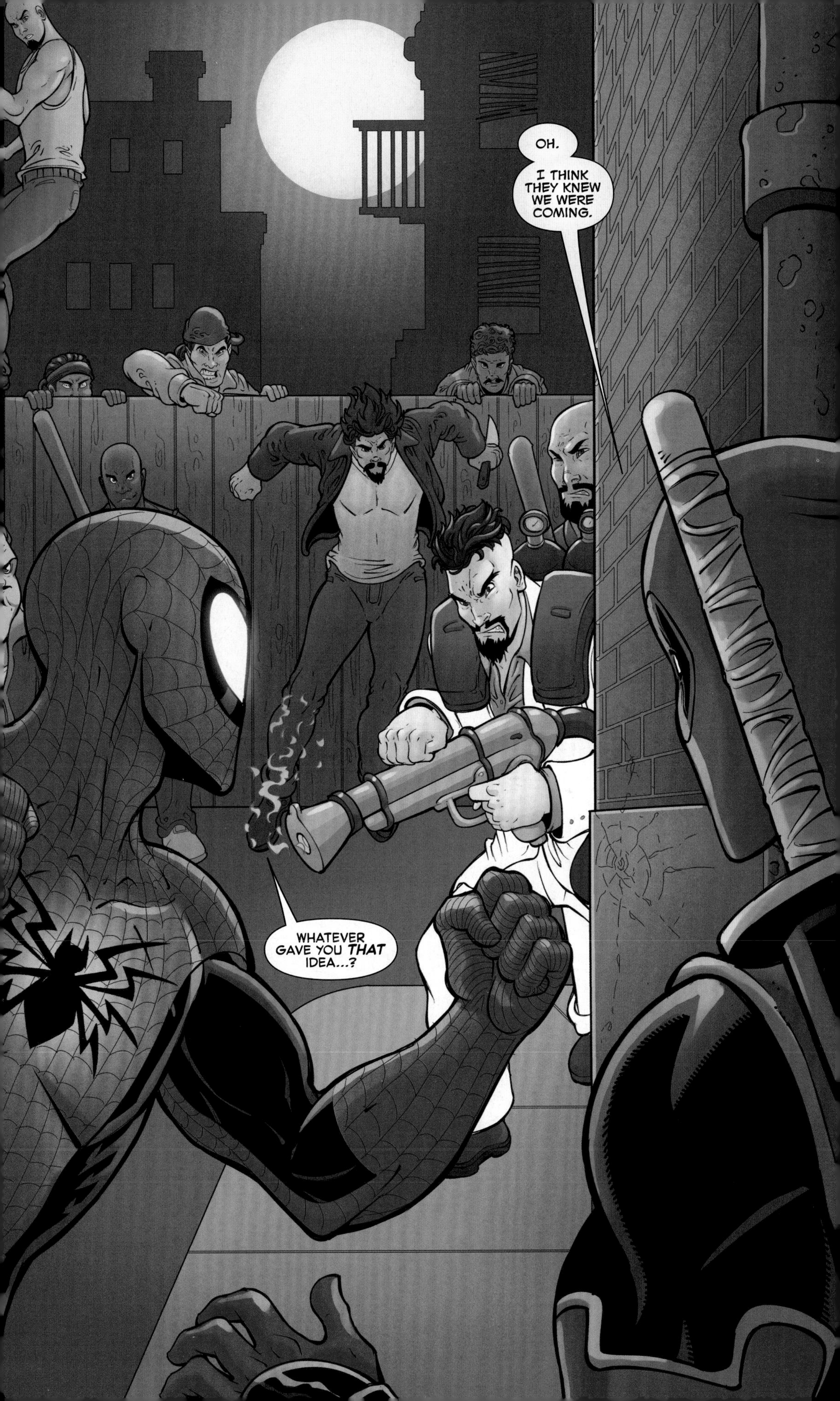

OH.
I THINK THEY KNEW WE WERE COMING.
WHATEVER GAVE YOU *THAT* IDEA...?

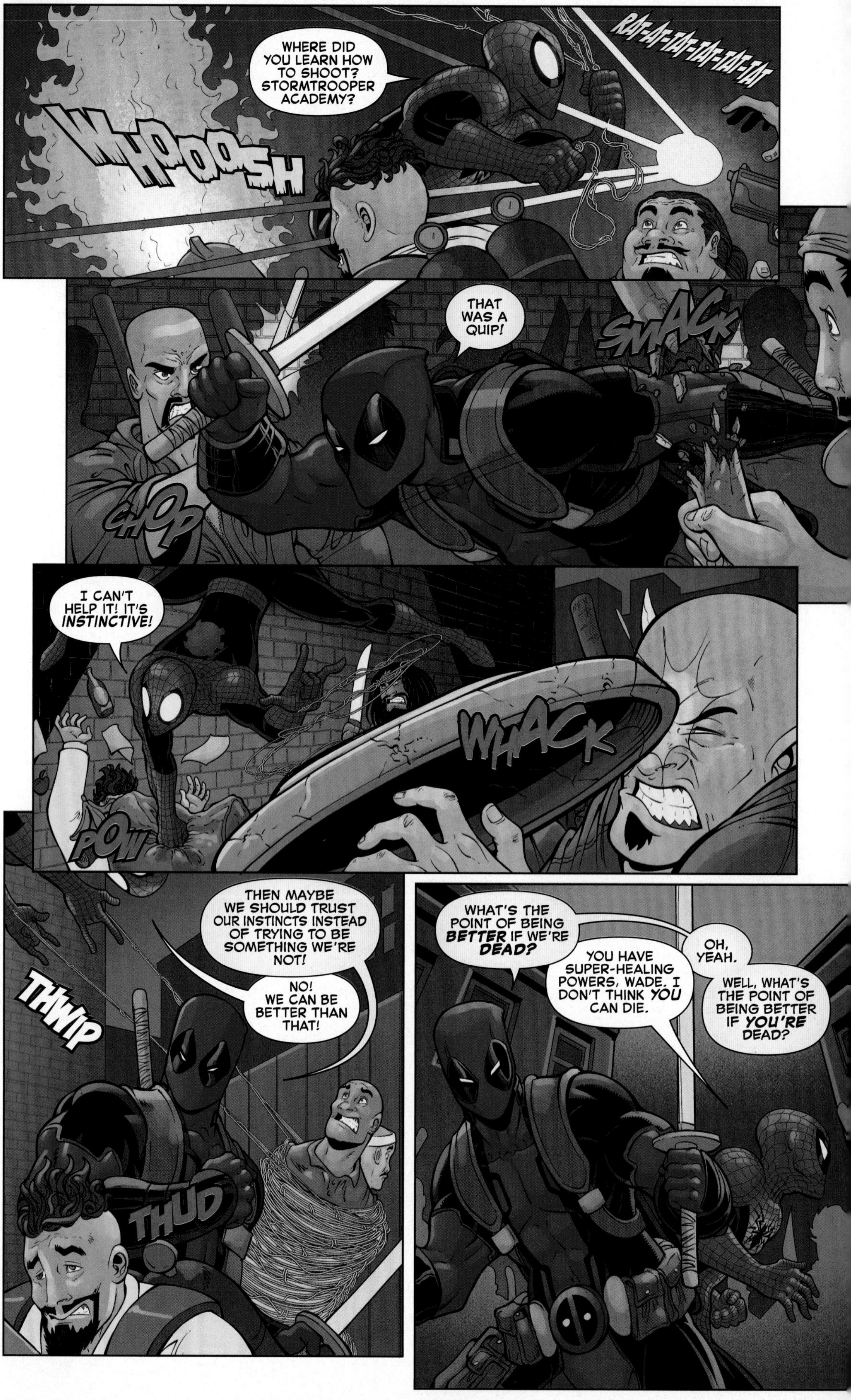
WHERE DID YOU LEARN HOW TO SHOOT? STORMTROOPER ACADEMY?
RAT-AT-TAT-TAT-TAT-TAT
WHOOOSH
THAT WAS A QUIP!
SMACK
CHOP
I CAN'T HELP IT! IT'S INSTINCTIVE!
WHACK
POW
THEN MAYBE WE SHOULD TRUST OUR INSTINCTS INSTEAD OF TRYING TO BE SOMETHING WE'RE NOT!
NO! WE CAN BE BETTER THAN THAT!
THWIP
THUD
WHAT'S THE POINT OF BEING BETTER IF WE'RE DEAD?
YOU HAVE SUPER-HEALING POWERS, WADE. I DON'T THINK YOU CAN DIE.
OH, YEAH.
WELL, WHAT'S THE POINT OF BEING BETTER IF YOU'RE DEAD?

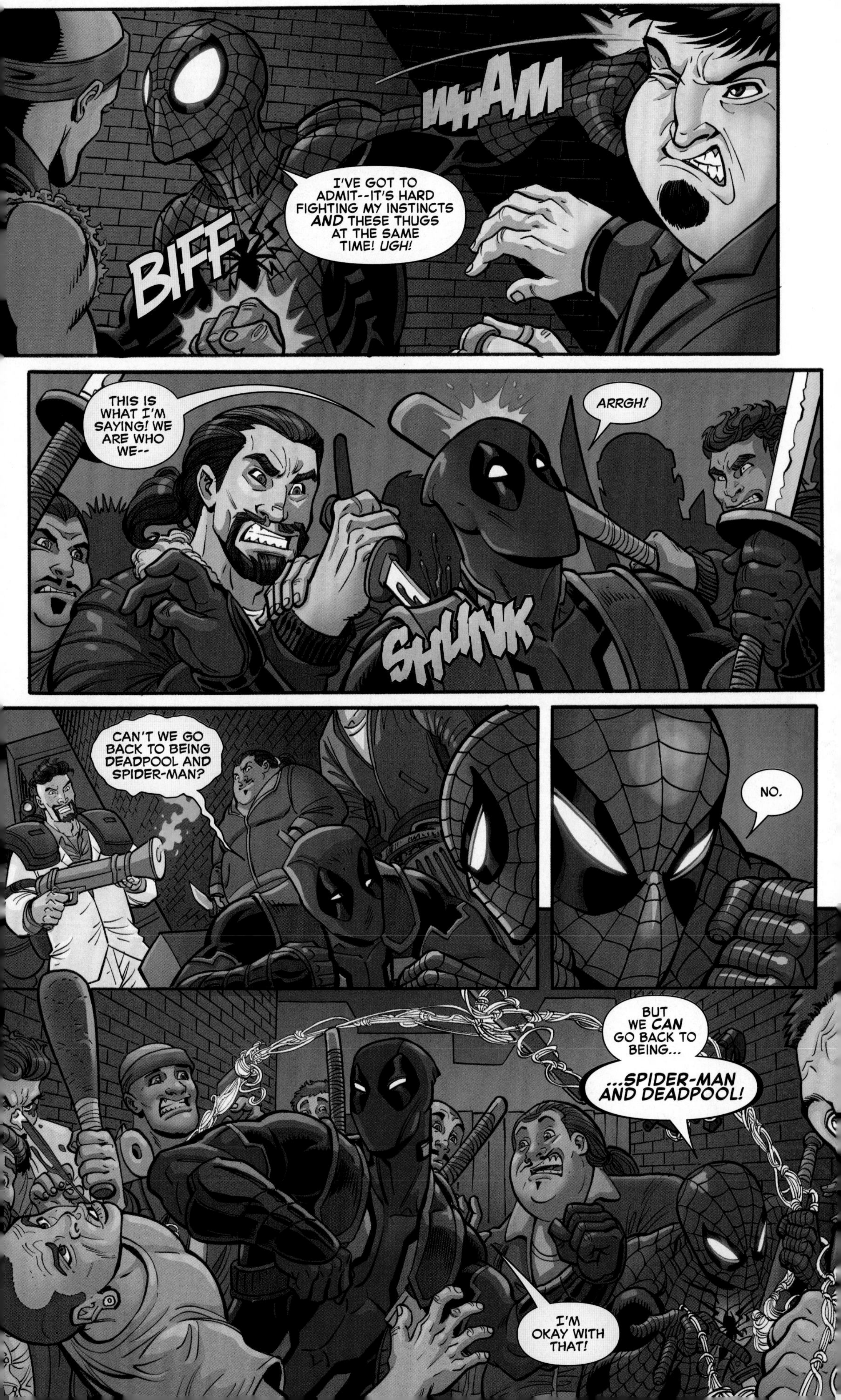
WHAM
I'VE GOT TO ADMIT--IT'S HARD FIGHTING MY INSTINCTS AND THESE THUGS AT THE SAME TIME! UGH!
BIFF
THIS IS WHAT I'M SAYING! WE ARE WHO WE--
ARRGH!
SHUNK
CAN'T WE GO BACK TO BEING DEADPOOL AND SPIDER-MAN?
NO.
BUT WE CAN GO BACK TO BEING...
...SPIDER-MAN AND DEADPOOL!
I'M OKAY WITH THAT!

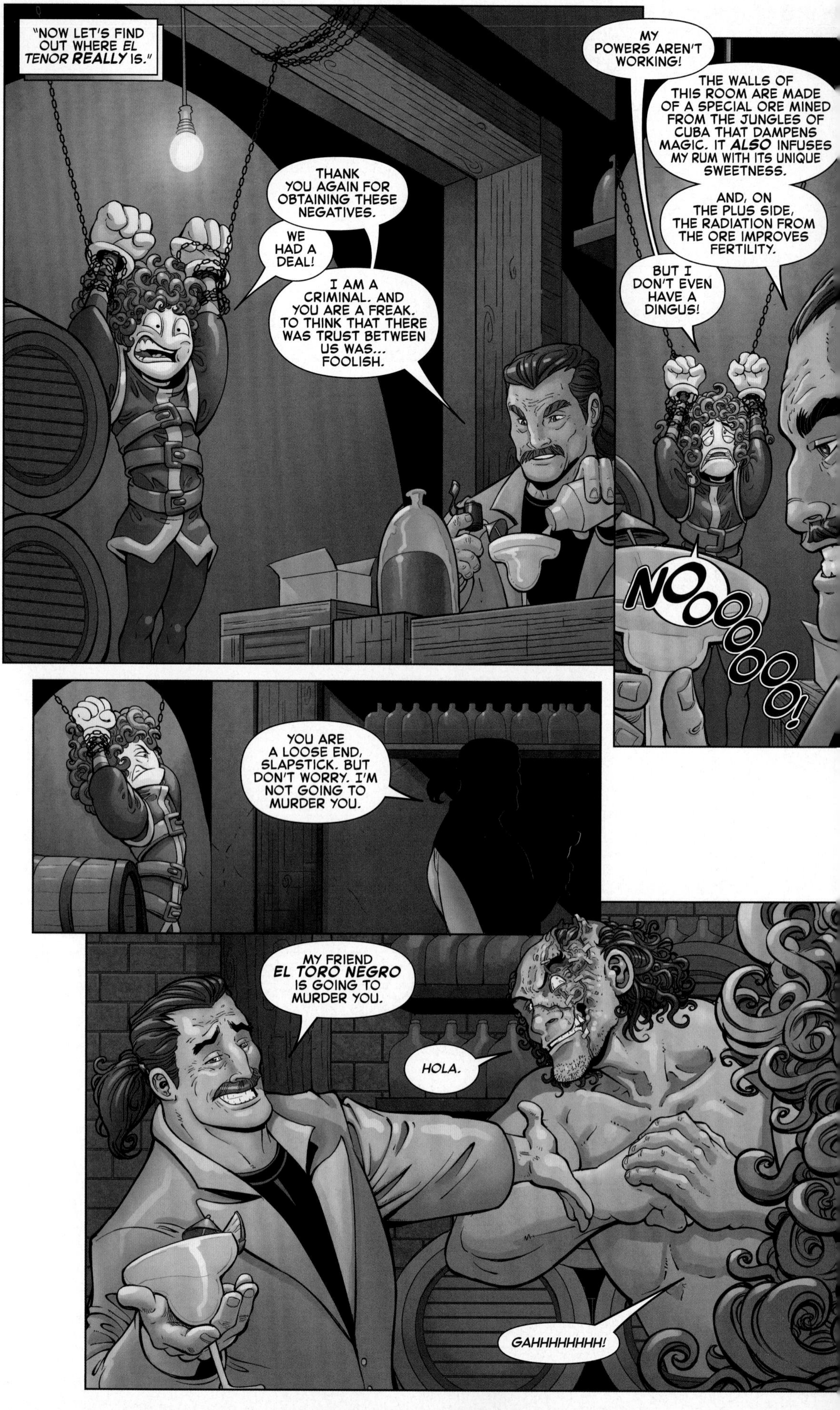

"NOW LET'S FIND OUT WHERE EL TENOR REALLY IS."
THANK YOU AGAIN FOR OBTAINING THESE NEGATIVES.
WE HAD A DEAL!
I AM A CRIMINAL. AND YOU ARE A FREAK. TO THINK THAT THERE WAS TRUST BETWEEN US WAS... FOOLISH.
MY POWERS AREN'T WORKING!
THE WALLS OF THIS ROOM ARE MADE OF A SPECIAL ORE MINED FROM THE JUNGLES OF CUBA THAT DAMPENS MAGIC. IT ALSO INFUSES MY RUM WITH ITS UNIQUE SWEETNESS.
AND, ON THE PLUS SIDE, THE RADIATION FROM THE ORE IMPROVES FERTILITY.
BUT I DON'T EVEN HAVE A DINGUS!
NOOOOOOO!
YOU ARE A LOOSE END, SLAPSTICK. BUT DON'T WORRY. I'M NOT GOING TO MURDER YOU.
MY FRIEND EL TORO NEGRO IS GOING TO MURDER YOU.
HOLA.
GAHHHHHHHH!

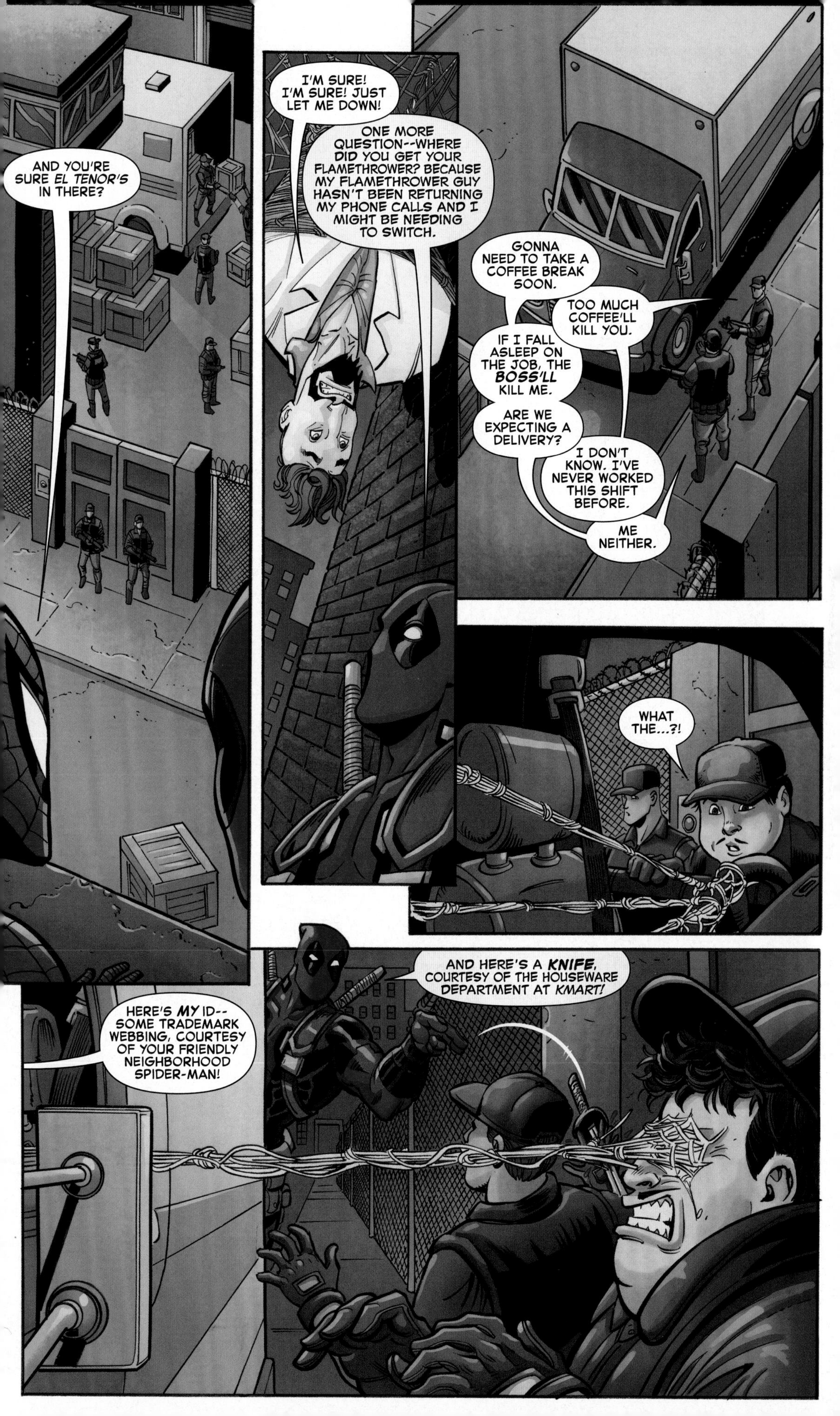
AND YOU'RE SURE EL TENOR'S IN THERE?
I'M SURE! I'M SURE! JUST LET ME DOWN!
ONE MORE QUESTION--WHERE DID YOU GET YOUR FLAMETHROWER? BECAUSE MY FLAMETHROWER GUY HASN'T BEEN RETURNING MY PHONE CALLS AND I MIGHT BE NEEDING TO SWITCH.
GONNA NEED TO TAKE A COFFEE BREAK SOON.
TOO MUCH COFFEE'LL KILL YOU.
IF I FALL ASLEEP ON THE JOB, THE BOSS'LL KILL ME.
ARE WE EXPECTING A DELIVERY?
I DON'T KNOW. I'VE NEVER WORKED THIS SHIFT BEFORE.
ME NEITHER.
WHAT THE...?!
HERE'S MY ID--SOME TRADEMARK WEBBING, COURTESY OF YOUR FRIENDLY NEIGHBORHOOD SPIDER-MAN!
AND HERE'S A KNIFE, COURTESY OF THE HOUSEWARE DEPARTMENT AT KMART!

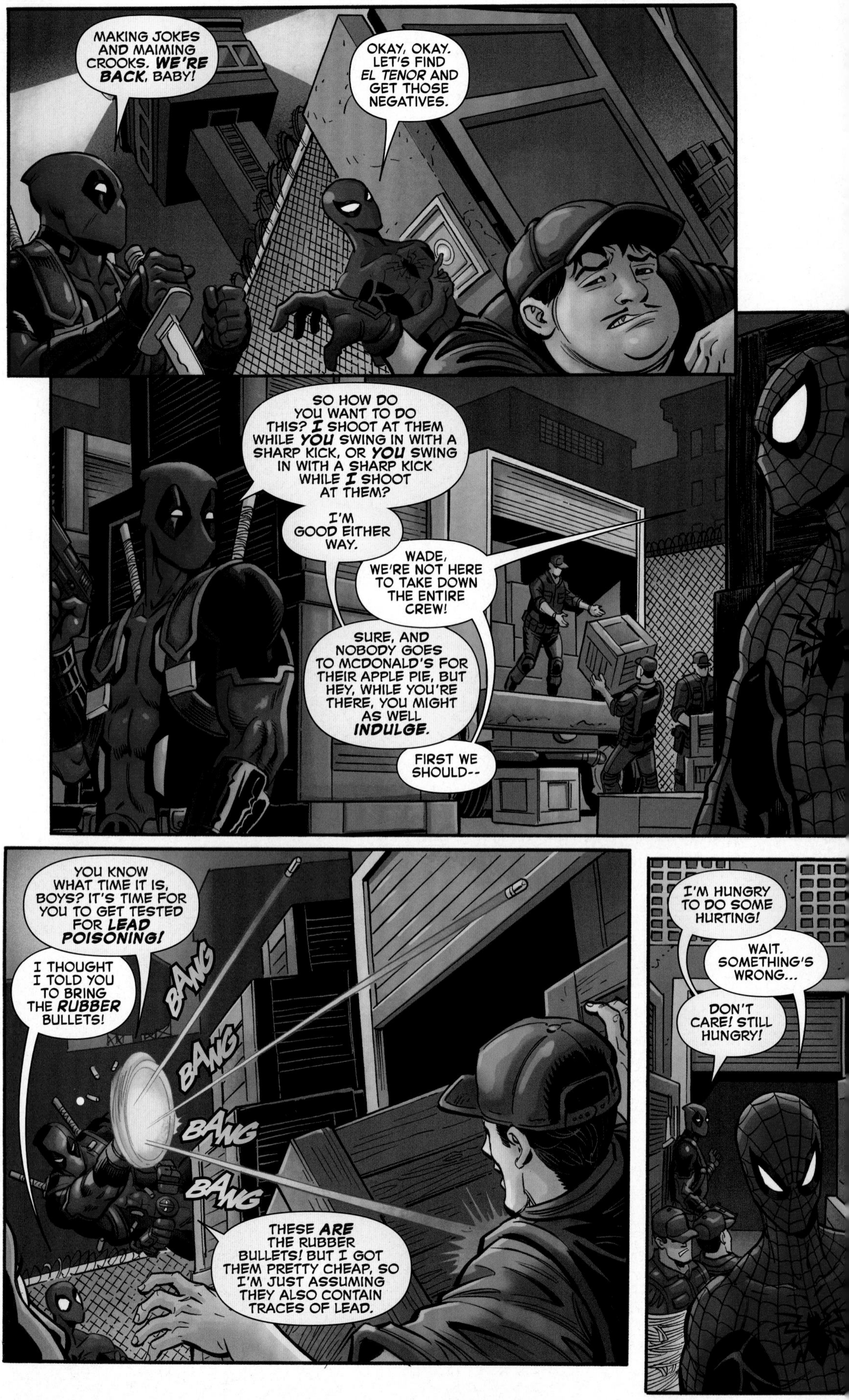
MAKING JOKES AND MAIMING CROOKS. WE'RE BACK, BABY!
OKAY, OKAY. LET'S FIND EL TENOR AND GET THOSE NEGATIVES.
SO HOW DO YOU WANT TO DO THIS? I SHOOT AT THEM WHILE YOU SWING IN WITH A SHARP KICK, OR YOU SWING IN WITH A SHARP KICK WHILE I SHOOT AT THEM?
I'M GOOD EITHER WAY.
WADE, WE'RE NOT HERE TO TAKE DOWN THE ENTIRE CREW!
SURE, AND NOBODY GOES TO MCDONALD'S FOR THEIR APPLE PIE, BUT HEY, WHILE YOU'RE THERE, YOU MIGHT AS WELL INDULGE.
FIRST WE SHOULD--
YOU KNOW WHAT TIME IT IS, BOYS? IT'S TIME FOR YOU TO GET TESTED FOR LEAD POISONING!
I THOUGHT I TOLD YOU TO BRING THE RUBBER BULLETS!
BANG
BANG
BANG
BANG
THESE ARE THE RUBBER BULLETS! BUT I GOT THEM PRETTY CHEAP, SO I'M JUST ASSUMING THEY ALSO CONTAIN TRACES OF LEAD.
I'M HUNGRY TO DO SOME HURTING!
WAIT. SOMETHING'S WRONG...
DON'T CARE! STILL HUNGRY!

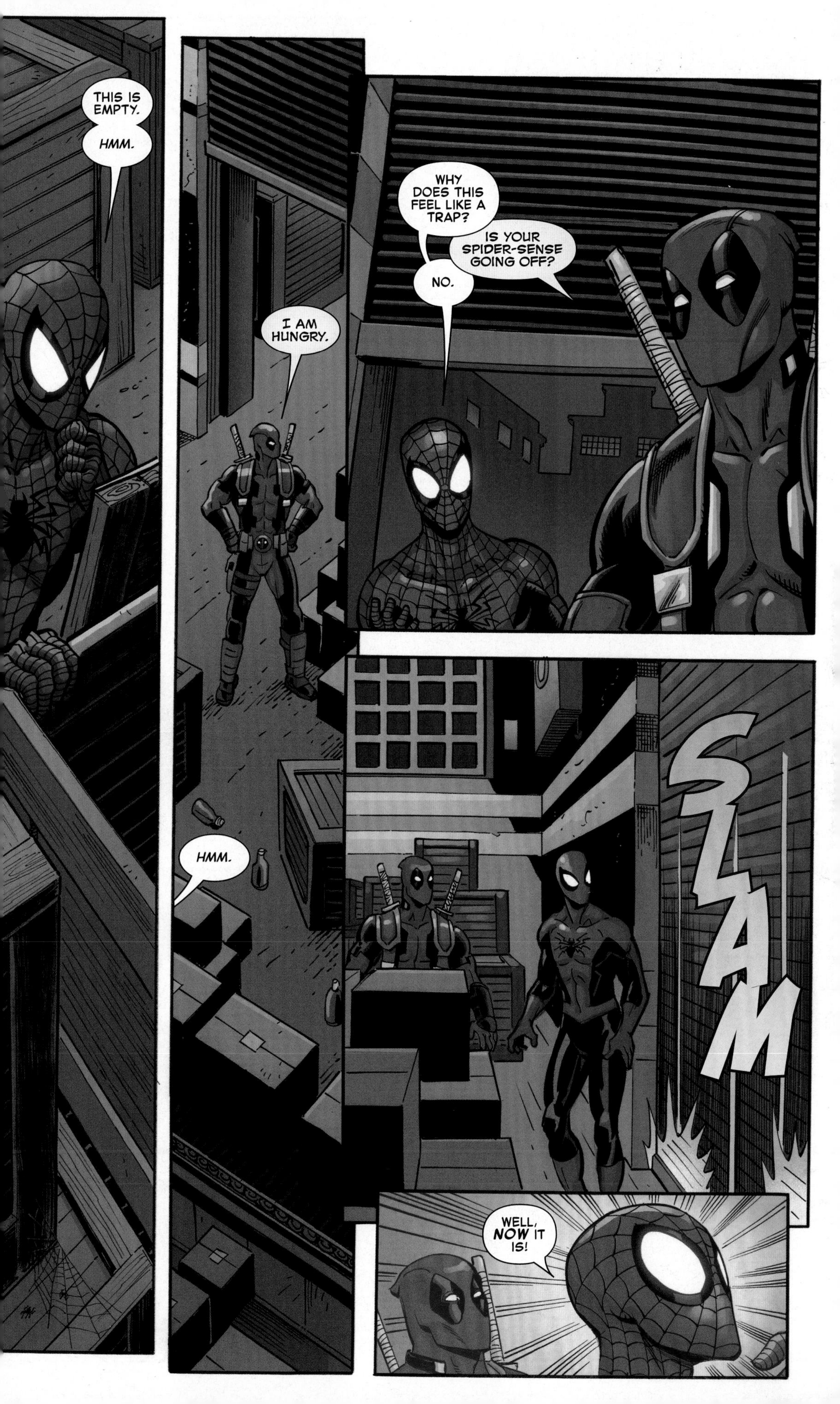
THIS IS EMPTY.
HMM.
I AM HUNGRY.
WHY DOES THIS FEEL LIKE A TRAP?
IS YOUR SPIDER-SENSE GOING OFF?
NO.
HMM.
SLAM
WELL, NOW IT IS!

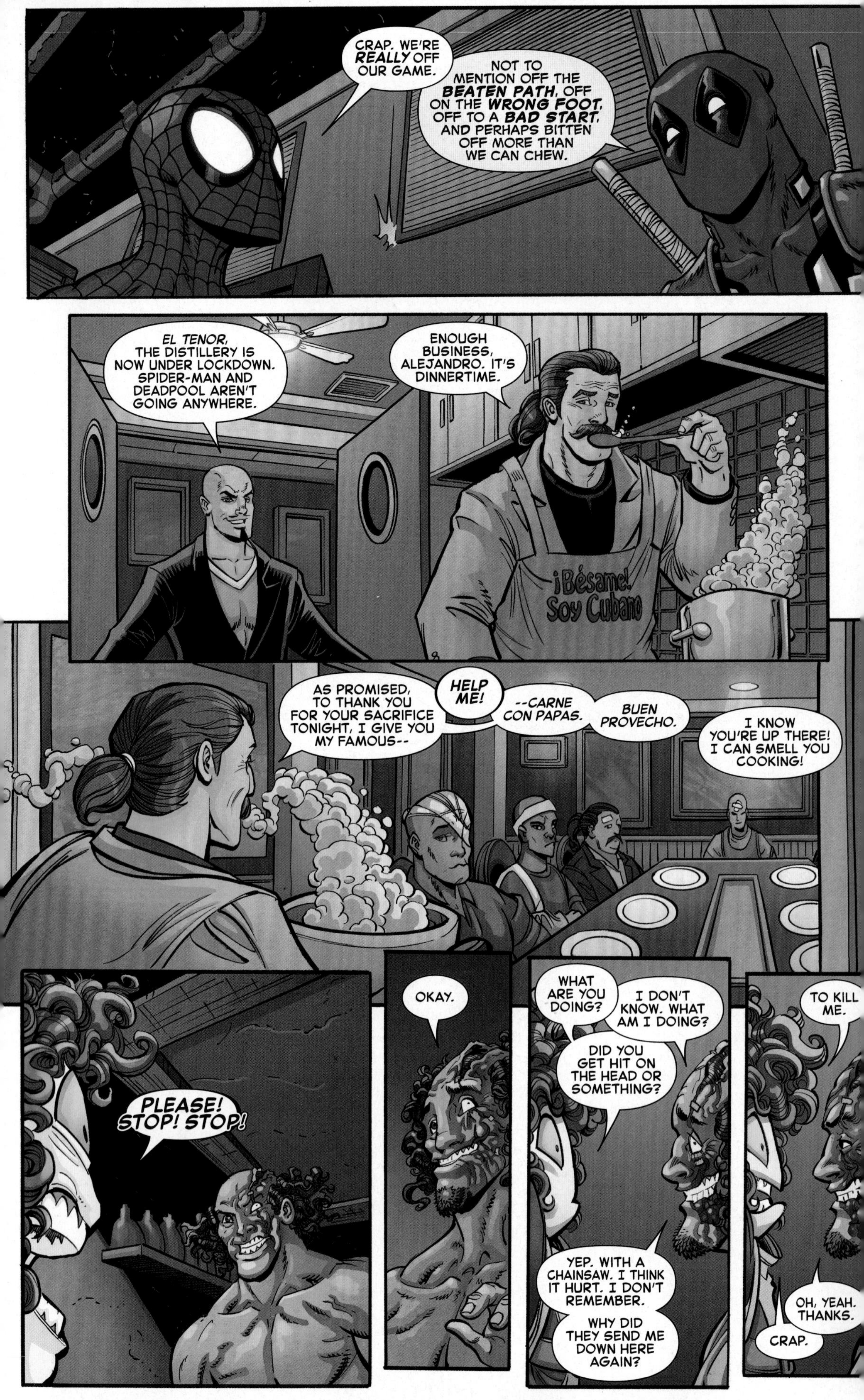

CRAP. WE'RE REALLY OFF OUR GAME.
NOT TO MENTION OFF THE BEATEN PATH, OFF ON THE WRONG FOOT, OFF TO A BAD START, AND PERHAPS BITTEN OFF MORE THAN WE CAN CHEW.
EL TENOR, THE DISTILLERY IS NOW UNDER LOCKDOWN. SPIDER-MAN AND DEADPOOL AREN'T GOING ANYWHERE.
ENOUGH BUSINESS, ALEJANDRO. IT'S DINNERTIME.
¡Bésame! Soy Cubano
AS PROMISED, TO THANK YOU FOR YOUR SACRIFICE TONIGHT, I GIVE YOU MY FAMOUS--
HELP ME!
--CARNE CON PAPAS.
BUEN PROVECHO.
I KNOW YOU'RE UP THERE! I CAN SMELL YOU COOKING!
PLEASE! STOP! STOP!
OKAY.
WHAT ARE YOU DOING?
I DON'T KNOW. WHAT AM I DOING?
DID YOU GET HIT ON THE HEAD OR SOMETHING?
YEP. WITH A CHAINSAW. I THINK IT HURT. I DON'T REMEMBER.
WHY DID THEY SEND ME DOWN HERE AGAIN?
TO KILL ME.
OH, YEAH. THANKS.
CRAP.

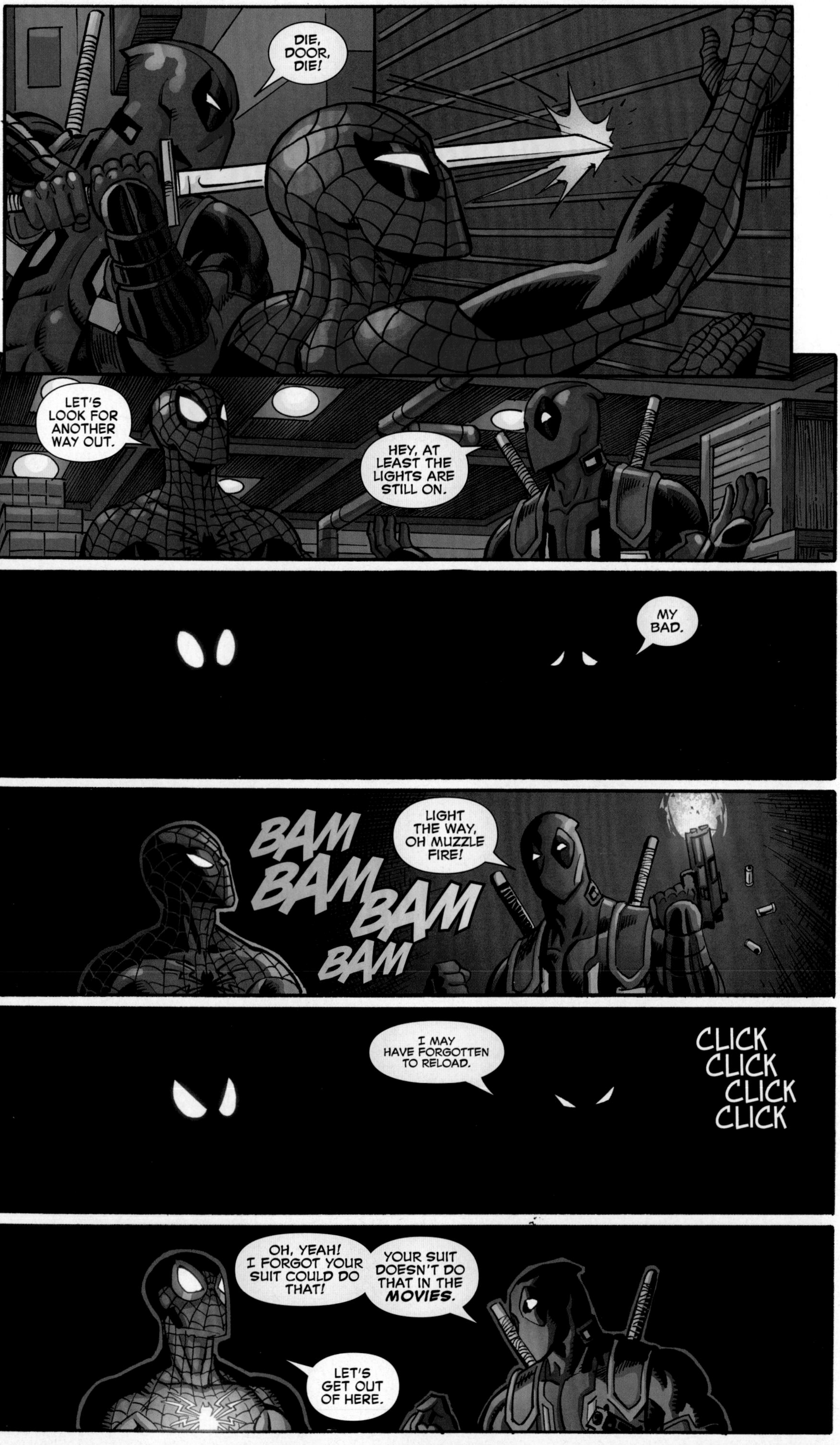
DIE, DOOR, DIE!
LET'S LOOK FOR ANOTHER WAY OUT.
HEY, AT LEAST THE LIGHTS ARE STILL ON.
MY BAD.
BAM BAM BAM BAM
LIGHT THE WAY, OH MUZZLE FIRE!
I MAY HAVE FORGOTTEN TO RELOAD.
CLICK CLICK CLICK CLICK
OH, YEAH! I FORGOT YOUR SUIT COULD DO THAT!
YOUR SUIT DOESN'T DO THAT IN THE MOVIES.
LET'S GET OUT OF HERE.

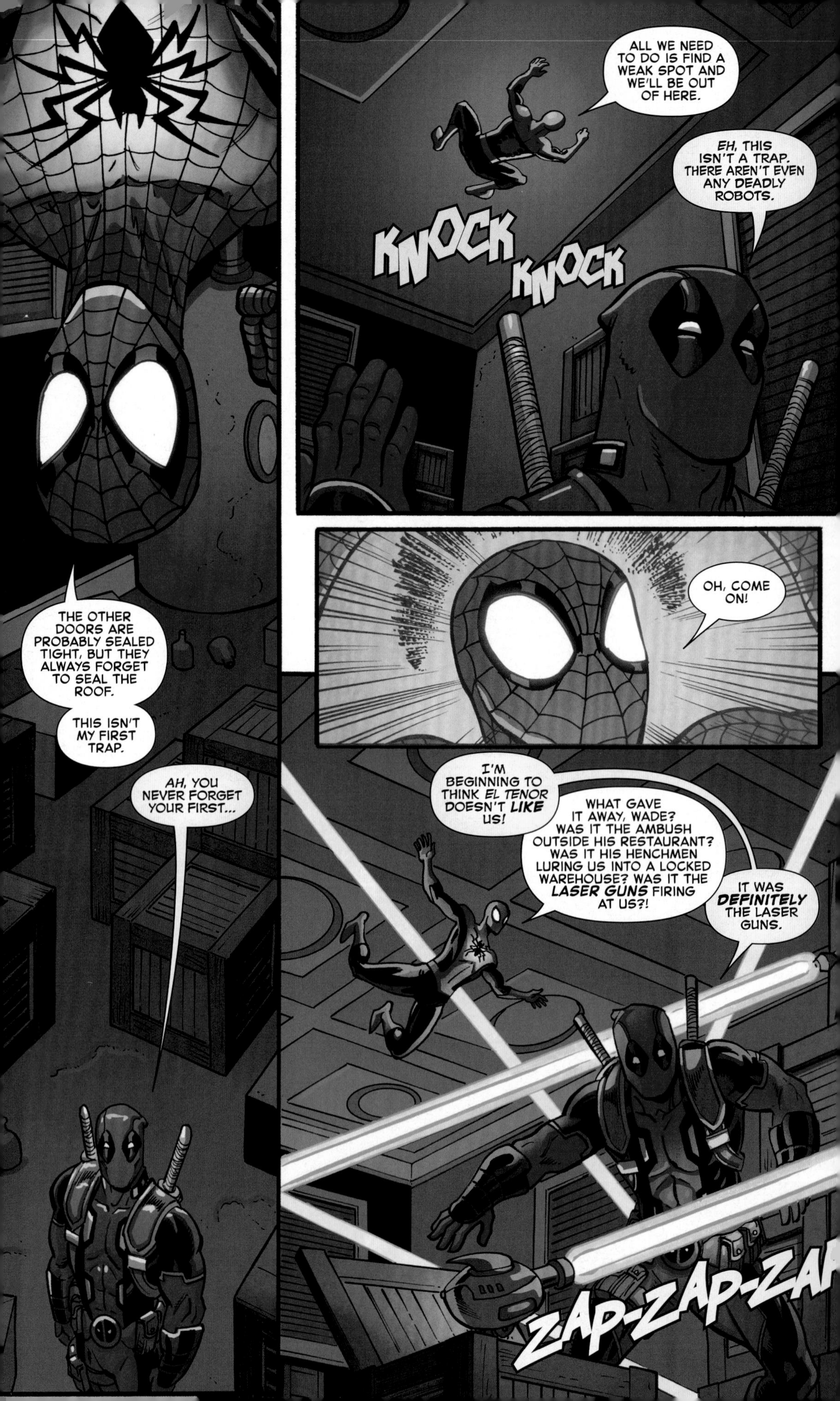
THE OTHER DOORS ARE PROBABLY SEALED TIGHT, BUT THEY ALWAYS FORGET TO SEAL THE ROOF.
THIS ISN'T MY FIRST TRAP.
AH, YOU NEVER FORGET YOUR FIRST...
ALL WE NEED TO DO IS FIND A WEAK SPOT AND WE'LL BE OUT OF HERE.
EH, THIS ISN'T A TRAP. THERE AREN'T EVEN ANY DEADLY ROBOTS.
KNOCK
KNOCK
OH, COME ON!
I'M BEGINNING TO THINK EL TENOR DOESN'T LIKE US!
WHAT GAVE IT AWAY, WADE? WAS IT THE AMBUSH OUTSIDE HIS RESTAURANT? WAS IT HIS HENCHMEN LURING US INTO A LOCKED WAREHOUSE? WAS IT THE LASER GUNS FIRING AT US?!
IT WAS DEFINITELY THE LASER GUNS.
ZAP-ZAP-ZAP

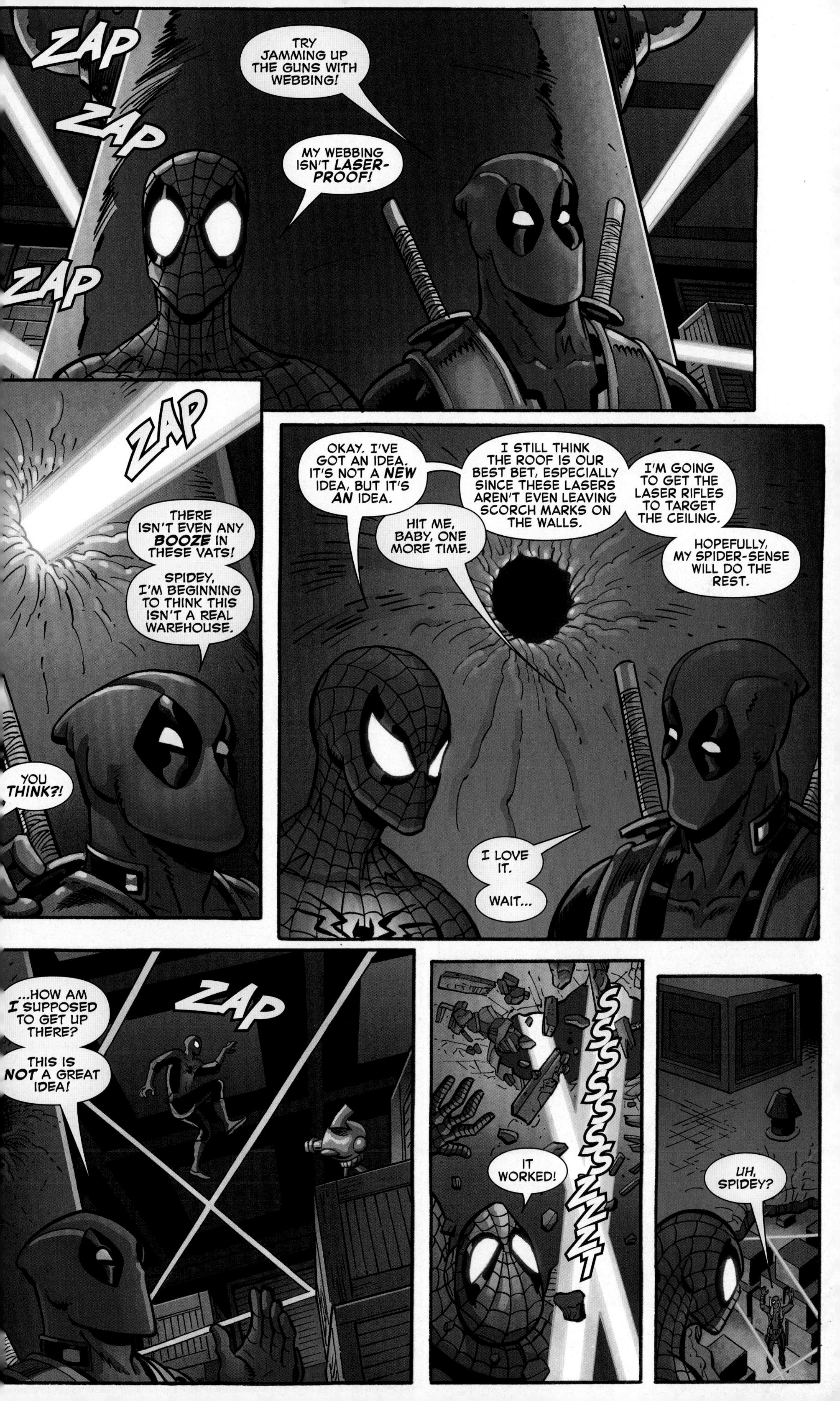
ZAP
ZAP
ZAP
TRY JAMMING UP THE GUNS WITH WEBBING!
MY WEBBING ISN'T LASER-PROOF!
ZAP
THERE ISN'T EVEN ANY BOOZE IN THESE VATS!
SPIDEY, I'M BEGINNING TO THINK THIS ISN'T A REAL WAREHOUSE.
YOU THINK?!
OKAY. I'VE GOT AN IDEA. IT'S NOT A NEW IDEA, BUT IT'S AN IDEA.
HIT ME, BABY, ONE MORE TIME.
I STILL THINK THE ROOF IS OUR BEST BET, ESPECIALLY SINCE THESE LASERS AREN'T EVEN LEAVING SCORCH MARKS ON THE WALLS.
I'M GOING TO GET THE LASER RIFLES TO TARGET THE CEILING.
HOPEFULLY, MY SPIDER-SENSE WILL DO THE REST.
I LOVE IT.
WAIT...
...HOW AM I SUPPOSED TO GET UP THERE?
THIS IS NOT A GREAT IDEA!
ZAP
SSSSSSZZZT
IT WORKED!
UH, SPIDEY?

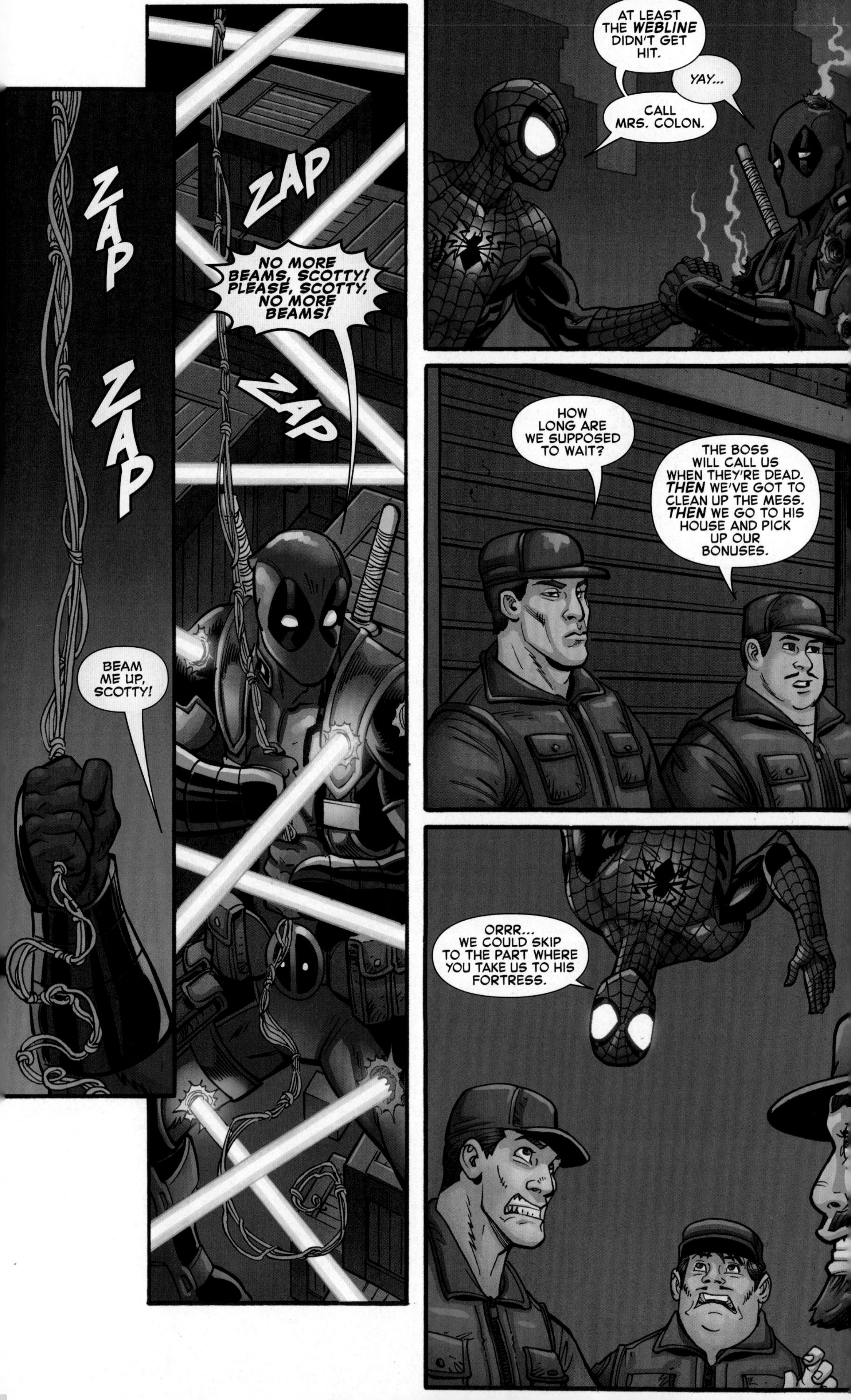
ZAP
ZAP
ZAP
NO MORE BEAMS, SCOTTY! PLEASE, SCOTTY, NO MORE BEAMS!
ZAP
BEAM ME UP, SCOTTY!
AT LEAST THE WEBLINE DIDN'T GET HIT.
YAY...
CALL MRS. COLON.
HOW LONG ARE WE SUPPOSED TO WAIT?
THE BOSS WILL CALL US WHEN THEY'RE DEAD. THEN WE'VE GOT TO CLEAN UP THE MESS. THEN WE GO TO HIS HOUSE AND PICK UP OUR BONUSES.
ORRR... WE COULD SKIP TO THE PART WHERE YOU TAKE US TO HIS FORTRESS.

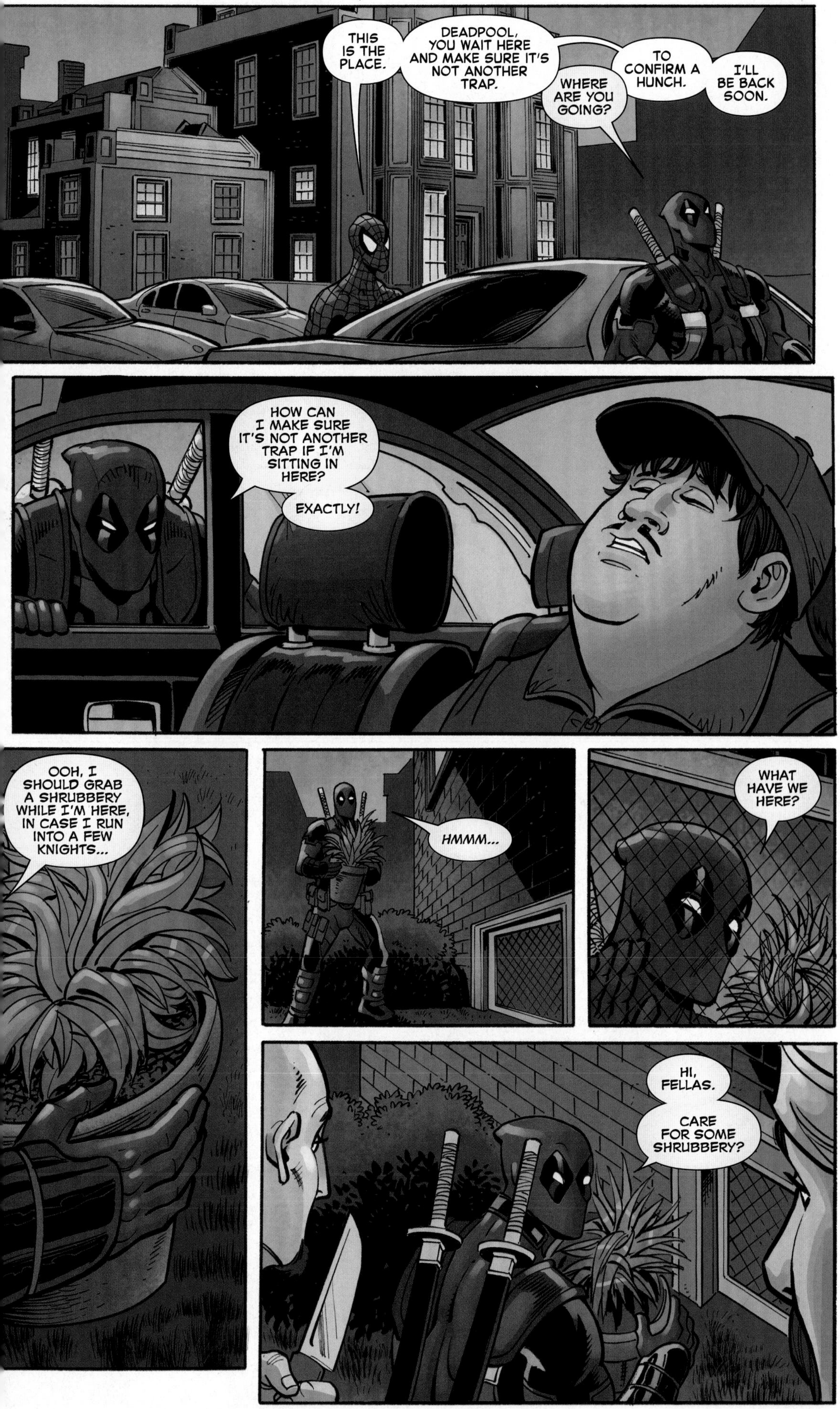
THIS IS THE PLACE.
DEADPOOL, YOU WAIT HERE AND MAKE SURE IT'S NOT ANOTHER TRAP.
WHERE ARE YOU GOING?
TO CONFIRM A HUNCH.
I'LL BE BACK SOON.
HOW CAN I MAKE SURE IT'S NOT ANOTHER TRAP IF I'M SITTING IN HERE?
EXACTLY!
OOH, I SHOULD GRAB A SHRUBBERY WHILE I'M HERE, IN CASE I RUN INTO A FEW KNIGHTS...
HMMM...
WHAT HAVE WE HERE?
HI, FELLAS.
CARE FOR SOME SHRUBBERY?

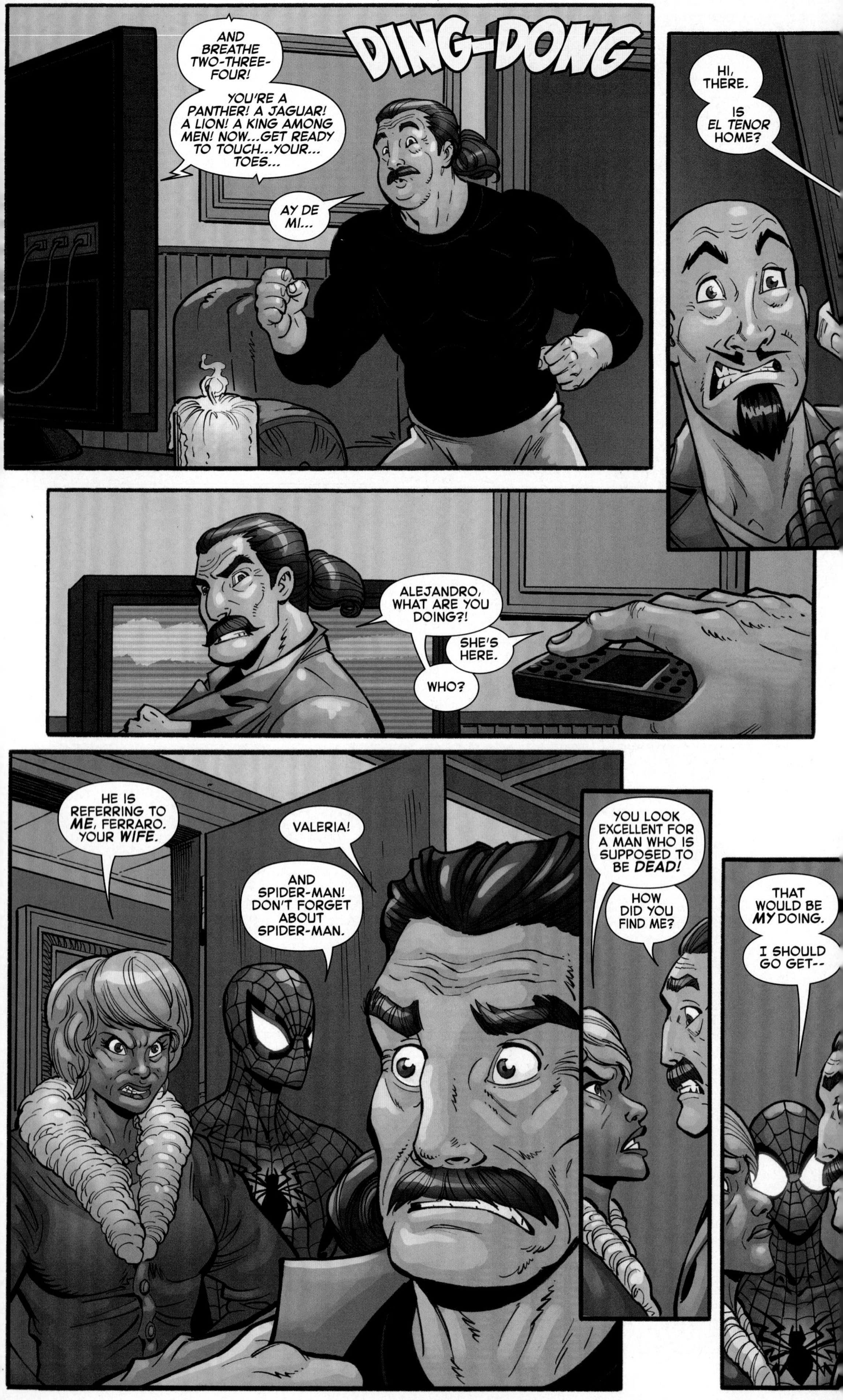
DING-DONG
AND BREATHE TWO-THREE-FOUR!
YOU'RE A PANTHER! A JAGUAR! A LION! A KING AMONG MEN! NOW...GET READY TO TOUCH...YOUR... TOES...
AY DE MI...
HI, THERE.
IS EL TENOR HOME?
ALEJANDRO, WHAT ARE YOU DOING?!
SHE'S HERE.
WHO?
HE IS REFERRING TO ME, FERRARO. YOUR WIFE.
VALERIA!
AND SPIDER-MAN! DON'T FORGET ABOUT SPIDER-MAN.
YOU LOOK EXCELLENT FOR A MAN WHO IS SUPPOSED TO BE DEAD!
HOW DID YOU FIND ME?
THAT WOULD BE MY DOING.
I SHOULD GO GET--

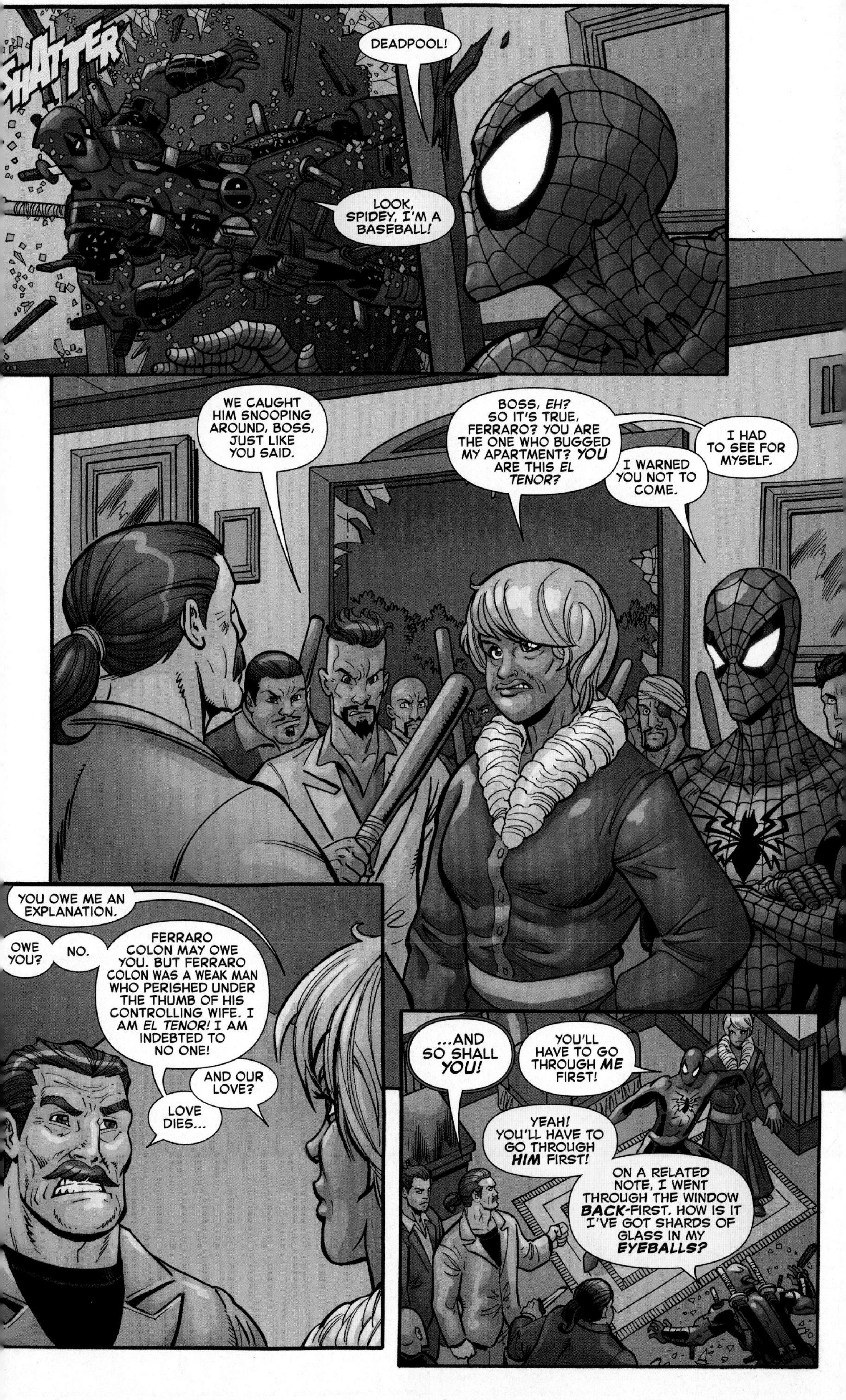

SHATTER
DEADPOOL!
LOOK, SPIDEY, I'M A BASEBALL!
WE CAUGHT HIM SNOOPING AROUND, BOSS, JUST LIKE YOU SAID.
BOSS, *EH?* SO IT'S TRUE, FERRARO? YOU ARE THE ONE WHO BUGGED MY APARTMENT? ***YOU*** ARE THIS *EL TENOR?*
I HAD TO SEE FOR MYSELF.
I WARNED YOU NOT TO COME.
YOU OWE ME AN EXPLANATION.
OWE YOU?
NO.
FERRARO COLON MAY OWE YOU. BUT FERRARO COLON WAS A WEAK MAN WHO PERISHED UNDER THE THUMB OF HIS CONTROLLING WIFE. I AM *EL TENOR!* I AM INDEBTED TO NO ONE!
AND OUR LOVE?
LOVE DIES...
...AND SO SHALL ***YOU!***
YOU'LL HAVE TO GO THROUGH ***ME*** FIRST!
YEAH! YOU'LL HAVE TO GO THROUGH ***HIM*** FIRST!
ON A RELATED NOTE, I WENT THROUGH THE WINDOW ***BACK***-FIRST. HOW IS IT I'VE GOT SHARDS OF GLASS IN MY ***EYEBALLS?***

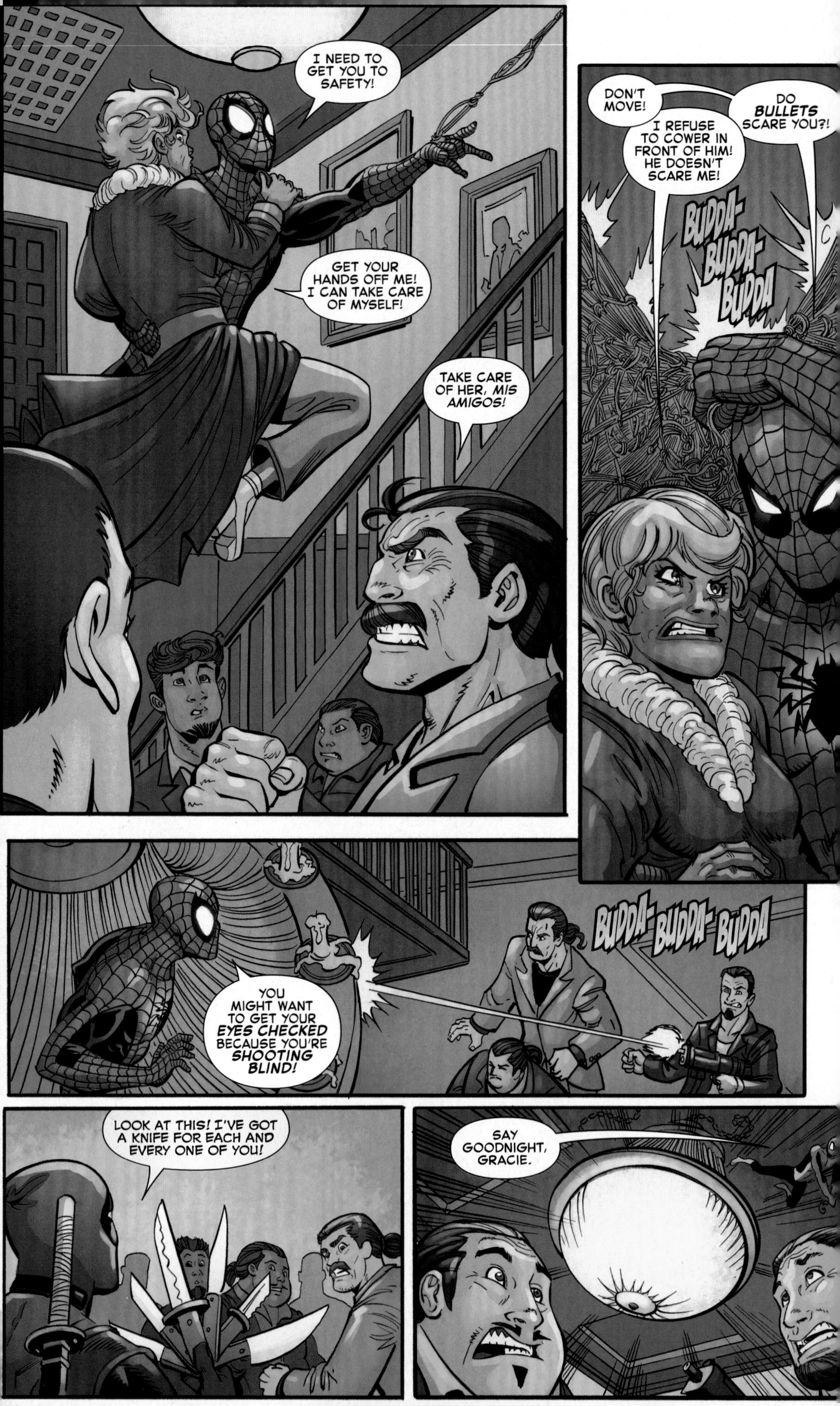
I NEED TO GET YOU TO SAFETY!
GET YOUR HANDS OFF ME! I CAN TAKE CARE OF MYSELF!
TAKE CARE OF HER, *MIS AMIGOS!*
DON'T MOVE!
I REFUSE TO COWER IN FRONT OF HIM! HE DOESN'T SCARE ME!
DO *BULLETS* SCARE YOU?!
BUDDA-BUDDA-BUDDA
BUDDA-BUDDA-BUDDA
YOU MIGHT WANT TO GET YOUR *EYES CHECKED* BECAUSE YOU'RE *SHOOTING BLIND!*
LOOK AT THIS! I'VE GOT A KNIFE FOR EACH AND EVERY ONE OF YOU!
SAY GOODNIGHT, GRACIE.

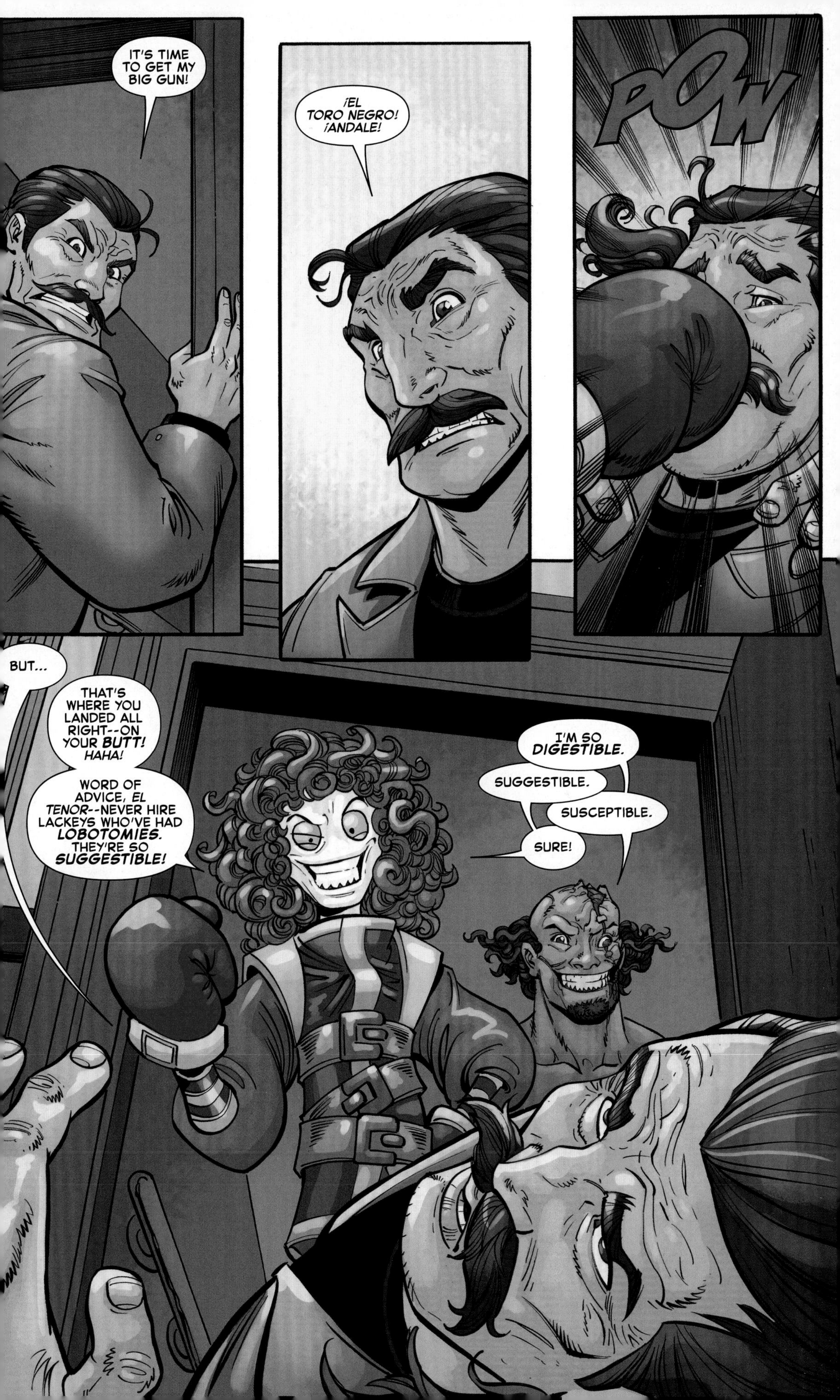
IT'S TIME TO GET MY BIG GUN!
¡EL TORO NEGRO! ¡ANDALE!
POW
BUT...
THAT'S WHERE YOU LANDED ALL RIGHT--ON YOUR BUTT! HAHA!
WORD OF ADVICE, EL TENOR--NEVER HIRE LACKEYS WHO'VE HAD LOBOTOMIES. THEY'RE SO SUGGESTIBLE!
I'M SO DIGESTIBLE.
SUGGESTIBLE.
SUSCEPTIBLE.
SURE!

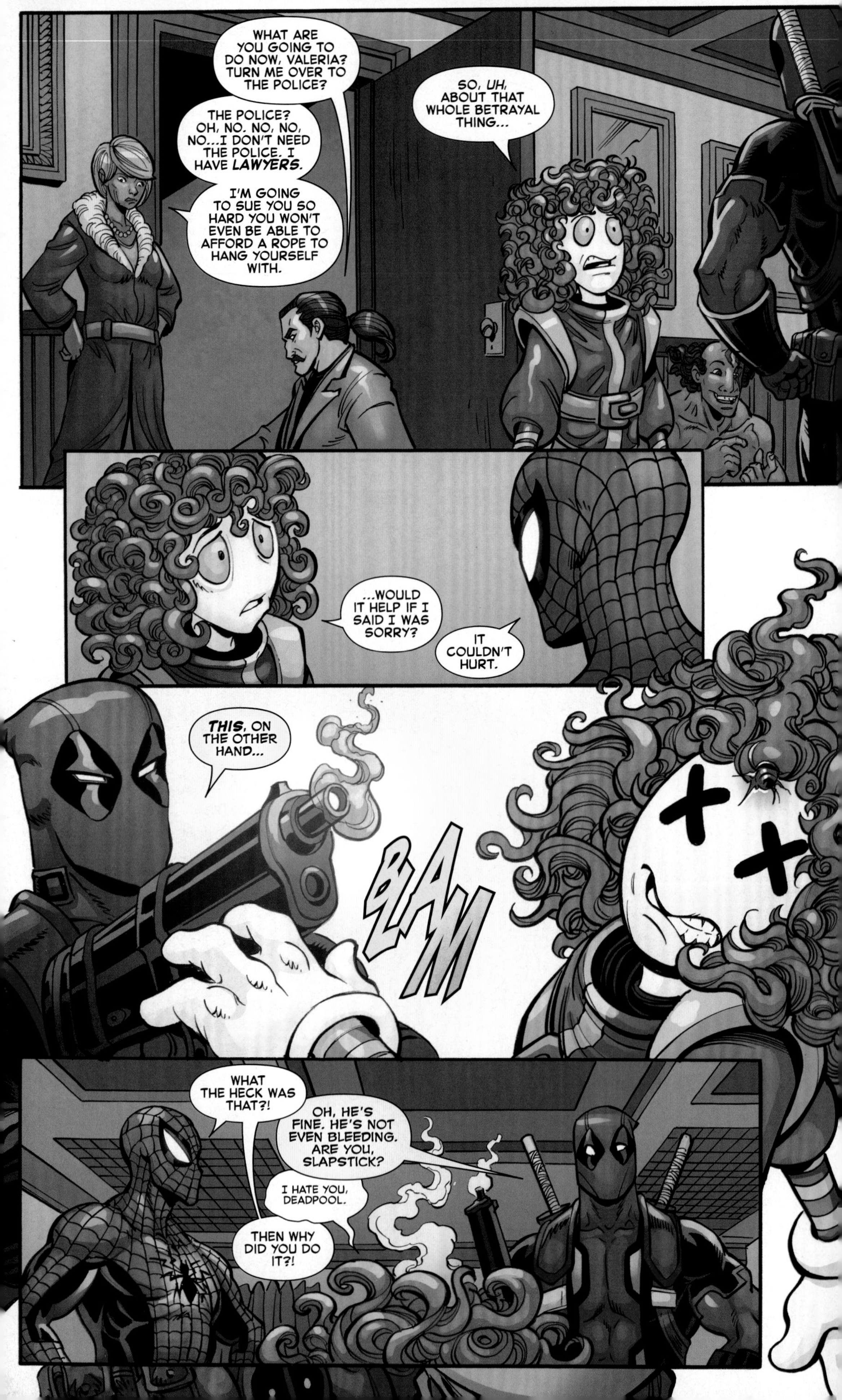

WHAT ARE YOU GOING TO DO NOW, VALERIA? TURN ME OVER TO THE POLICE?
THE POLICE? OH, NO. NO, NO, NO...I DON'T NEED THE POLICE. I HAVE *LAWYERS.*
I'M GOING TO SUE YOU SO HARD YOU WON'T EVEN BE ABLE TO AFFORD A ROPE TO HANG YOURSELF WITH.
SO, *UH,* ABOUT THAT WHOLE BETRAYAL THING...
...WOULD IT HELP IF I SAID I WAS SORRY?
IT COULDN'T HURT.
THIS, ON THE OTHER HAND...
BLAM
WHAT THE HECK WAS THAT?!
OH, HE'S FINE. HE'S NOT EVEN BLEEDING. ARE YOU, SLAPSTICK?
I HATE YOU, DEADPOOL.
THEN WHY DID YOU DO IT?!

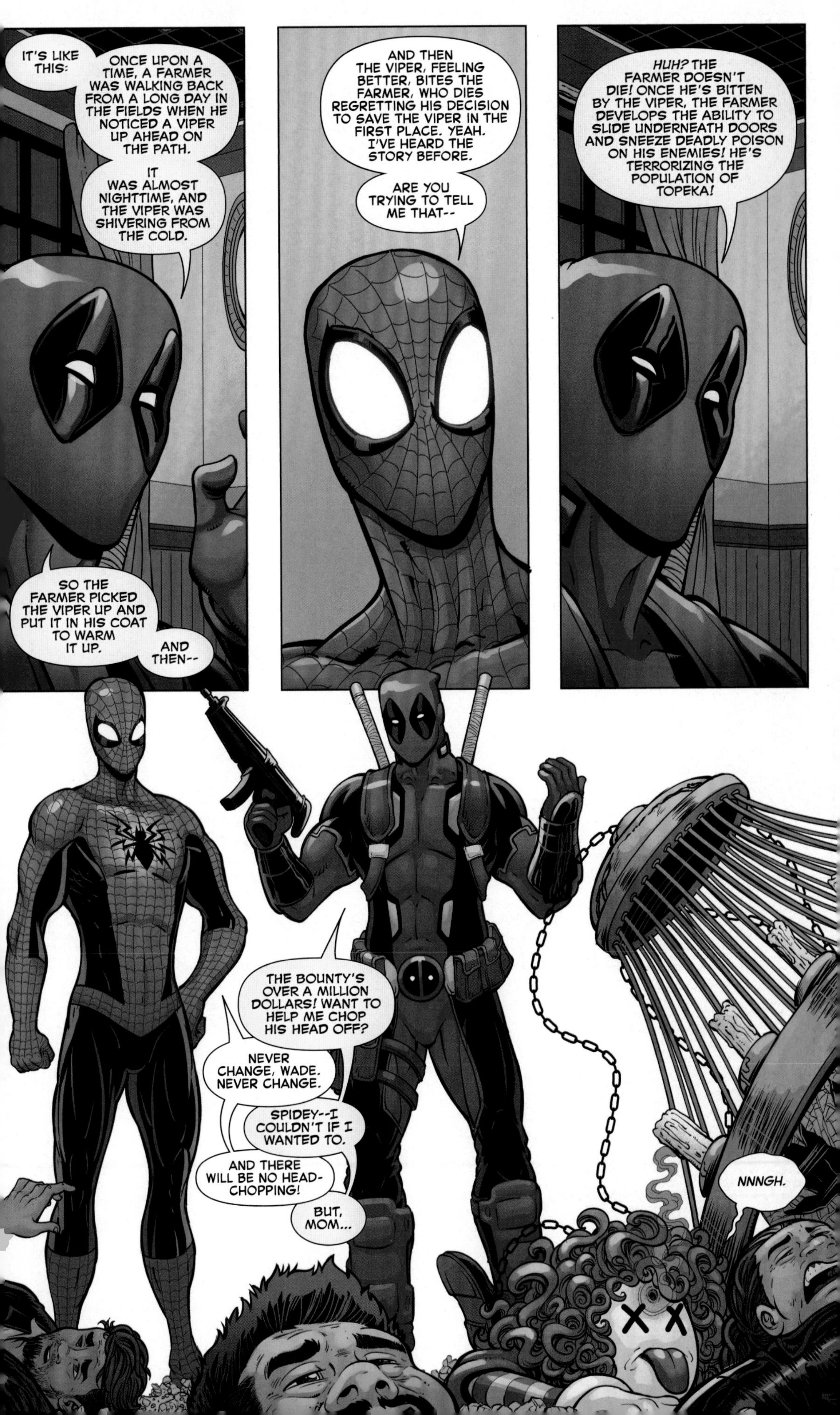
IT'S LIKE THIS:
ONCE UPON A TIME, A FARMER WAS WALKING BACK FROM A LONG DAY IN THE FIELDS WHEN HE NOTICED A VIPER UP AHEAD ON THE PATH.
IT WAS ALMOST NIGHTTIME, AND THE VIPER WAS SHIVERING FROM THE COLD.
SO THE FARMER PICKED THE VIPER UP AND PUT IT IN HIS COAT TO WARM IT UP.
AND THEN--
AND THEN THE VIPER, FEELING BETTER, BITES THE FARMER, WHO DIES REGRETTING HIS DECISION TO SAVE THE VIPER IN THE FIRST PLACE. YEAH. I'VE HEARD THE STORY BEFORE.
ARE YOU TRYING TO TELL ME THAT--
HUH? THE FARMER DOESN'T DIE! ONCE HE'S BITTEN BY THE VIPER, THE FARMER DEVELOPS THE ABILITY TO SLIDE UNDERNEATH DOORS AND SNEEZE DEADLY POISON ON HIS ENEMIES! HE'S TERRORIZING THE POPULATION OF TOPEKA!
THE BOUNTY'S OVER A MILLION DOLLARS! WANT TO HELP ME CHOP HIS HEAD OFF?
NEVER CHANGE, WADE. NEVER CHANGE.
SPIDEY--I COULDN'T IF I WANTED TO.
AND THERE WILL BE NO HEAD-CHOPPING!
BUT, MOM...
NNNGH.

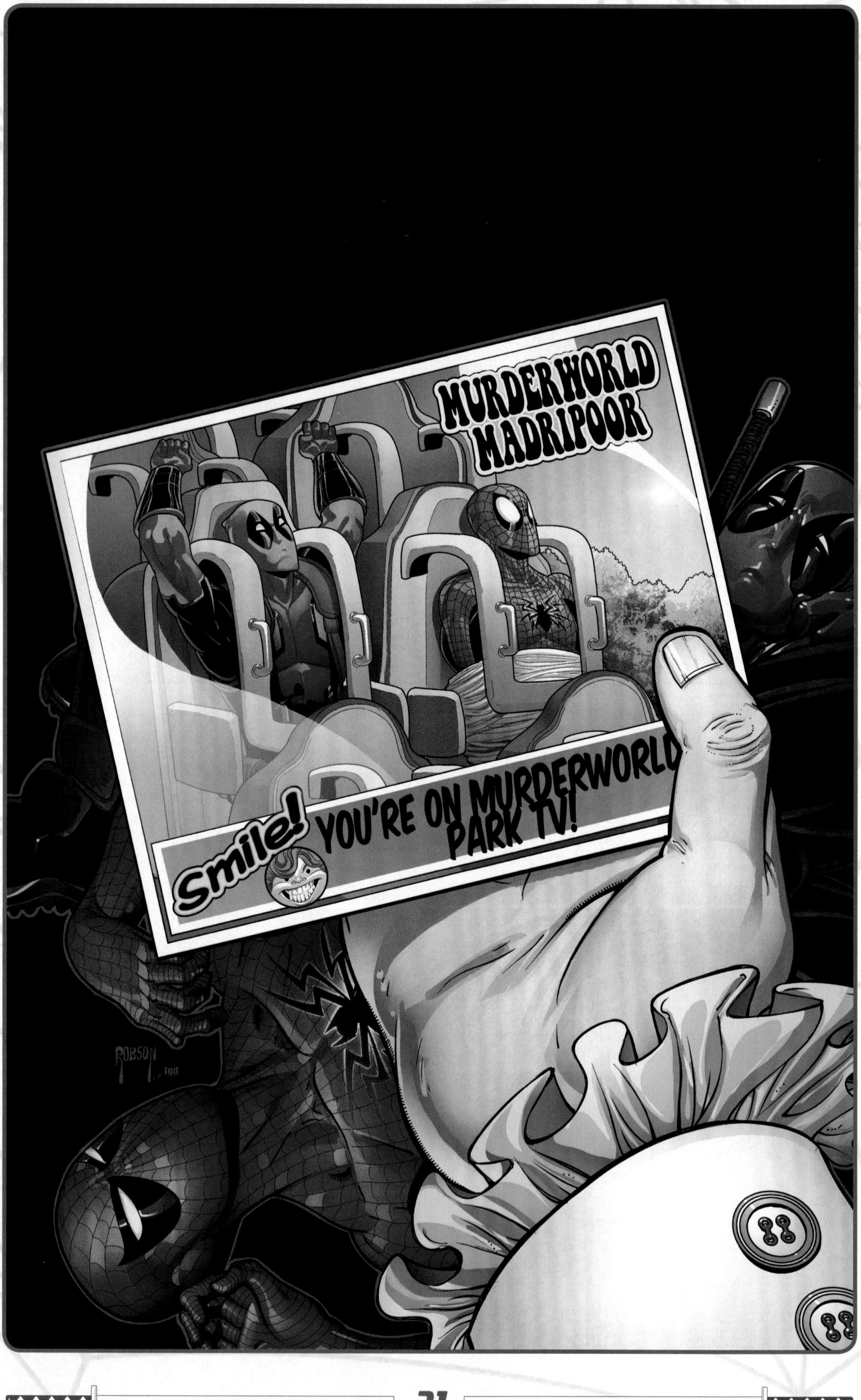
MURDERWORLD MADRIPOOR
Smile! YOU'RE ON MURDERWORLD PARK TV!
ROBSON

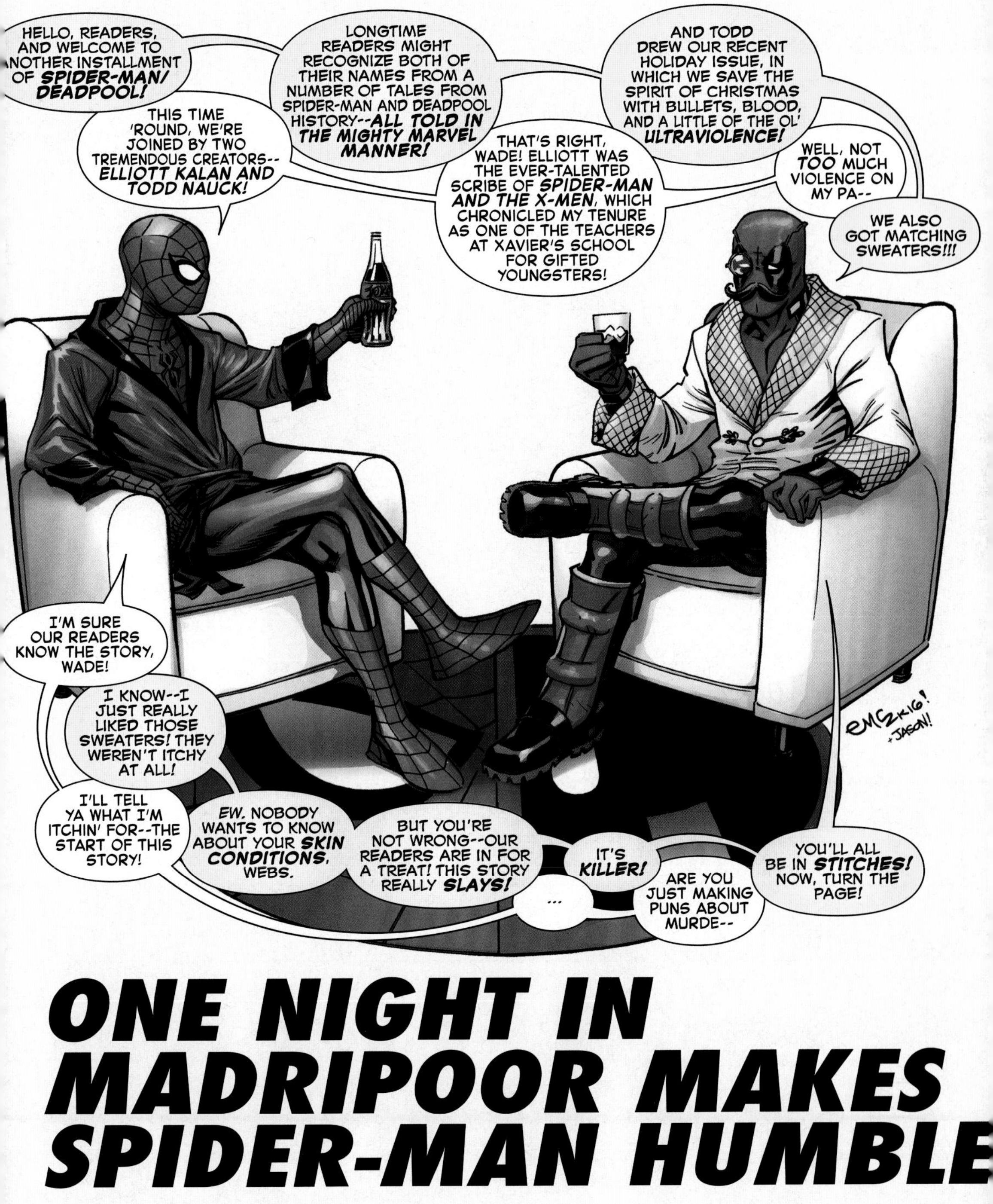
HELLO, READERS, AND WELCOME TO ANOTHER INSTALLMENT OF SPIDER-MAN/ DEADPOOL!
THIS TIME 'ROUND, WE'RE JOINED BY TWO TREMENDOUS CREATORS-- ELLIOTT KALAN AND TODD NAUCK!
LONGTIME READERS MIGHT RECOGNIZE BOTH OF THEIR NAMES FROM A NUMBER OF TALES FROM SPIDER-MAN AND DEADPOOL HISTORY--ALL TOLD IN THE MIGHTY MARVEL MANNER!
THAT'S RIGHT, WADE! ELLIOTT WAS THE EVER-TALENTED SCRIBE OF SPIDER-MAN AND THE X-MEN, WHICH CHRONICLED MY TENURE AS ONE OF THE TEACHERS AT XAVIER'S SCHOOL FOR GIFTED YOUNGSTERS!
AND TODD DREW OUR RECENT HOLIDAY ISSUE, IN WHICH WE SAVE THE SPIRIT OF CHRISTMAS WITH BULLETS, BLOOD, AND A LITTLE OF THE OL' ULTRAVIOLENCE!
WELL, NOT TOO MUCH VIOLENCE ON MY PA--
WE ALSO GOT MATCHING SWEATERS!!!
I'M SURE OUR READERS KNOW THE STORY, WADE!
I KNOW--I JUST REALLY LIKED THOSE SWEATERS! THEY WEREN'T ITCHY AT ALL!
I'LL TELL YA WHAT I'M ITCHIN' FOR--THE START OF THIS STORY!
EW. NOBODY WANTS TO KNOW ABOUT YOUR SKIN CONDITIONS, WEBS.
BUT YOU'RE NOT WRONG--OUR READERS ARE IN FOR A TREAT! THIS STORY REALLY SLAYS!
IT'S KILLER!
...
ARE YOU JUST MAKING PUNS ABOUT MURDE--
YOU'LL ALL BE IN STITCHES! NOW, TURN THE PAGE!

ONE NIGHT IN MADRIPOOR MAKES SPIDER-MAN HUMBLE

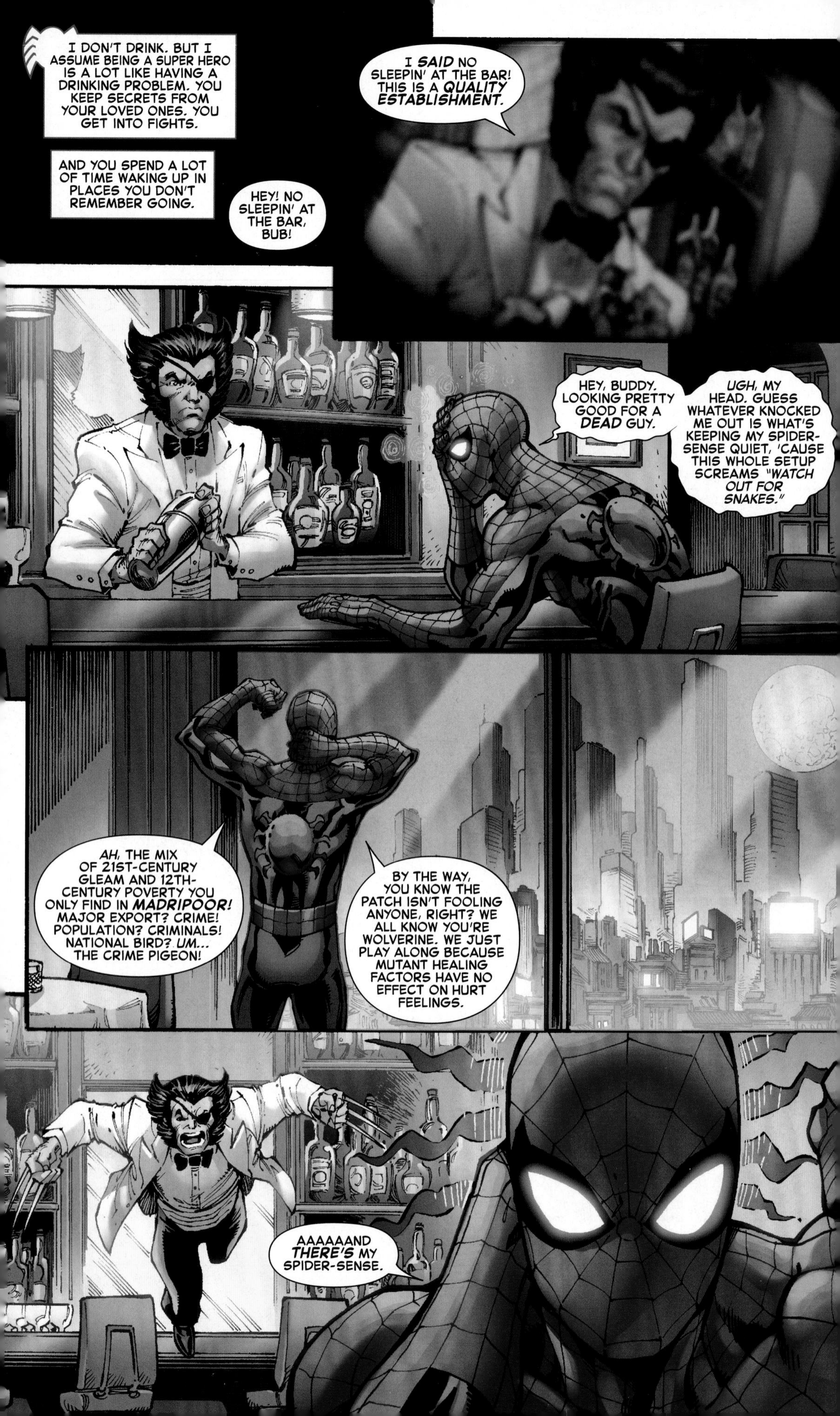
I DON'T DRINK. BUT I ASSUME BEING A SUPER HERO IS A LOT LIKE HAVING A DRINKING PROBLEM. YOU KEEP SECRETS FROM YOUR LOVED ONES. YOU GET INTO FIGHTS.
AND YOU SPEND A LOT OF TIME WAKING UP IN PLACES YOU DON'T REMEMBER GOING.
HEY! NO SLEEPIN' AT THE BAR, BUB!
I SAID NO SLEEPIN' AT THE BAR! THIS IS A QUALITY ESTABLISHMENT.
HEY, BUDDY. LOOKING PRETTY GOOD FOR A DEAD GUY.
UGH, MY HEAD. GUESS WHATEVER KNOCKED ME OUT IS WHAT'S KEEPING MY SPIDER-SENSE QUIET, 'CAUSE THIS WHOLE SETUP SCREAMS "WATCH OUT FOR SNAKES."
AH, THE MIX OF 21ST-CENTURY GLEAM AND 12TH-CENTURY POVERTY YOU ONLY FIND IN MADRIPOOR! MAJOR EXPORT? CRIME! POPULATION? CRIMINALS! NATIONAL BIRD? UM... THE CRIME PIGEON!
BY THE WAY, YOU KNOW THE PATCH ISN'T FOOLING ANYONE, RIGHT? WE ALL KNOW YOU'RE WOLVERINE. WE JUST PLAY ALONG BECAUSE MUTANT HEALING FACTORS HAVE NO EFFECT ON HURT FEELINGS.
AAAAAAND THERE'S MY SPIDER-SENSE.

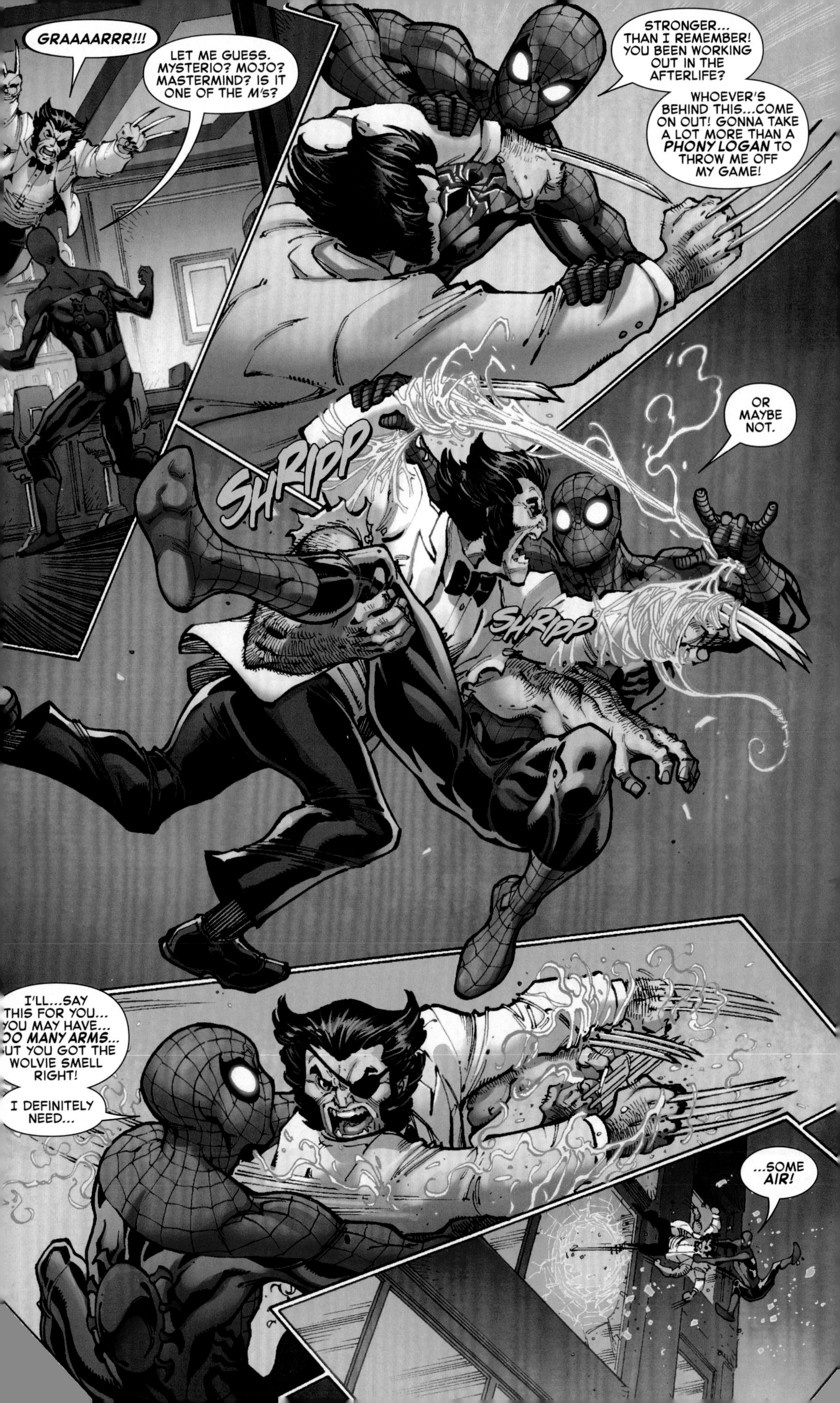
GRAAAARRR!!!
LET ME GUESS. MYSTERIO? MOJO? MASTERMIND? IS IT ONE OF THE M's?
STRONGER... THAN I REMEMBER! YOU BEEN WORKING OUT IN THE AFTERLIFE?
WHOEVER'S BEHIND THIS...COME ON OUT! GONNA TAKE A LOT MORE THAN A PHONY LOGAN TO THROW ME OFF MY GAME!
SHRIPP
OR MAYBE NOT.
SHRIPP
I'LL...SAY THIS FOR YOU... YOU MAY HAVE... TOO MANY ARMS... BUT YOU GOT THE WOLVIE SMELL RIGHT!
I DEFINITELY NEED...
...SOME AIR!

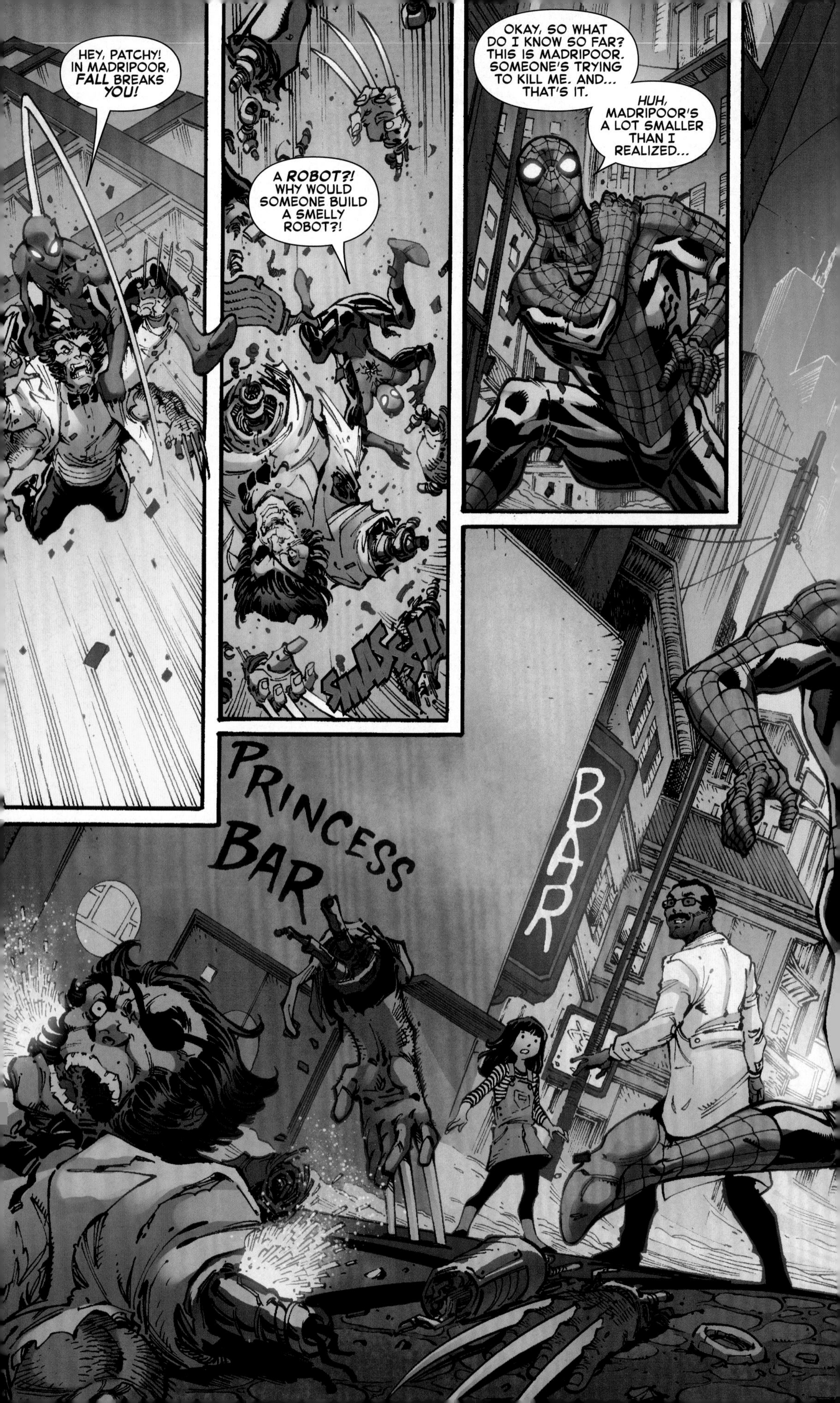
HEY, PATCHY! IN MADRIPOOR, FALL BREAKS YOU!
A ROBOT?! WHY WOULD SOMEONE BUILD A SMELLY ROBOT?!
SMASH
OKAY, SO WHAT DO I KNOW SO FAR? THIS IS MADRIPOOR. SOMEONE'S TRYING TO KILL ME. AND... THAT'S IT.
HUH, MADRIPOOR'S A LOT SMALLER THAN I REALIZED...
PRINCESS BAR
BAR

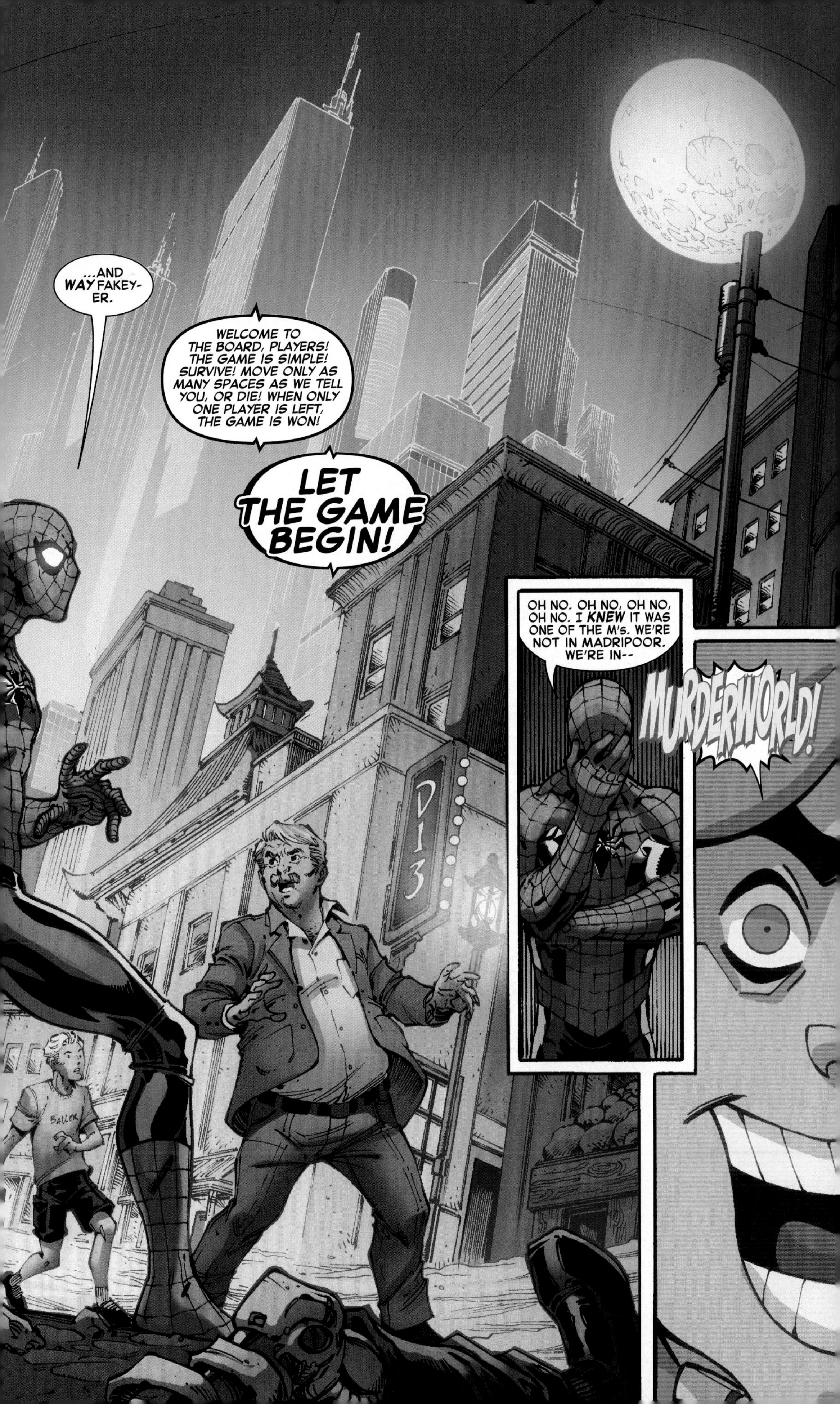

...AND WAY FAKEY-ER.
WELCOME TO THE BOARD, PLAYERS! THE GAME IS SIMPLE! SURVIVE! MOVE ONLY AS MANY SPACES AS WE TELL YOU, OR DIE! WHEN ONLY ONE PLAYER IS LEFT, THE GAME IS WON!
LET THE GAME BEGIN!
D13
OH NO. OH NO, OH NO, OH NO. I KNEW IT WAS ONE OF THE M's. WE'RE NOT IN MADRIPOOR. WE'RE IN--
MURDERWORLD!

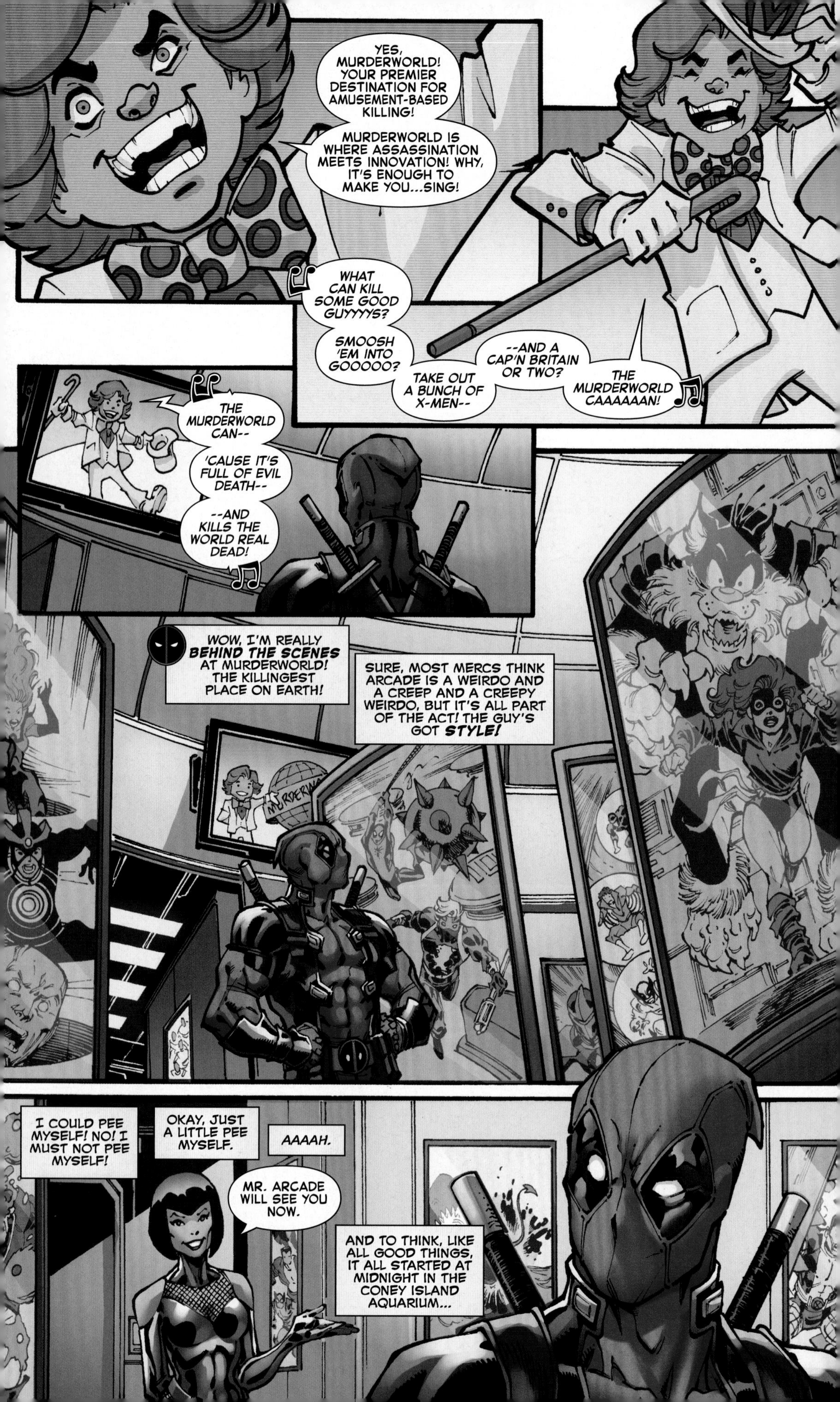

YES, MURDERWORLD! YOUR PREMIER DESTINATION FOR AMUSEMENT-BASED KILLING!
MURDERWORLD IS WHERE ASSASSINATION MEETS INNOVATION! WHY, IT'S ENOUGH TO MAKE YOU...SING!
WHAT CAN KILL SOME GOOD GUYYYYS?
SMOOSH 'EM INTO GOOOOO?
TAKE OUT A BUNCH OF X-MEN--
--AND A CAP'N BRITAIN OR TWO?
THE MURDERWORLD CAAAAAAN!
THE MURDERWORLD CAN--
'CAUSE IT'S FULL OF EVIL DEATH--
--AND KILLS THE WORLD REAL DEAD!
WOW, I'M REALLY **BEHIND THE SCENES** AT MURDERWORLD! THE KILLINGEST PLACE ON EARTH!
SURE, MOST MERCS THINK ARCADE IS A WEIRDO AND A CREEP AND A CREEPY WEIRDO, BUT IT'S ALL PART OF THE ACT! THE GUY'S GOT **STYLE!**
I COULD PEE MYSELF! NO! I MUST NOT PEE MYSELF!
OKAY, JUST A LITTLE PEE MYSELF.
AAAAH.
MR. ARCADE WILL SEE YOU NOW.
AND TO THINK, LIKE ALL GOOD THINGS, IT ALL STARTED AT MIDNIGHT IN THE CONEY ISLAND AQUARIUM...

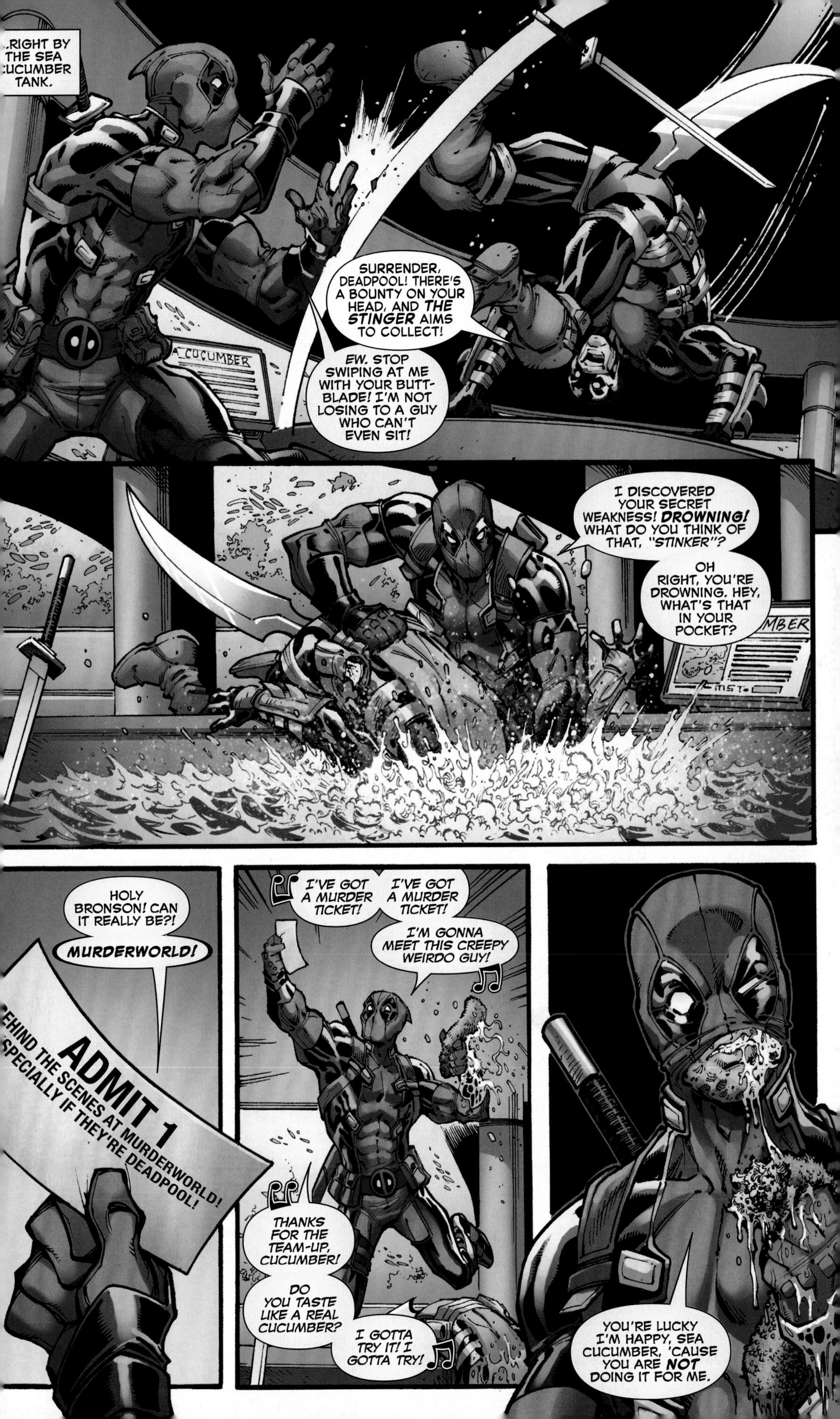

...RIGHT BY THE SEA CUCUMBER TANK.
SURRENDER, DEADPOOL! THERE'S A BOUNTY ON YOUR HEAD, AND THE STINGER AIMS TO COLLECT!
EW. STOP SWIPING AT ME WITH YOUR BUTT-BLADE! I'M NOT LOSING TO A GUY WHO CAN'T EVEN SIT!
A CUCUMBER
I DISCOVERED YOUR SECRET WEAKNESS! DROWNING! WHAT DO YOU THINK OF THAT, "STINKER"?
OH RIGHT, YOU'RE DROWNING. HEY, WHAT'S THAT IN YOUR POCKET?
MBER
HOLY BRONSON! CAN IT REALLY BE?!
MURDERWORLD!
ADMIT 1
EHIND THE SCENES AT MURDERWORLD!
SPECIALLY IF THEY'RE DEADPOOL!
I'VE GOT A MURDER TICKET!
I'VE GOT A MURDER TICKET!
I'M GONNA MEET THIS CREEPY WEIRDO GUY!
THANKS FOR THE TEAM-UP, CUCUMBER!
DO YOU TASTE LIKE A REAL CUCUMBER?
I GOTTA TRY IT! I GOTTA TRY!
YOU'RE LUCKY I'M HAPPY, SEA CUCUMBER, 'CAUSE YOU ARE NOT DOING IT FOR ME.

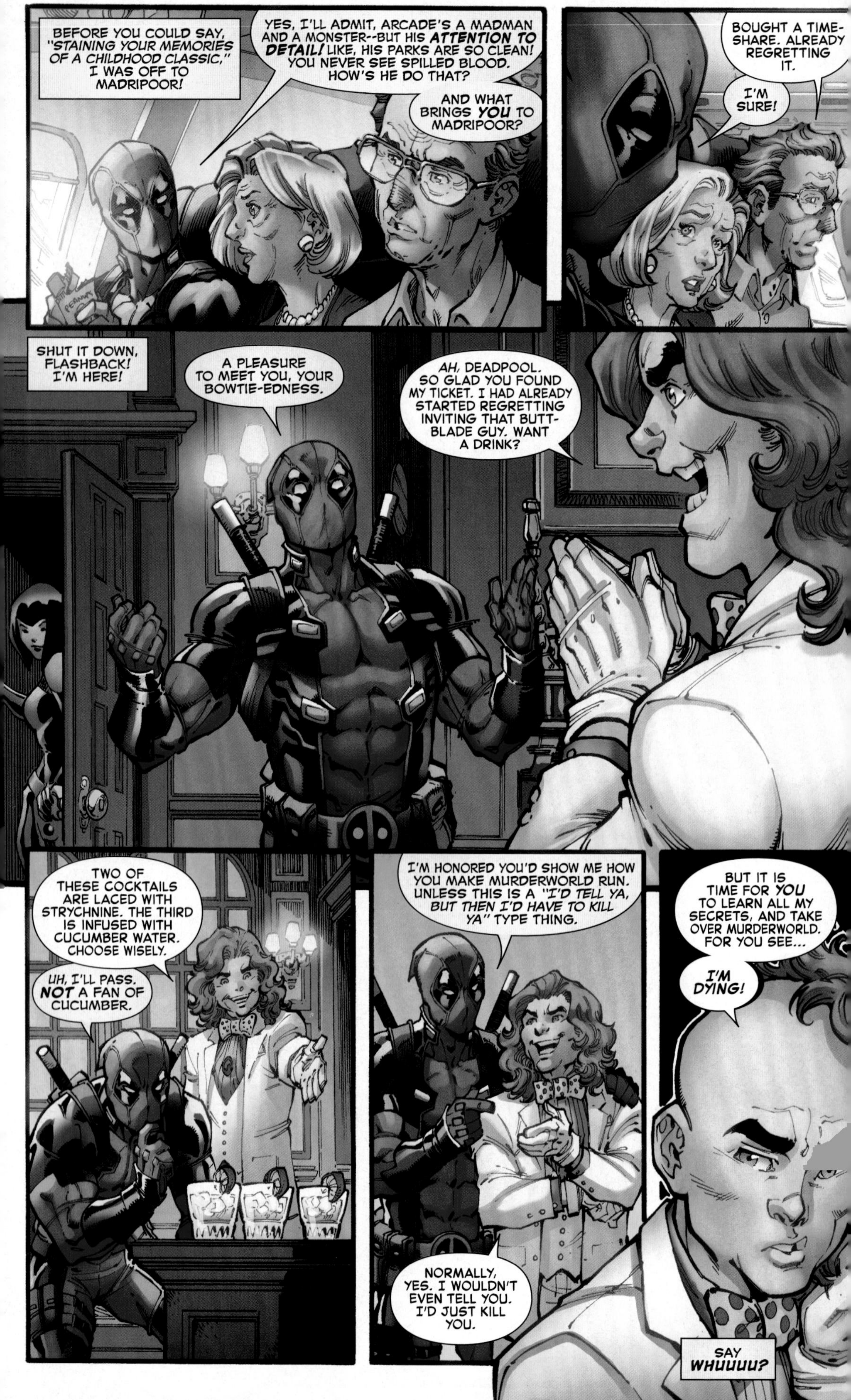

BEFORE YOU COULD SAY, "STAINING YOUR MEMORIES OF A CHILDHOOD CLASSIC," I WAS OFF TO MADRIPOOR!
YES, I'LL ADMIT, ARCADE'S A MADMAN AND A MONSTER--BUT HIS ATTENTION TO DETAIL! LIKE, HIS PARKS ARE SO CLEAN! YOU NEVER SEE SPILLED BLOOD. HOW'S HE DO THAT?
AND WHAT BRINGS YOU TO MADRIPOOR?
BOUGHT A TIME-SHARE. ALREADY REGRETTING IT.
I'M SURE!
SHUT IT DOWN, FLASHBACK! I'M HERE!
A PLEASURE TO MEET YOU, YOUR BOWTIE-EDNESS.
AH, DEADPOOL. SO GLAD YOU FOUND MY TICKET. I HAD ALREADY STARTED REGRETTING INVITING THAT BUTT-BLADE GUY. WANT A DRINK?
TWO OF THESE COCKTAILS ARE LACED WITH STRYCHNINE. THE THIRD IS INFUSED WITH CUCUMBER WATER. CHOOSE WISELY.
UH, I'LL PASS. NOT A FAN OF CUCUMBER.
I'M HONORED YOU'D SHOW ME HOW YOU MAKE MURDERWORLD RUN. UNLESS THIS IS A "I'D TELL YA, BUT THEN I'D HAVE TO KILL YA" TYPE THING.
NORMALLY, YES. I WOULDN'T EVEN TELL YOU. I'D JUST KILL YOU.
BUT IT IS TIME FOR YOU TO LEARN ALL MY SECRETS, AND TAKE OVER MURDERWORLD. FOR YOU SEE...
I'M DYING!
SAY WHUUUU?

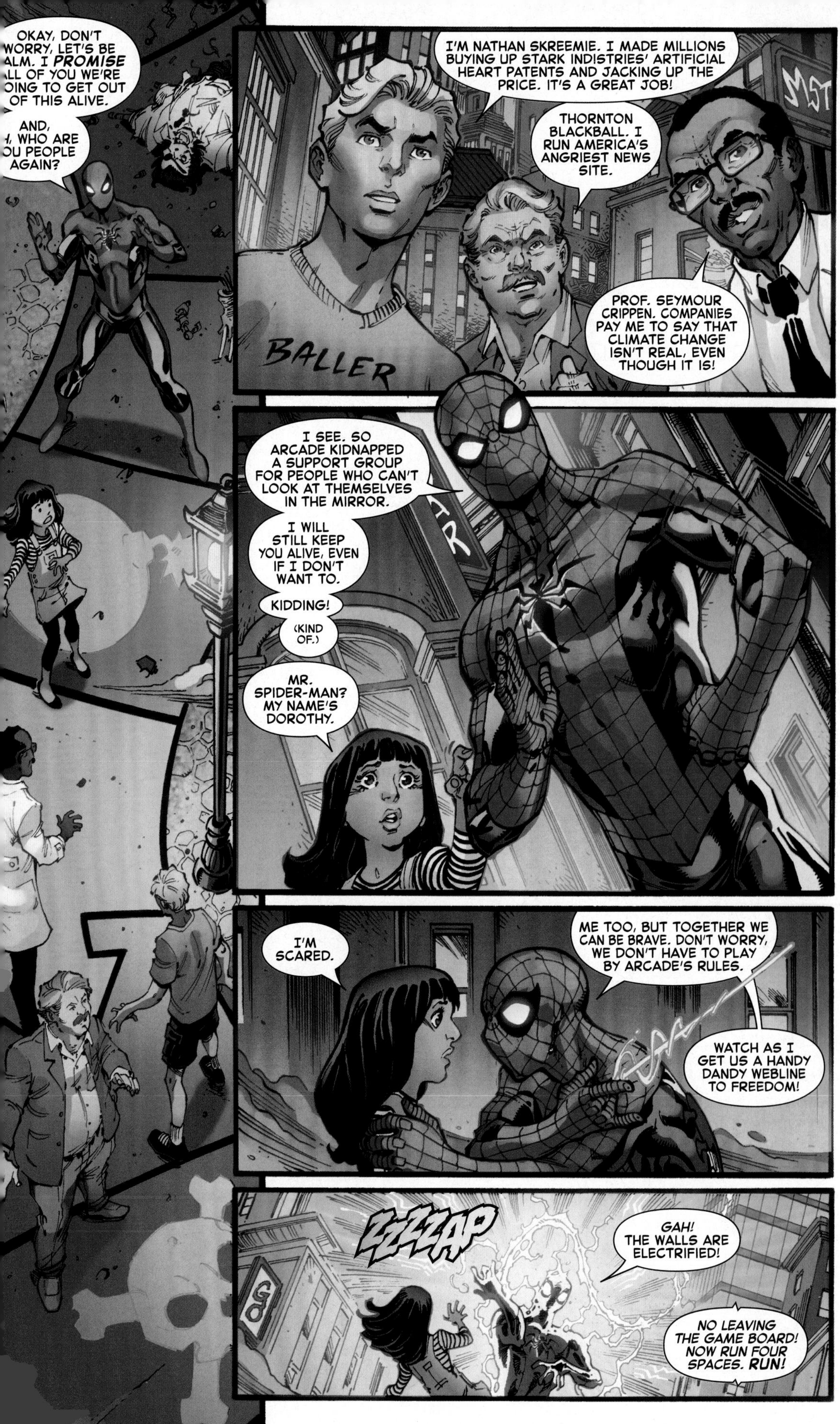
OKAY, DON'T WORRY, LET'S BE ALM. I PROMISE LL OF YOU WE'RE OING TO GET OUT OF THIS ALIVE.
AND, , WHO ARE OU PEOPLE AGAIN?
I'M NATHAN SKREEMIE. I MADE MILLIONS BUYING UP STARK INDISTRIES' ARTIFICIAL HEART PATENTS AND JACKING UP THE PRICE. IT'S A GREAT JOB!
THORNTON BLACKBALL. I RUN AMERICA'S ANGRIEST NEWS SITE.
PROF. SEYMOUR CRIPPEN. COMPANIES PAY ME TO SAY THAT CLIMATE CHANGE ISN'T REAL, EVEN THOUGH IT IS!
BALLER
I SEE. SO ARCADE KIDNAPPED A SUPPORT GROUP FOR PEOPLE WHO CAN'T LOOK AT THEMSELVES IN THE MIRROR.
I WILL STILL KEEP YOU ALIVE, EVEN IF I DON'T WANT TO.
KIDDING!
(KIND OF.)
MR. SPIDER-MAN? MY NAME'S DOROTHY.
I'M SCARED.
ME TOO, BUT TOGETHER WE CAN BE BRAVE. DON'T WORRY, WE DON'T HAVE TO PLAY BY ARCADE'S RULES.
WATCH AS I GET US A HANDY DANDY WEBLINE TO FREEDOM!
ZZZZAP
GAH! THE WALLS ARE ELECTRIFIED!
NO LEAVING THE GAME BOARD! NOW RUN FOUR SPACES. RUN!

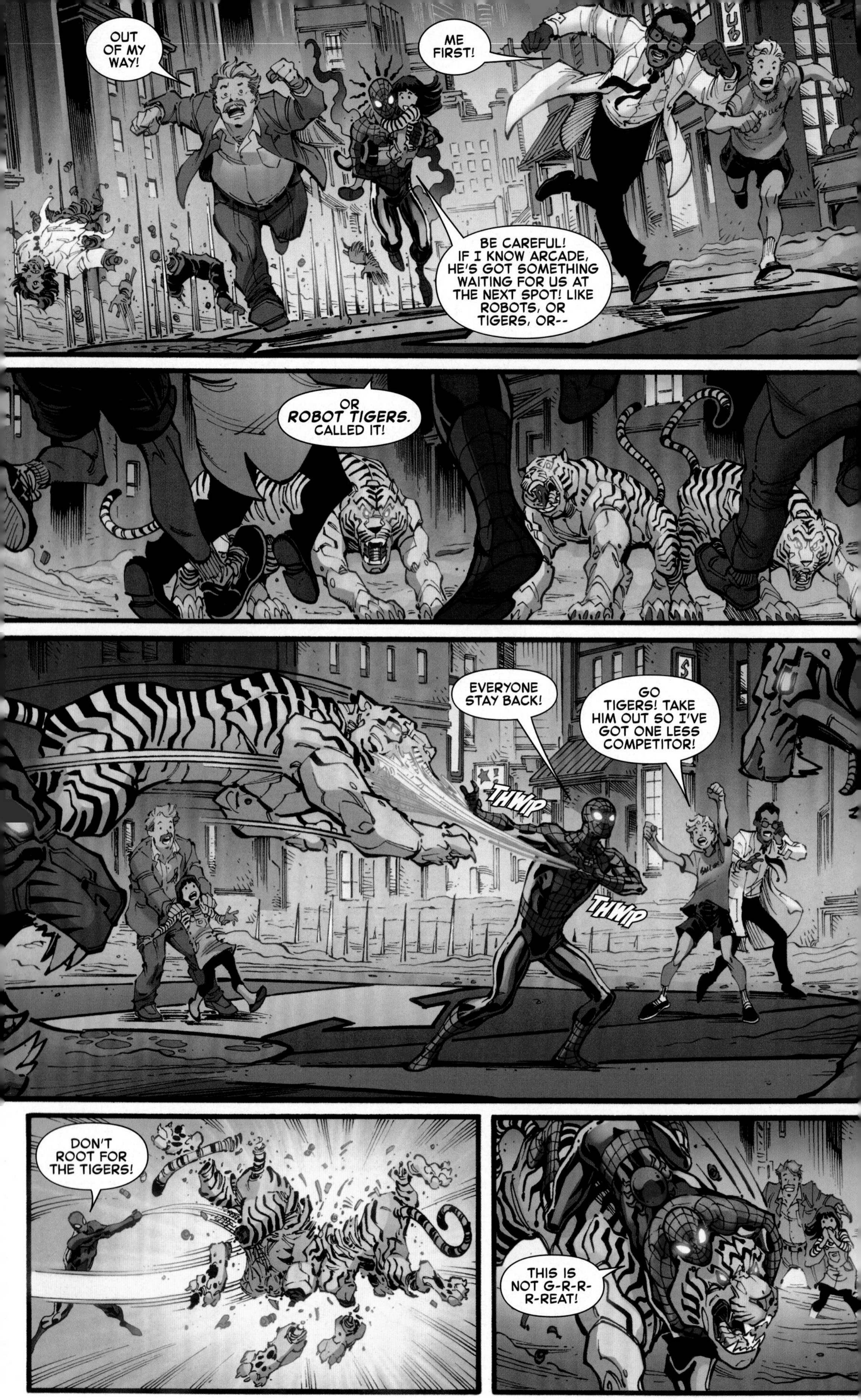
OUT OF MY WAY!
ME FIRST!
BE CAREFUL! IF I KNOW ARCADE, HE'S GOT SOMETHING WAITING FOR US AT THE NEXT SPOT! LIKE ROBOTS, OR TIGERS, OR--
OR *ROBOT TIGERS.* CALLED IT!
EVERYONE STAY BACK!
GO TIGERS! TAKE HIM OUT SO I'VE GOT ONE LESS COMPETITOR!
THWIP
THWIP
DON'T ROOT FOR THE TIGERS!
THIS IS NOT G-R-R-R-REAT!

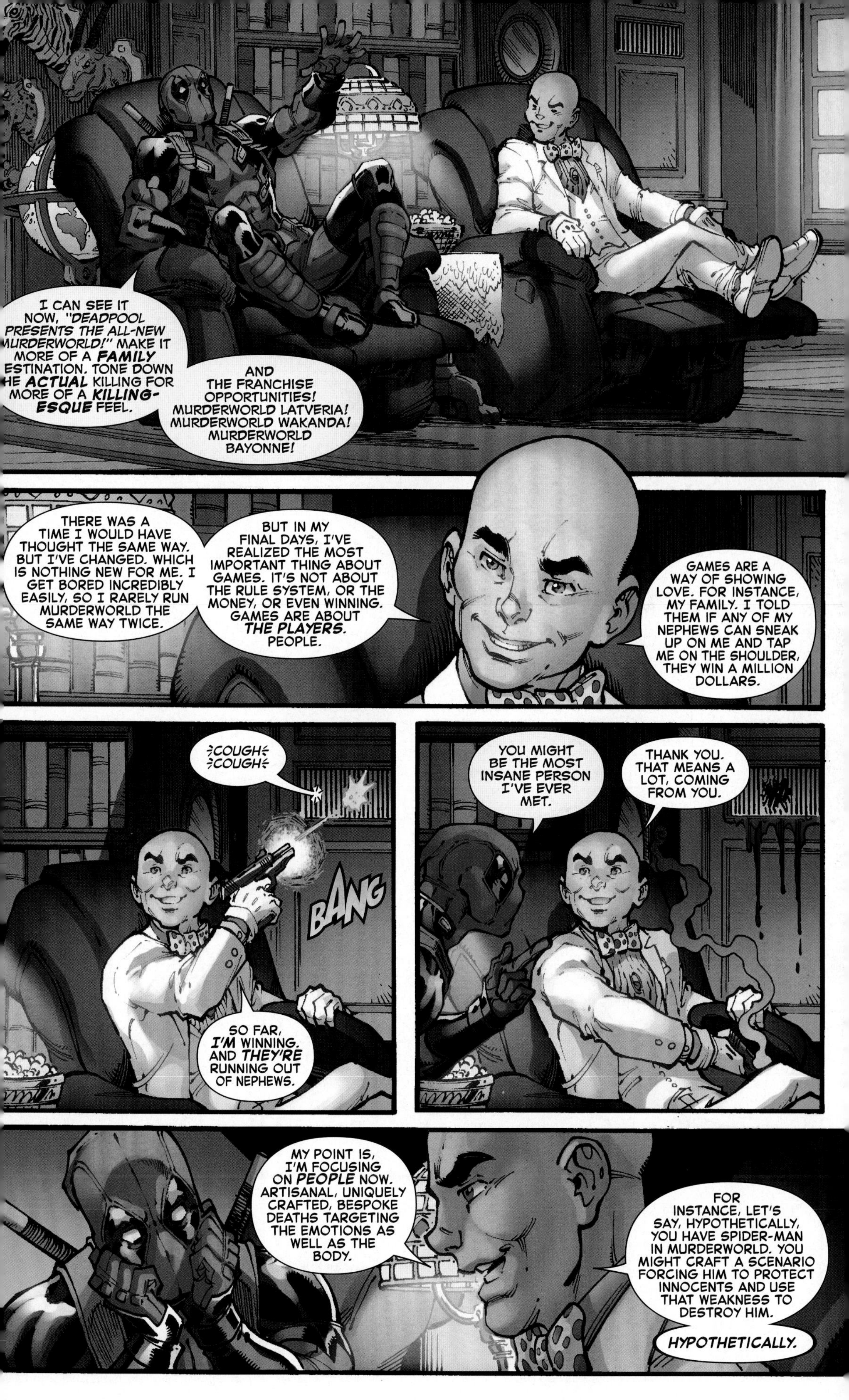

I CAN SEE IT NOW, "DEADPOOL PRESENTS THE ALL-NEW MURDERWORLD!" MAKE IT MORE OF A FAMILY ESTINATION. TONE DOWN HE ACTUAL KILLING FOR MORE OF A KILLING-ESQUE FEEL.
AND THE FRANCHISE OPPORTUNITIES! MURDERWORLD LATVERIA! MURDERWORLD WAKANDA! MURDERWORLD BAYONNE!
THERE WAS A TIME I WOULD HAVE THOUGHT THE SAME WAY. BUT I'VE CHANGED. WHICH IS NOTHING NEW FOR ME. I GET BORED INCREDIBLY EASILY, SO I RARELY RUN MURDERWORLD THE SAME WAY TWICE.
BUT IN MY FINAL DAYS, I'VE REALIZED THE MOST IMPORTANT THING ABOUT GAMES. IT'S NOT ABOUT THE RULE SYSTEM, OR THE MONEY, OR EVEN WINNING. GAMES ARE ABOUT THE PLAYERS. PEOPLE.
GAMES ARE A WAY OF SHOWING LOVE. FOR INSTANCE, MY FAMILY. I TOLD THEM IF ANY OF MY NEPHEWS CAN SNEAK UP ON ME AND TAP ME ON THE SHOULDER, THEY WIN A MILLION DOLLARS.
COUGH COUGH
BANG
SO FAR, I'M WINNING. AND THEY'RE RUNNING OUT OF NEPHEWS.
YOU MIGHT BE THE MOST INSANE PERSON I'VE EVER MET.
THANK YOU. THAT MEANS A LOT, COMING FROM YOU.
MY POINT IS, I'M FOCUSING ON PEOPLE NOW. ARTISANAL, UNIQUELY CRAFTED, BESPOKE DEATHS TARGETING THE EMOTIONS AS WELL AS THE BODY.
FOR INSTANCE, LET'S SAY, HYPOTHETICALLY, YOU HAVE SPIDER-MAN IN MURDERWORLD. YOU MIGHT CRAFT A SCENARIO FORCING HIM TO PROTECT INNOCENTS AND USE THAT WEAKNESS TO DESTROY HIM.
HYPOTHETICALLY.

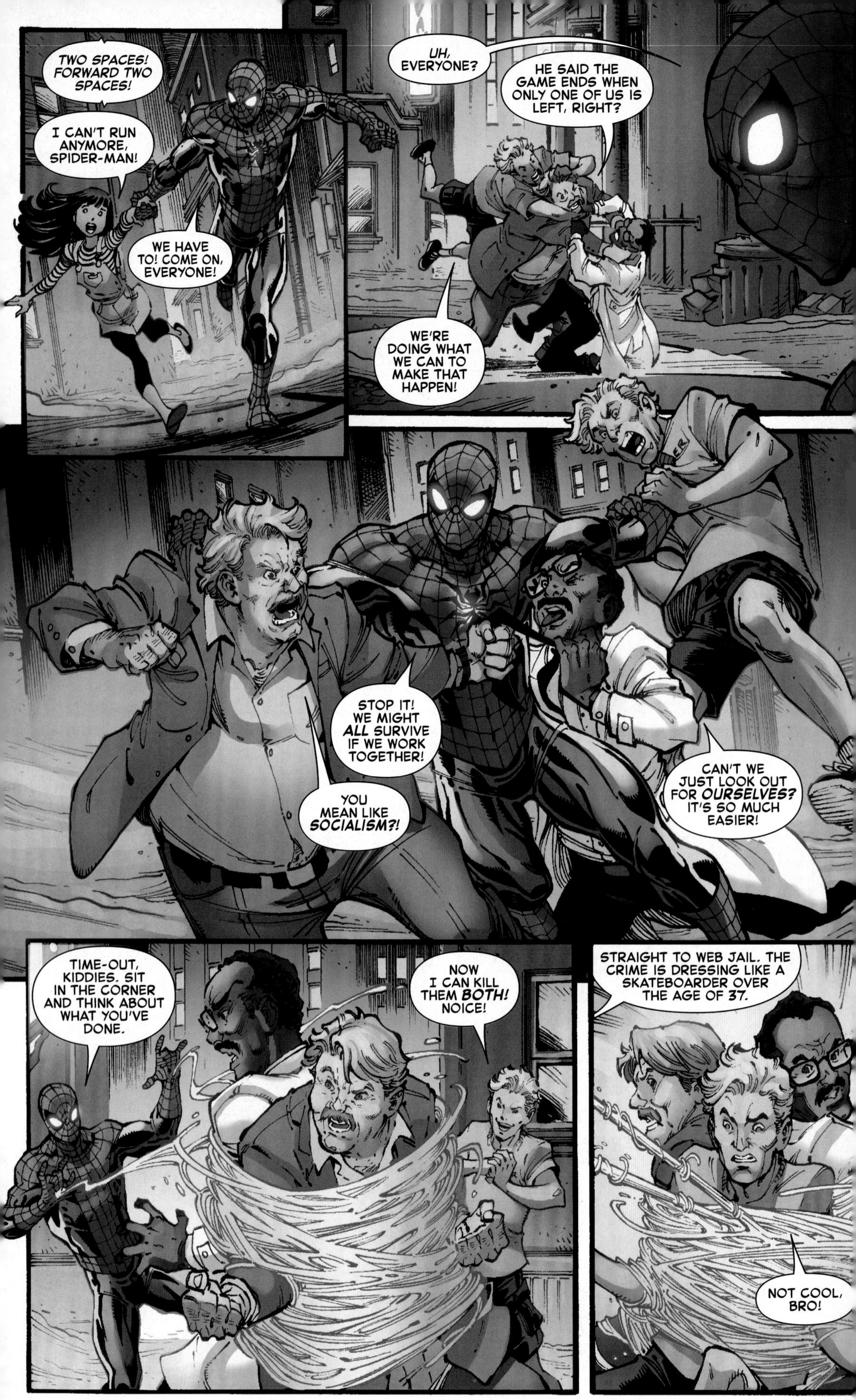
TWO SPACES! FORWARD TWO SPACES!
I CAN'T RUN ANYMORE, SPIDER-MAN!
WE HAVE TO! COME ON, EVERYONE!
UH, EVERYONE?
HE SAID THE GAME ENDS WHEN ONLY ONE OF US IS LEFT, RIGHT?
WE'RE DOING WHAT WE CAN TO MAKE THAT HAPPEN!
STOP IT! WE MIGHT ALL SURVIVE IF WE WORK TOGETHER!
YOU MEAN LIKE SOCIALISM?!
CAN'T WE JUST LOOK OUT FOR OURSELVES? IT'S SO MUCH EASIER!
TIME-OUT, KIDDIES. SIT IN THE CORNER AND THINK ABOUT WHAT YOU'VE DONE.
NOW I CAN KILL THEM BOTH! NOICE!
STRAIGHT TO WEB JAIL. THE CRIME IS DRESSING LIKE A SKATEBOARDER OVER THE AGE OF 37.
NOT COOL, BRO!

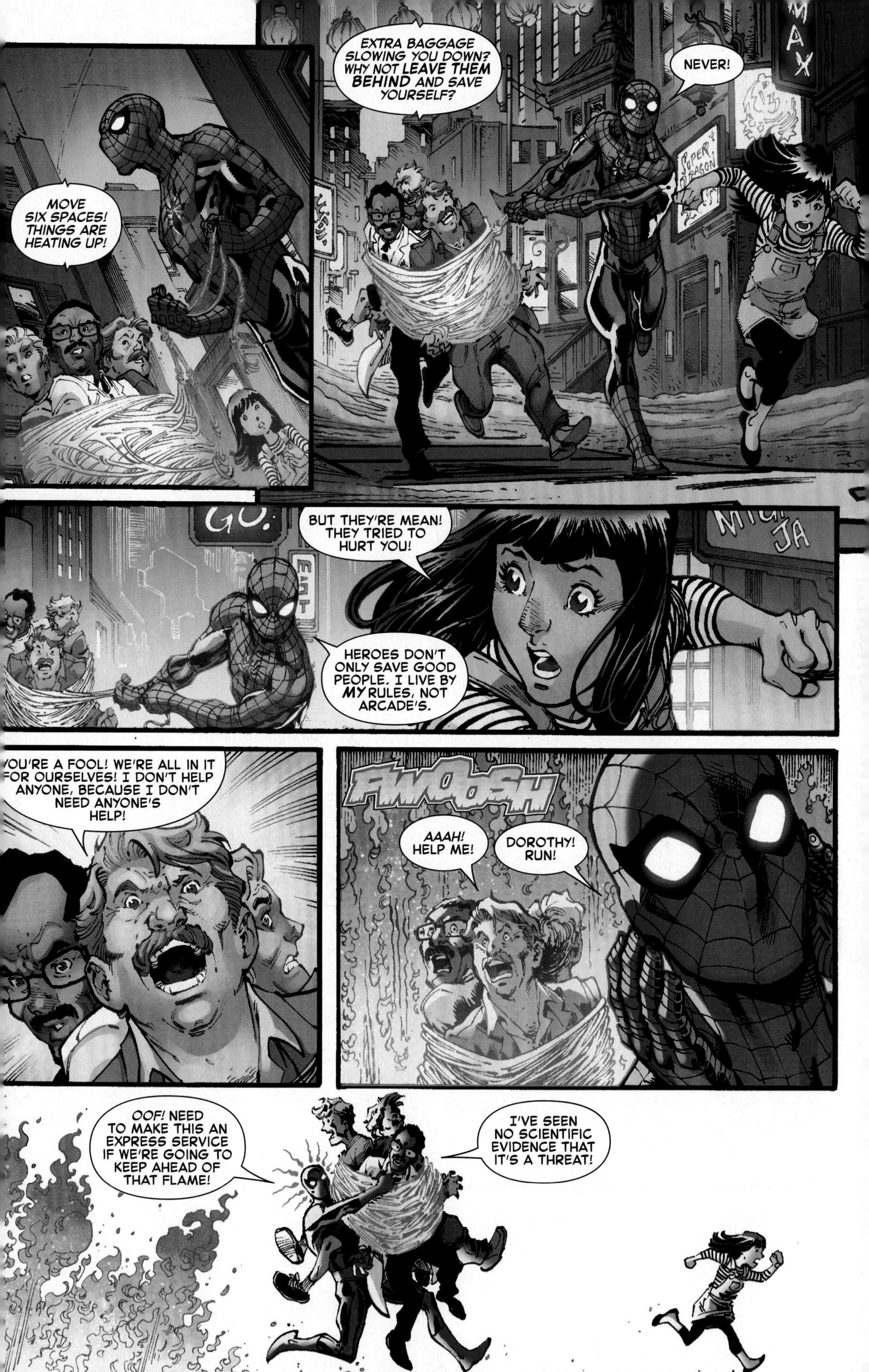

MOVE SIX SPACES! THINGS ARE HEATING UP!
EXTRA BAGGAGE SLOWING YOU DOWN? WHY NOT LEAVE THEM BEHIND AND SAVE YOURSELF?
NEVER!
SUPER DRAGON
BUT THEY'RE MEAN! THEY TRIED TO HURT YOU!
HEROES DON'T ONLY SAVE GOOD PEOPLE. I LIVE BY MY RULES, NOT ARCADE'S.
YOU'RE A FOOL! WE'RE ALL IN IT FOR OURSELVES! I DON'T HELP ANYONE, BECAUSE I DON'T NEED ANYONE'S HELP!
FWOOSH
AAAH! HELP ME!
DOROTHY! RUN!
OOF! NEED TO MAKE THIS AN EXPRESS SERVICE IF WE'RE GOING TO KEEP AHEAD OF THAT FLAME!
I'VE SEEN NO SCIENTIFIC EVIDENCE THAT IT'S A THREAT!

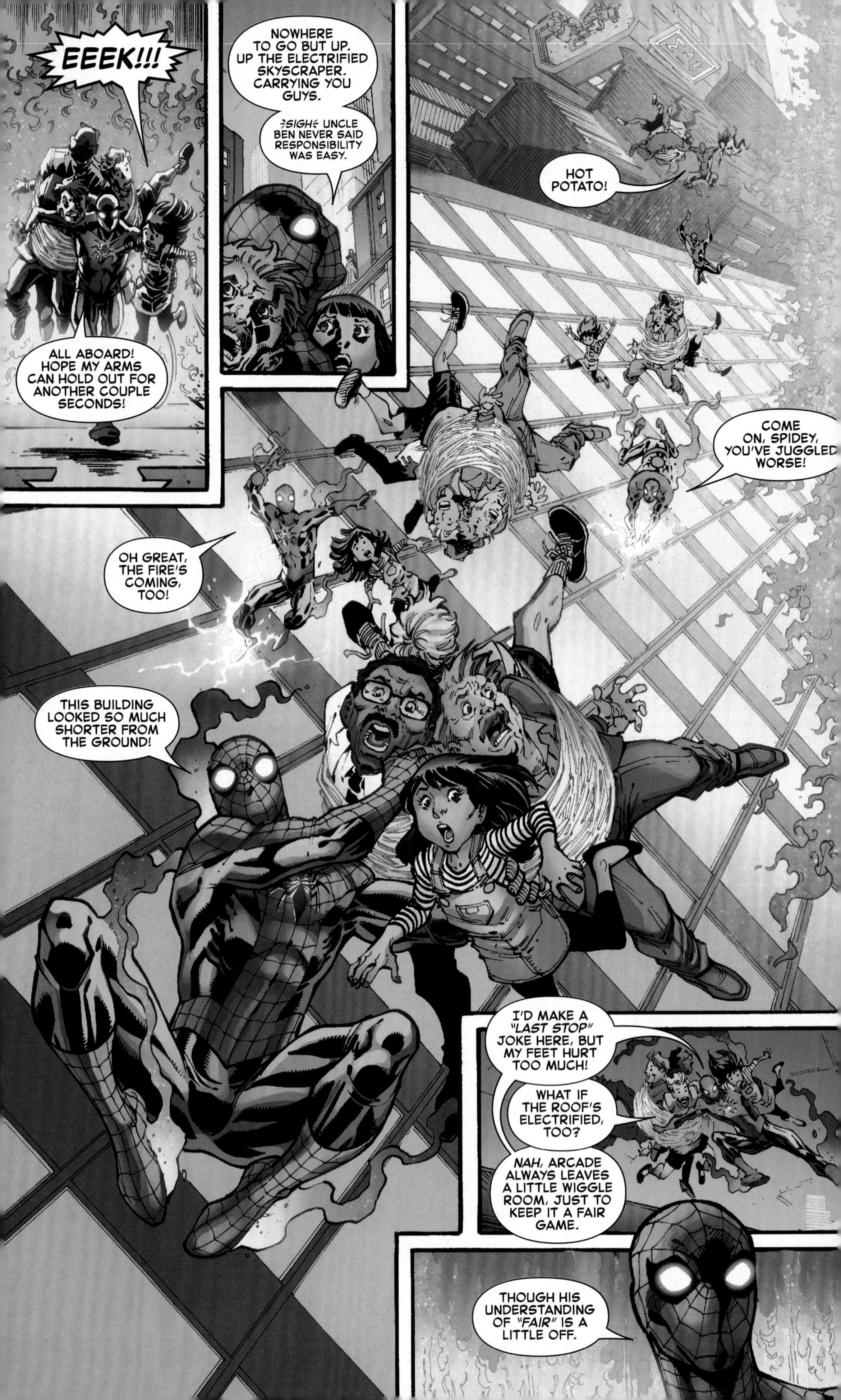
EEEK!!!
ALL ABOARD! HOPE MY ARMS CAN HOLD OUT FOR ANOTHER COUPLE SECONDS!
NOWHERE TO GO BUT UP. UP THE ELECTRIFIED SKYSCRAPER. CARRYING YOU GUYS.
SIGH UNCLE BEN NEVER SAID RESPONSIBILITY WAS EASY.
HOT POTATO!
COME ON, SPIDEY, YOU'VE JUGGLED WORSE!
OH GREAT, THE FIRE'S COMING, TOO!
THIS BUILDING LOOKED SO MUCH SHORTER FROM THE GROUND!
I'D MAKE A "LAST STOP" JOKE HERE, BUT MY FEET HURT TOO MUCH!
WHAT IF THE ROOF'S ELECTRIFIED, TOO?
NAH, ARCADE ALWAYS LEAVES A LITTLE WIGGLE ROOM, JUST TO KEEP IT A FAIR GAME.
THOUGH HIS UNDERSTANDING OF "FAIR" IS A LITTLE OFF.

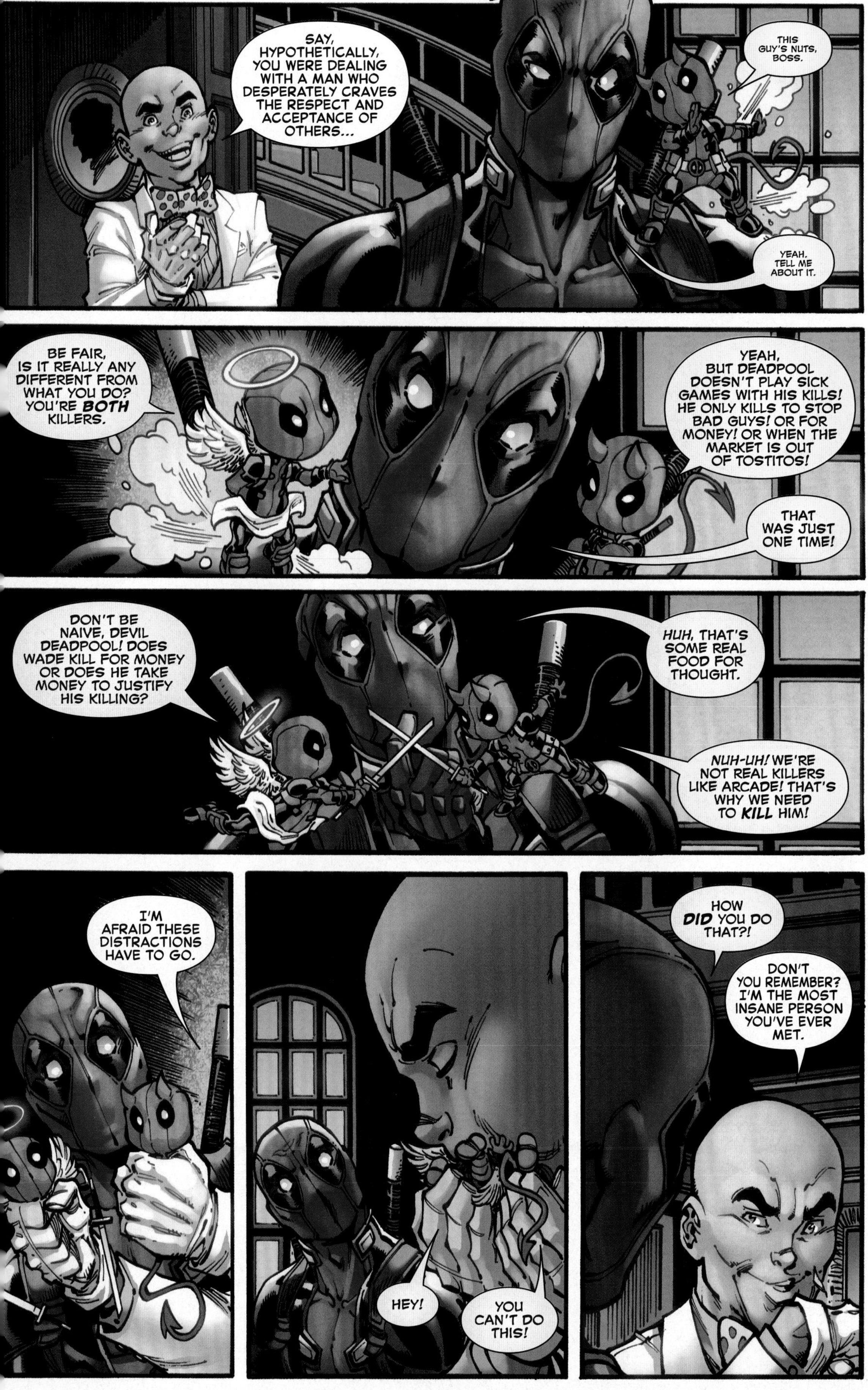
SAY, HYPOTHETICALLY, YOU WERE DEALING WITH A MAN WHO DESPERATELY CRAVES THE RESPECT AND ACCEPTANCE OF OTHERS...
THIS GUY'S NUTS, BOSS.
YEAH. TELL ME ABOUT IT.
BE FAIR, IS IT REALLY ANY DIFFERENT FROM WHAT YOU DO? YOU'RE BOTH KILLERS.
YEAH, BUT DEADPOOL DOESN'T PLAY SICK GAMES WITH HIS KILLS! HE ONLY KILLS TO STOP BAD GUYS! OR FOR MONEY! OR WHEN THE MARKET IS OUT OF TOSTITOS!
THAT WAS JUST ONE TIME!
DON'T BE NAIVE, DEVIL DEADPOOL! DOES WADE KILL FOR MONEY OR DOES HE TAKE MONEY TO JUSTIFY HIS KILLING?
HUH, THAT'S SOME REAL FOOD FOR THOUGHT.
NUH-UH! WE'RE NOT REAL KILLERS LIKE ARCADE! THAT'S WHY WE NEED TO KILL HIM!
I'M AFRAID THESE DISTRACTIONS HAVE TO GO.
HEY!
YOU CAN'T DO THIS!
HOW DID YOU DO THAT?!
DON'T YOU REMEMBER? I'M THE MOST INSANE PERSON YOU'VE EVER MET.

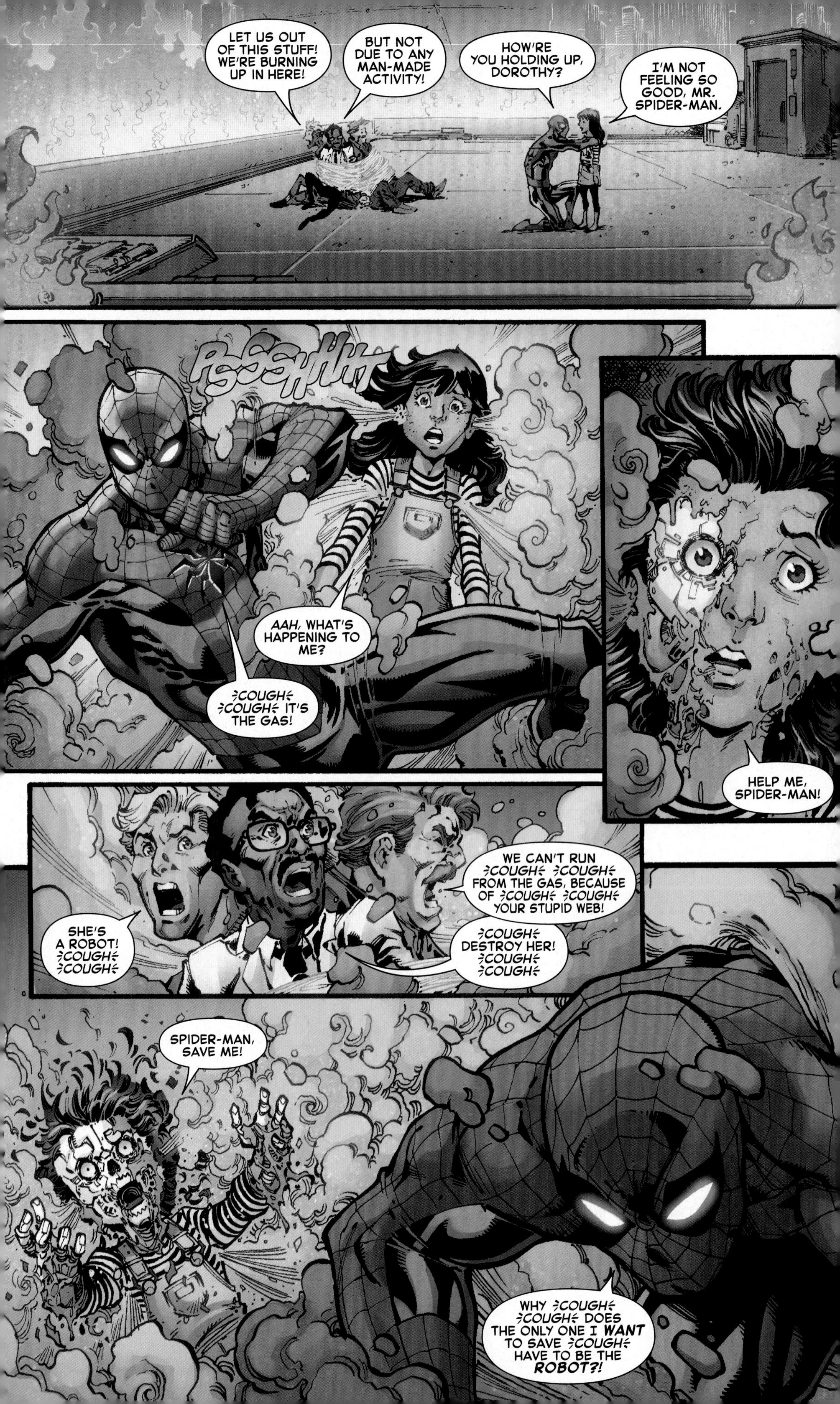
LET US OUT OF THIS STUFF! WE'RE BURNING UP IN HERE!
BUT NOT DUE TO ANY MAN-MADE ACTIVITY!
HOW'RE YOU HOLDING UP, DOROTHY?
I'M NOT FEELING SO GOOD, MR. SPIDER-MAN.
PSSSHHHT
AAH, WHAT'S HAPPENING TO ME?
COUGH COUGH IT'S THE GAS!
HELP ME, SPIDER-MAN!
WE CAN'T RUN COUGH COUGH FROM THE GAS, BECAUSE OF COUGH COUGH YOUR STUPID WEB!
SHE'S A ROBOT! COUGH COUGH
COUGH DESTROY HER! COUGH COUGH
SPIDER-MAN, SAVE ME!
WHY COUGH COUGH DOES THE ONLY ONE I WANT TO SAVE COUGH HAVE TO BE THE ROBOT?!

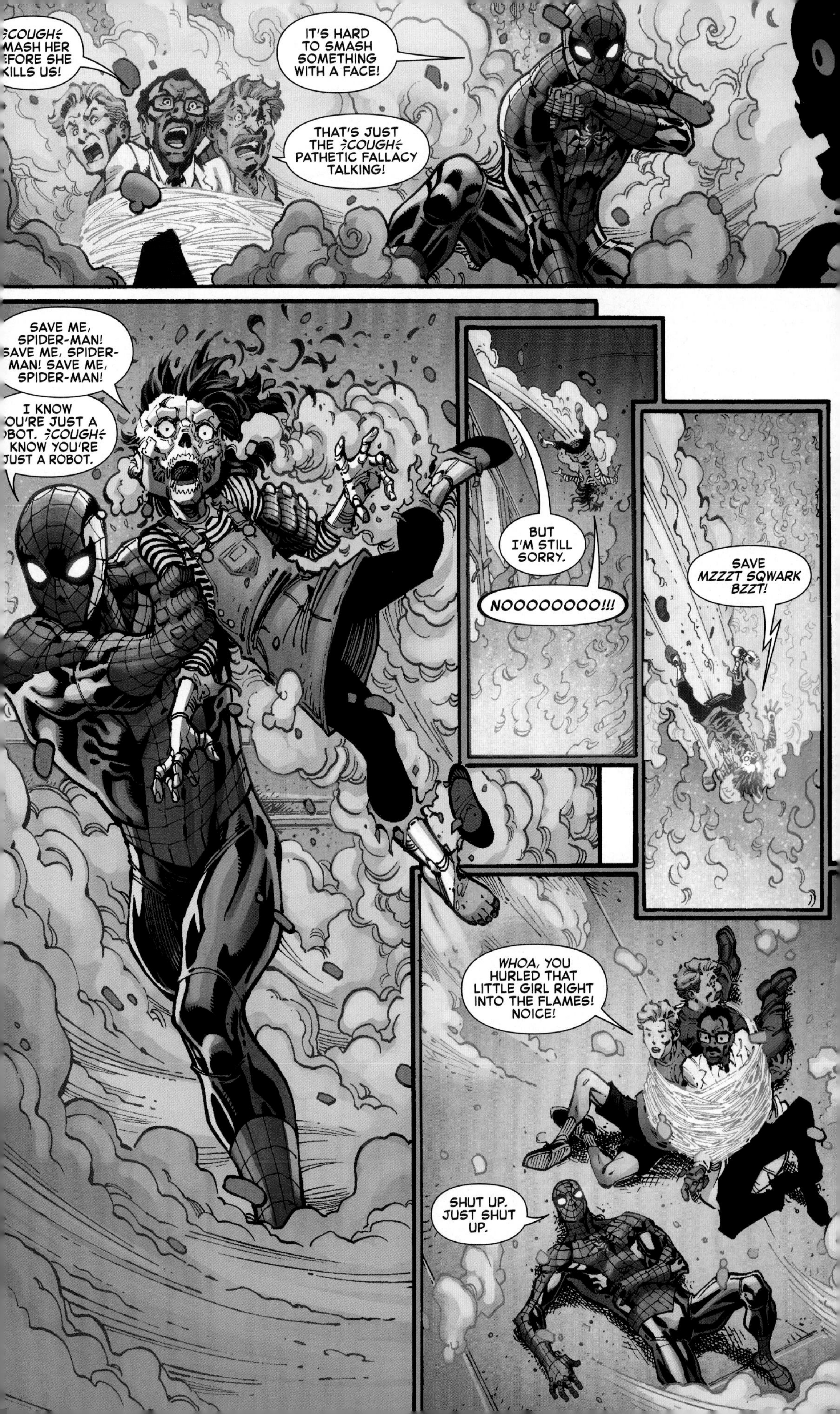

COUGH MASH HER EFORE SHE KILLS US!
IT'S HARD TO SMASH SOMETHING WITH A FACE!
THAT'S JUST THE COUGH PATHETIC FALLACY TALKING!
SAVE ME, SPIDER-MAN! SAVE ME, SPIDER-MAN! SAVE ME, SPIDER-MAN!
I KNOW YOU'RE JUST A OBOT. COUGH KNOW YOU'RE JUST A ROBOT.
BUT I'M STILL SORRY.
NOOOOOOOO!!!
SAVE MZZZT SQWARK BZZT!
WHOA, YOU HURLED THAT LITTLE GIRL RIGHT INTO THE FLAMES! NOICE!
SHUT UP. JUST SHUT UP.

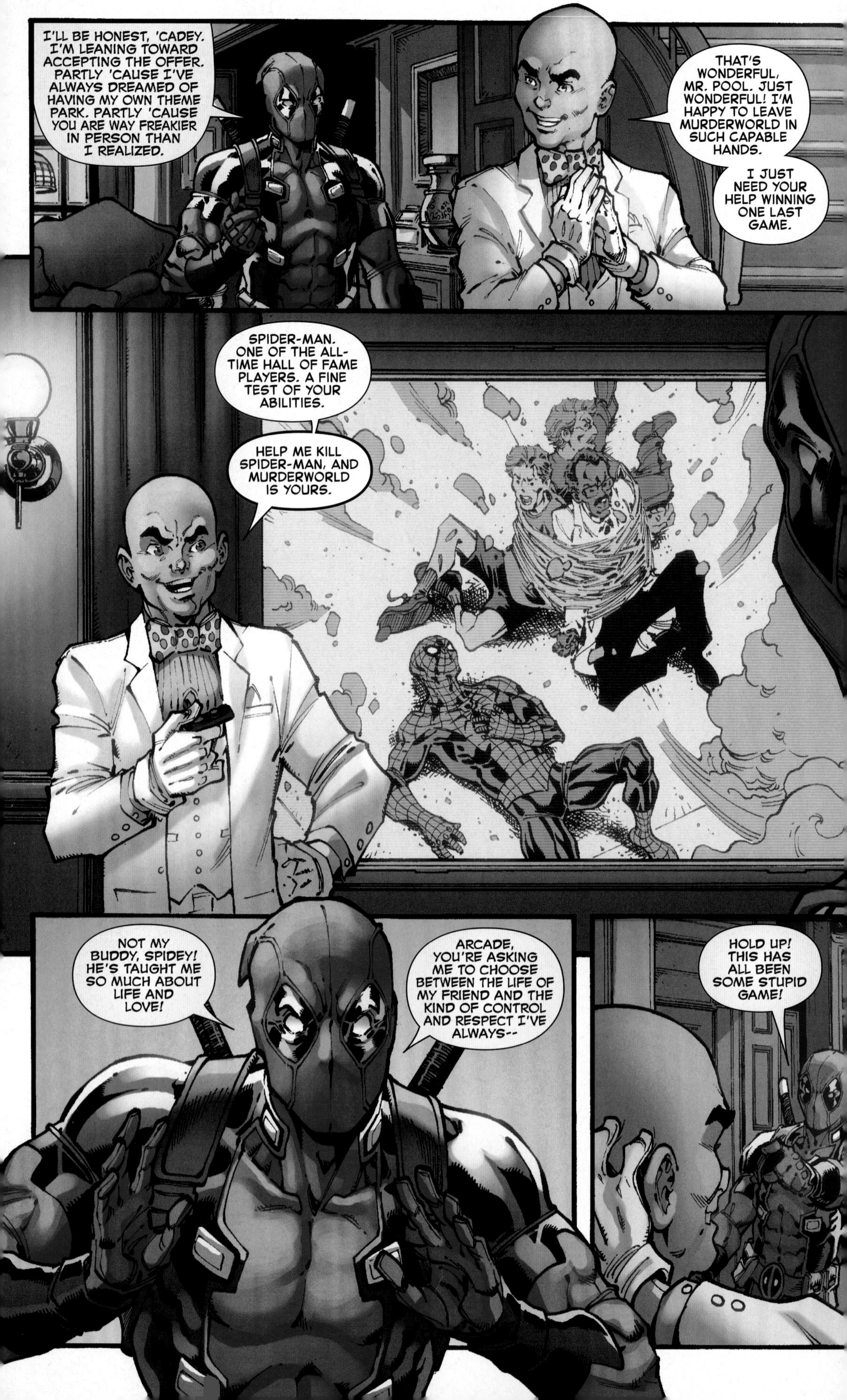
I'LL BE HONEST, 'CADEY. I'M LEANING TOWARD ACCEPTING THE OFFER. PARTLY 'CAUSE I'VE ALWAYS DREAMED OF HAVING MY OWN THEME PARK. PARTLY 'CAUSE YOU ARE WAY FREAKIER IN PERSON THAN I REALIZED.
THAT'S WONDERFUL, MR. POOL. JUST WONDERFUL! I'M HAPPY TO LEAVE MURDERWORLD IN SUCH CAPABLE HANDS.
I JUST NEED YOUR HELP WINNING ONE LAST GAME.
SPIDER-MAN. ONE OF THE ALL-TIME HALL OF FAME PLAYERS. A FINE TEST OF YOUR ABILITIES.
HELP ME KILL SPIDER-MAN, AND MURDERWORLD IS YOURS.
NOT MY BUDDY, SPIDEY! HE'S TAUGHT ME SO MUCH ABOUT LIFE AND LOVE!
ARCADE, YOU'RE ASKING ME TO CHOOSE BETWEEN THE LIFE OF MY FRIEND AND THE KIND OF CONTROL AND RESPECT I'VE ALWAYS--
HOLD UP! THIS HAS ALL BEEN SOME STUPID GAME!

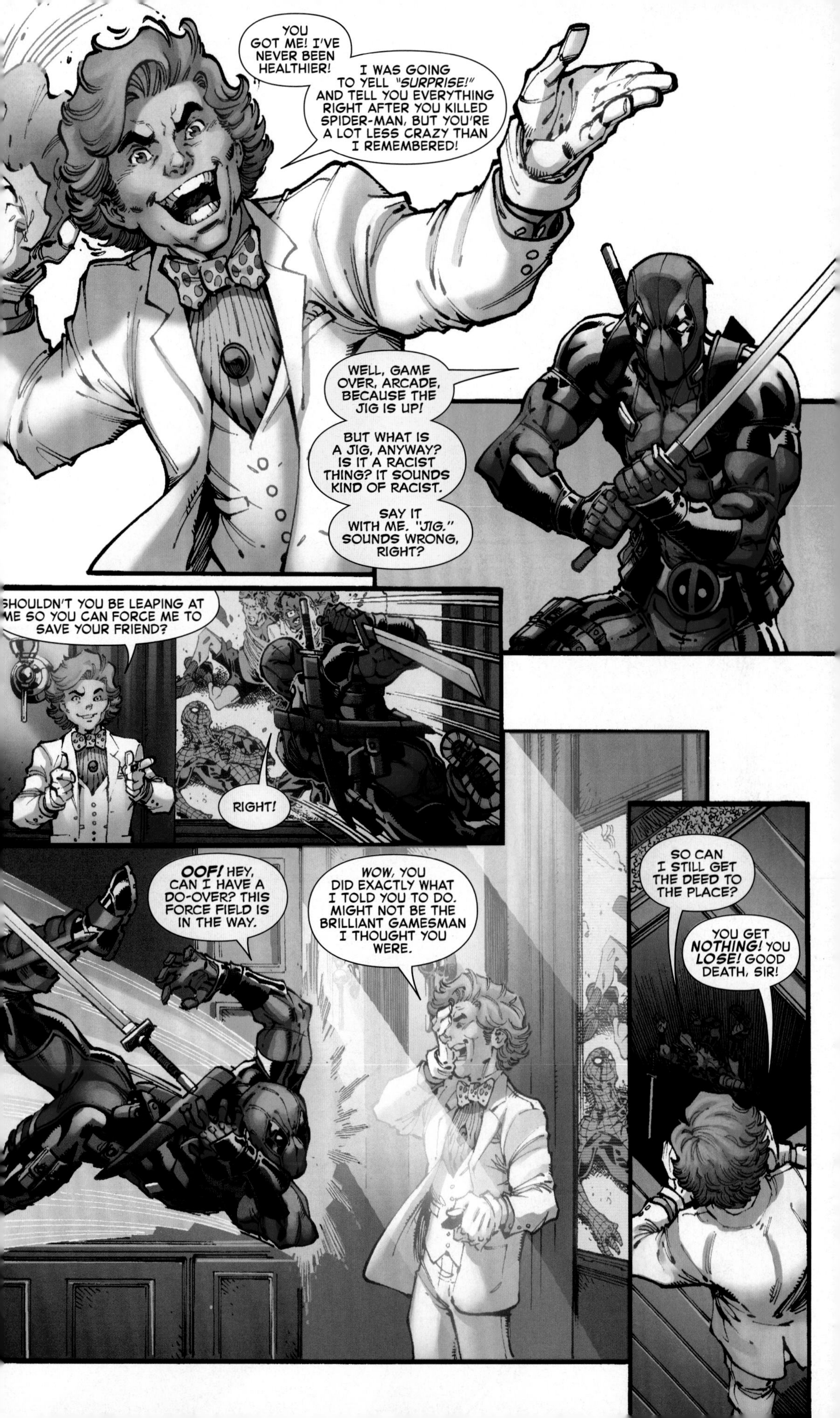
YOU GOT ME! I'VE NEVER BEEN HEALTHIER!
I WAS GOING TO YELL "SURPRISE!" AND TELL YOU EVERYTHING RIGHT AFTER YOU KILLED SPIDER-MAN, BUT YOU'RE A LOT LESS CRAZY THAN I REMEMBERED!
WELL, GAME OVER, ARCADE, BECAUSE THE JIG IS UP!
BUT WHAT IS A JIG, ANYWAY? IS IT A RACIST THING? IT SOUNDS KIND OF RACIST.
SAY IT WITH ME. "JIG." SOUNDS WRONG, RIGHT?
SHOULDN'T YOU BE LEAPING AT ME SO YOU CAN FORCE ME TO SAVE YOUR FRIEND?
RIGHT!
OOF! HEY, CAN I HAVE A DO-OVER? THIS FORCE FIELD IS IN THE WAY.
WOW, YOU DID EXACTLY WHAT I TOLD YOU TO DO. MIGHT NOT BE THE BRILLIANT GAMESMAN I THOUGHT YOU WERE.
SO CAN I STILL GET THE DEED TO THE PLACE?
YOU GET NOTHING! YOU LOSE! GOOD DEATH, SIR!

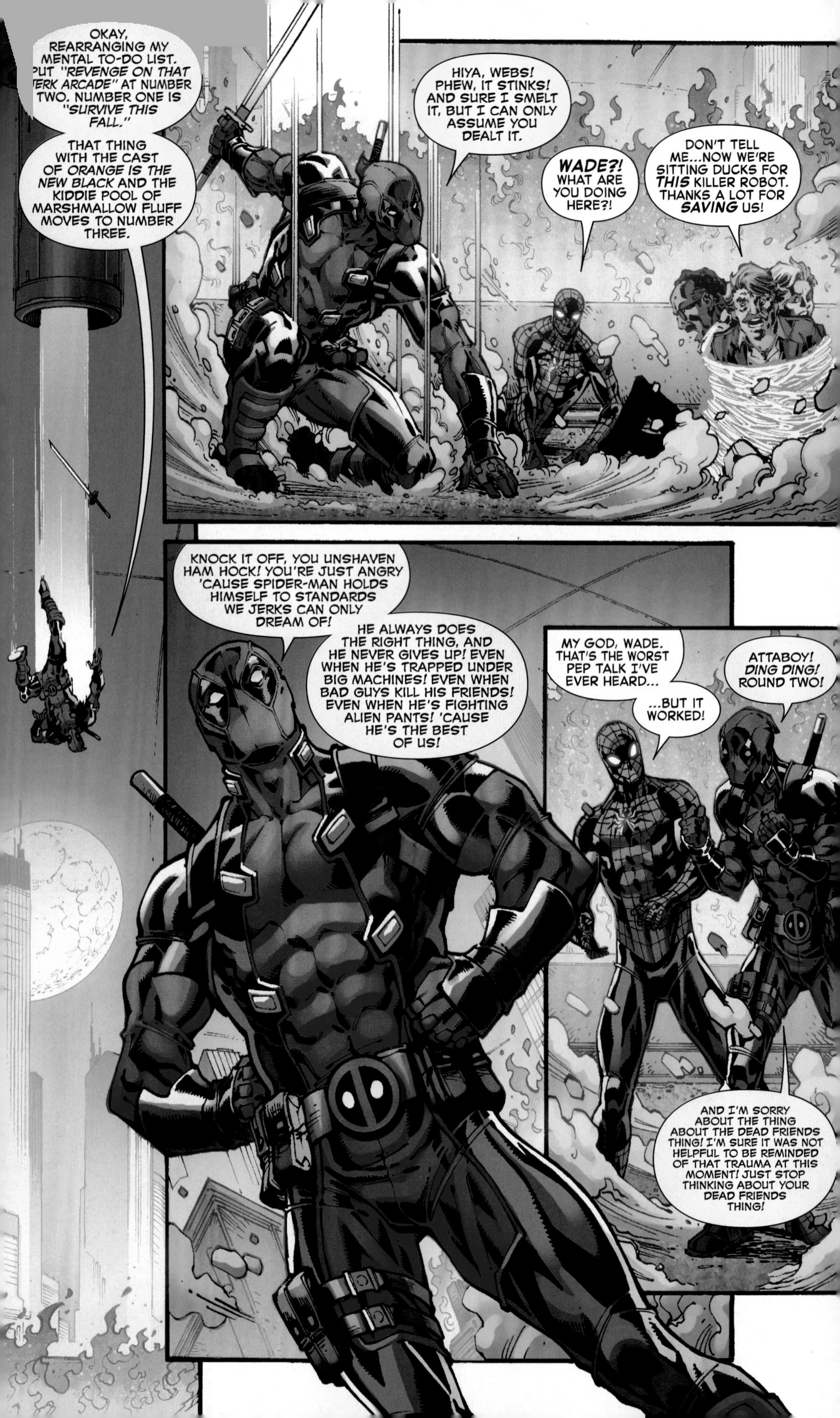
OKAY, REARRANGING MY MENTAL TO-DO LIST. PUT "REVENGE ON THAT JERK ARCADE" AT NUMBER TWO. NUMBER ONE IS "SURVIVE THIS FALL."
THAT THING WITH THE CAST OF ORANGE IS THE NEW BLACK AND THE KIDDIE POOL OF MARSHMALLOW FLUFF MOVES TO NUMBER THREE.
HIYA, WEBS! PHEW, IT STINKS! AND SURE I SMELT IT, BUT I CAN ONLY ASSUME YOU DEALT IT.
WADE?! WHAT ARE YOU DOING HERE?!
DON'T TELL ME...NOW WE'RE SITTING DUCKS FOR THIS KILLER ROBOT. THANKS A LOT FOR SAVING US!
KNOCK IT OFF, YOU UNSHAVEN HAM HOCK! YOU'RE JUST ANGRY 'CAUSE SPIDER-MAN HOLDS HIMSELF TO STANDARDS WE JERKS CAN ONLY DREAM OF!
HE ALWAYS DOES THE RIGHT THING, AND HE NEVER GIVES UP! EVEN WHEN HE'S TRAPPED UNDER BIG MACHINES! EVEN WHEN BAD GUYS KILL HIS FRIENDS! EVEN WHEN HE'S FIGHTING ALIEN PANTS! 'CAUSE HE'S THE BEST OF US!
MY GOD, WADE. THAT'S THE WORST PEP TALK I'VE EVER HEARD...
...BUT IT WORKED!
ATTABOY! DING DING! ROUND TWO!
AND I'M SORRY ABOUT THE THING ABOUT THE DEAD FRIENDS THING! I'M SURE IT WAS NOT HELPFUL TO BE REMINDED OF THAT TRAUMA AT THIS MOMENT! JUST STOP THINKING ABOUT YOUR DEAD FRIENDS THING!

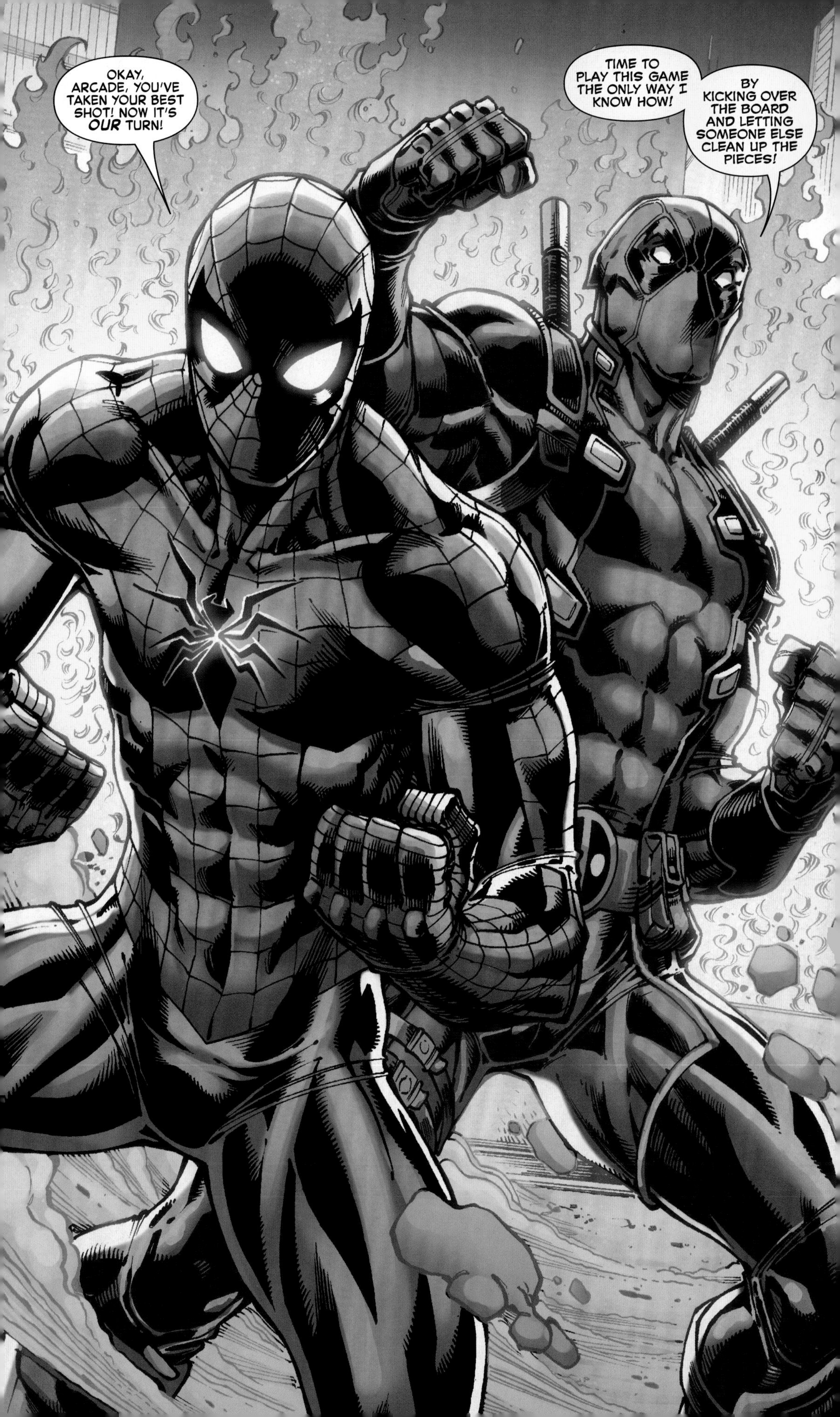
OKAY, ARCADE, YOU'VE TAKEN YOUR BEST SHOT! NOW IT'S **OUR** TURN!
TIME TO PLAY THIS GAME THE ONLY WAY I KNOW HOW!
BY KICKING OVER THE BOARD AND LETTING SOMEONE ELSE CLEAN UP THE PIECES!

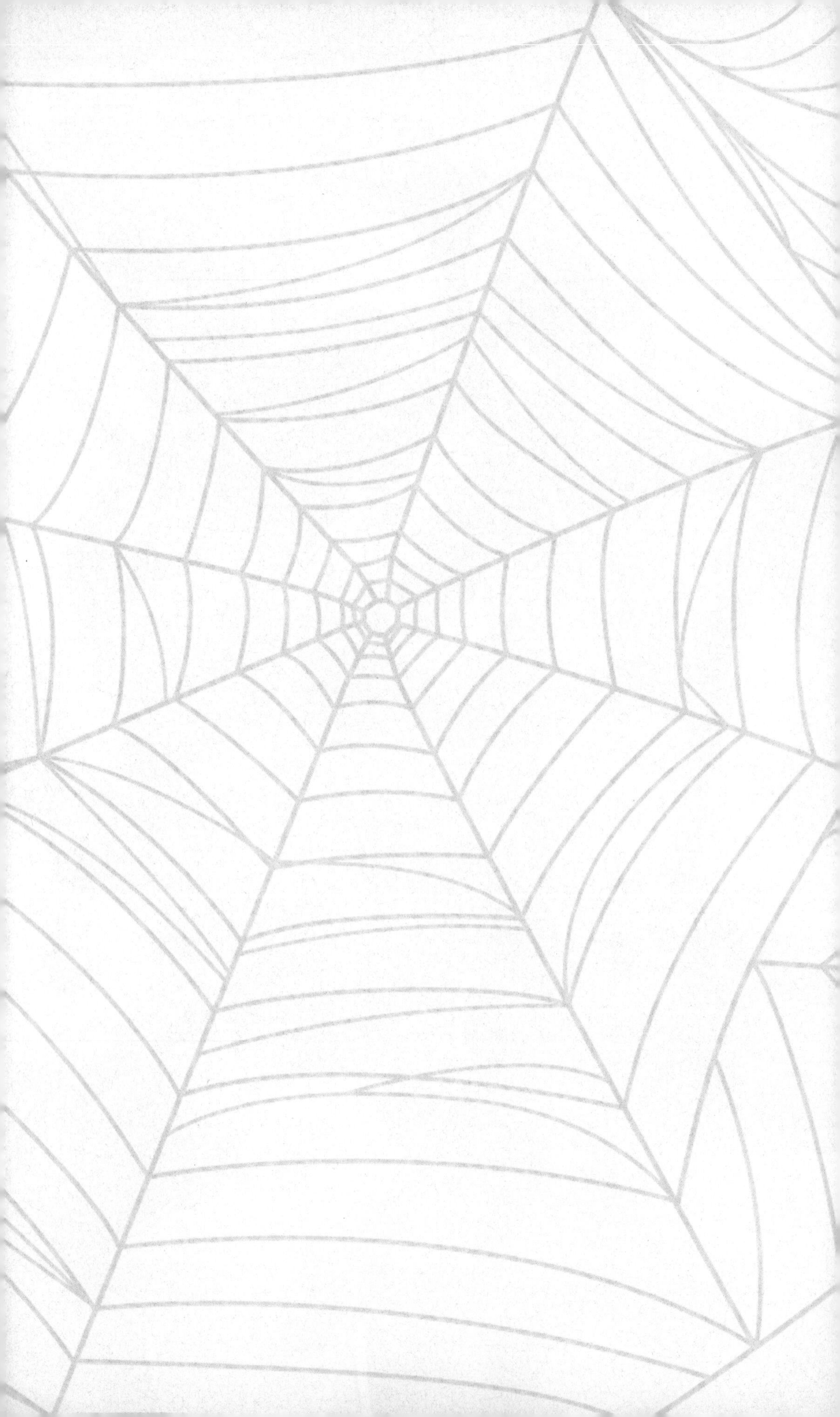

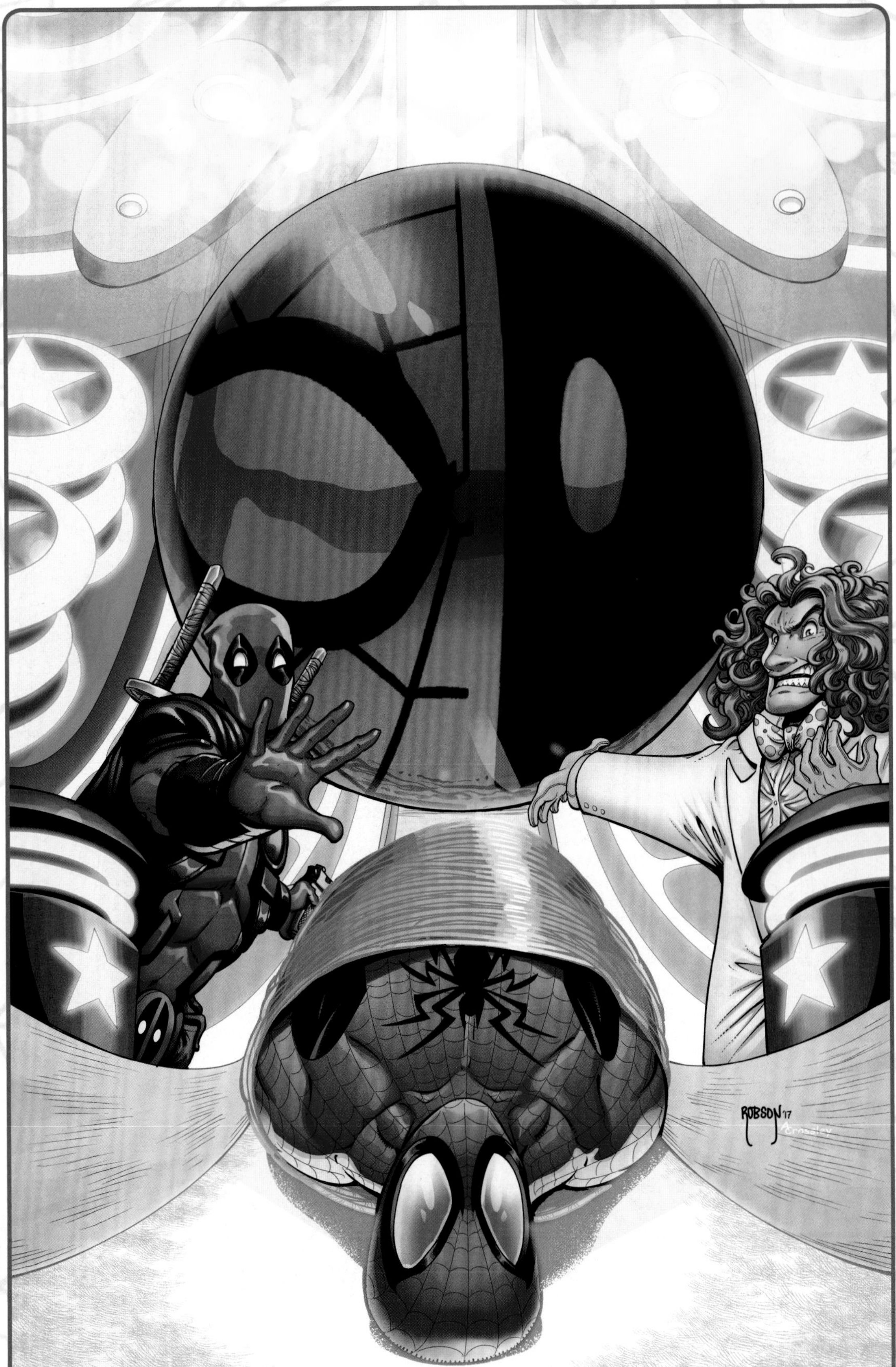
ROBSON '17

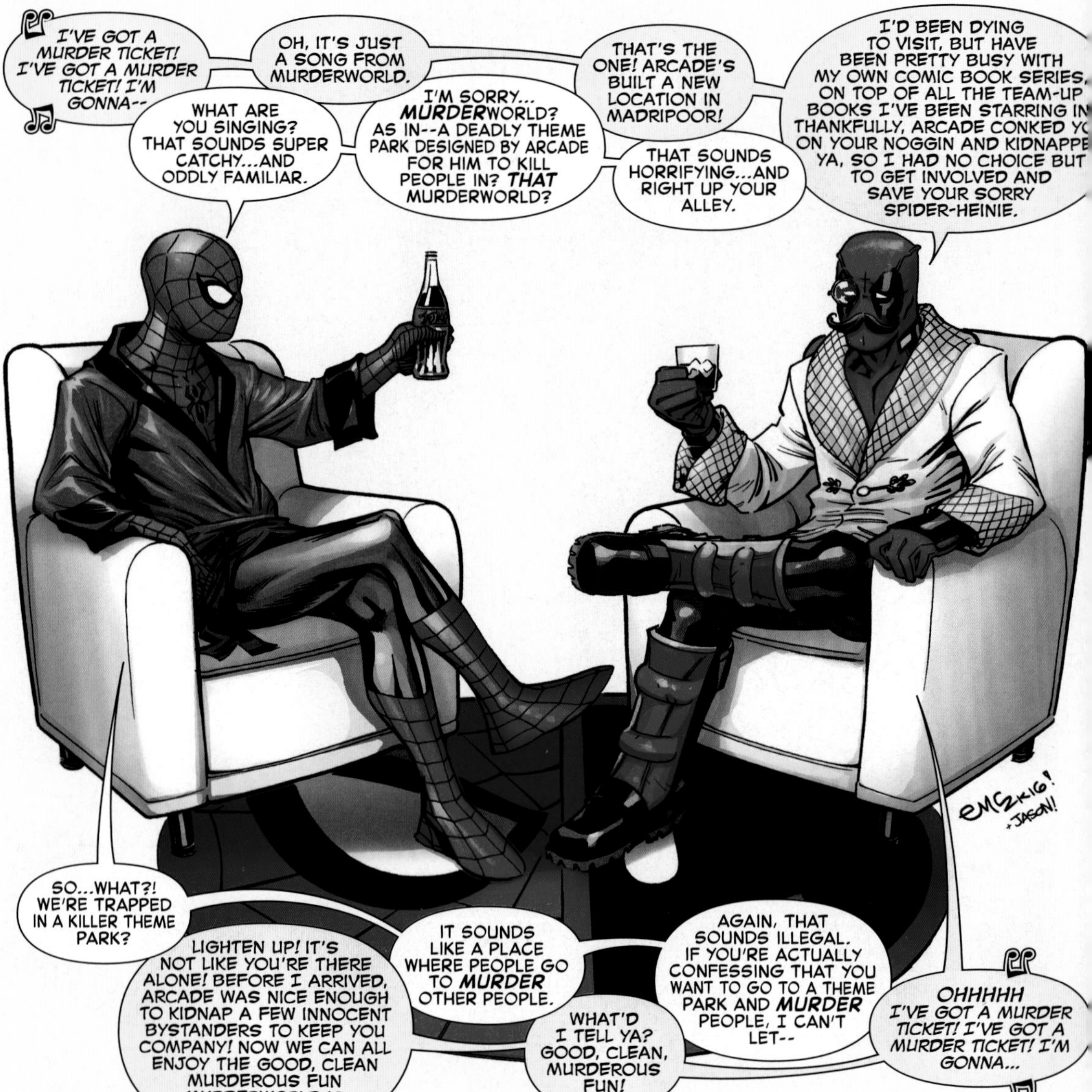

I'VE GOT A MURDER TICKET! I'VE GOT A MURDER TICKET! I'M GONNA--
WHAT ARE YOU SINGING? THAT SOUNDS SUPER CATCHY...AND ODDLY FAMILIAR.
OH, IT'S JUST A SONG FROM MURDERWORLD.
I'M SORRY... MURDERWORLD? AS IN--A DEADLY THEME PARK DESIGNED BY ARCADE FOR HIM TO KILL PEOPLE IN? THAT MURDERWORLD?
THAT'S THE ONE! ARCADE'S BUILT A NEW LOCATION IN MADRIPOOR!
THAT SOUNDS HORRIFYING...AND RIGHT UP YOUR ALLEY.
I'D BEEN DYING TO VISIT, BUT HAVE BEEN PRETTY BUSY WITH MY OWN COMIC BOOK SERIES, ON TOP OF ALL THE TEAM-UP BOOKS I'VE BEEN STARRING IN THANKFULLY, ARCADE CONKED Y ON YOUR NOGGIN AND KIDNAPPE YA, SO I HAD NO CHOICE BUT TO GET INVOLVED AND SAVE YOUR SORRY SPIDER-HEINIE.
SO...WHAT?! WE'RE TRAPPED IN A KILLER THEME PARK?
LIGHTEN UP! IT'S NOT LIKE YOU'RE THERE ALONE! BEFORE I ARRIVED, ARCADE WAS NICE ENOUGH TO KIDNAP A FEW INNOCENT BYSTANDERS TO KEEP YOU COMPANY! NOW WE CAN ALL ENJOY THE GOOD, CLEAN MURDEROUS FUN MURDERWORLD IS KNOWN FOR.
IT SOUNDS LIKE A PLACE WHERE PEOPLE GO TO MURDER OTHER PEOPLE.
WHAT'D I TELL YA? GOOD, CLEAN, MURDEROUS FUN!
AGAIN, THAT SOUNDS ILLEGAL. IF YOU'RE ACTUALLY CONFESSING THAT YOU WANT TO GO TO A THEME PARK AND MURDER PEOPLE, I CAN'T LET--
OHHHHH I'VE GOT A MURDER TICKET! I'VE GOT A MURDER TICKET! I'M GONNA...

IT'S A MURDER, MURDER, MURDER, MURDER WORLD

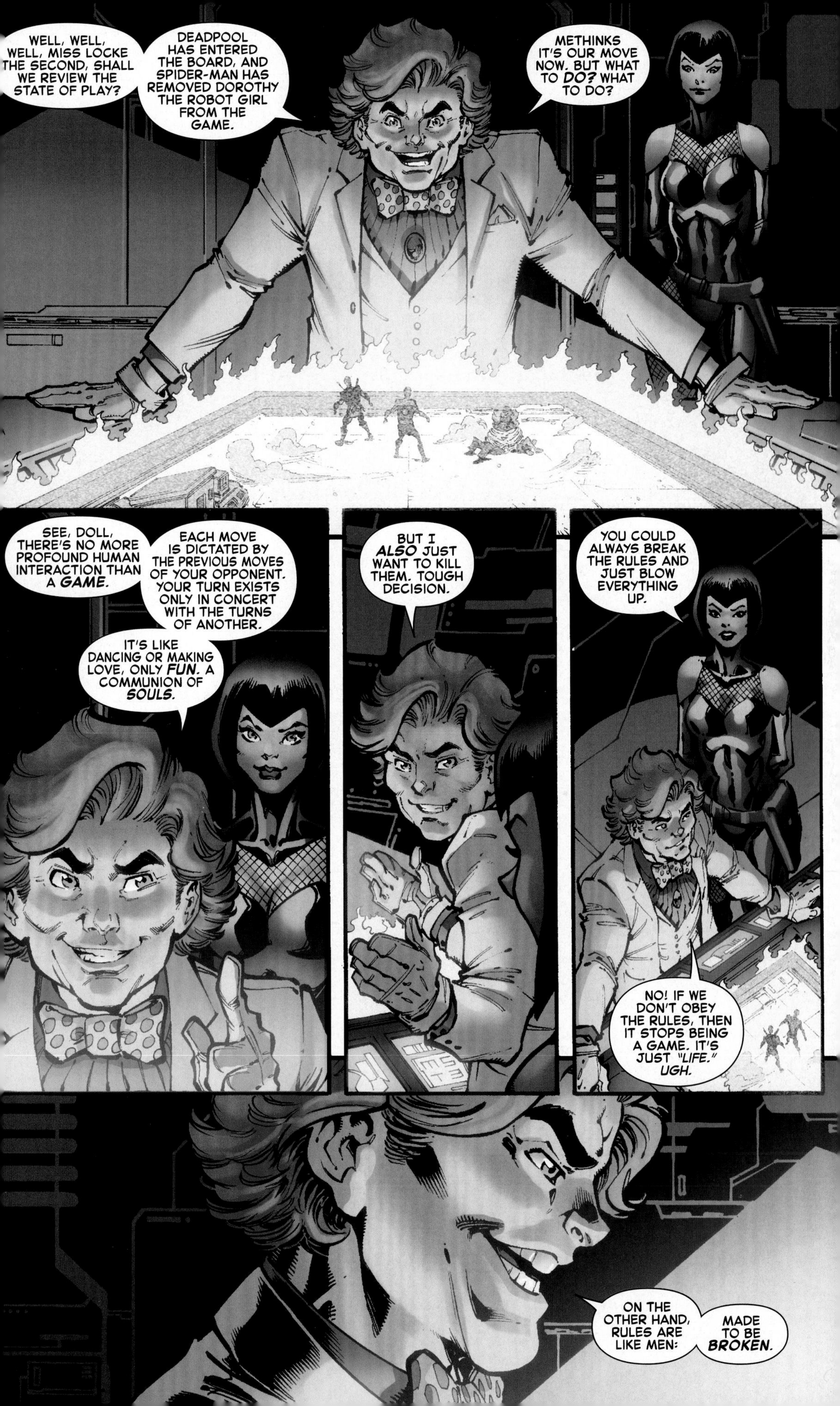
WELL, WELL, WELL, MISS LOCKE THE SECOND, SHALL WE REVIEW THE STATE OF PLAY?
DEADPOOL HAS ENTERED THE BOARD, AND SPIDER-MAN HAS REMOVED DOROTHY THE ROBOT GIRL FROM THE GAME.
METHINKS IT'S OUR MOVE NOW. BUT WHAT TO DO? WHAT TO DO?
SEE, DOLL, THERE'S NO MORE PROFOUND HUMAN INTERACTION THAN A GAME.
EACH MOVE IS DICTATED BY THE PREVIOUS MOVES OF YOUR OPPONENT. YOUR TURN EXISTS ONLY IN CONCERT WITH THE TURNS OF ANOTHER.
IT'S LIKE DANCING OR MAKING LOVE, ONLY FUN. A COMMUNION OF SOULS.
BUT I ALSO JUST WANT TO KILL THEM. TOUGH DECISION.
YOU COULD ALWAYS BREAK THE RULES AND JUST BLOW EVERYTHING UP.
NO! IF WE DON'T OBEY THE RULES, THEN IT STOPS BEING A GAME. IT'S JUST "LIFE." UGH.
ON THE OTHER HAND, RULES ARE LIKE MEN:
MADE TO BE BROKEN.

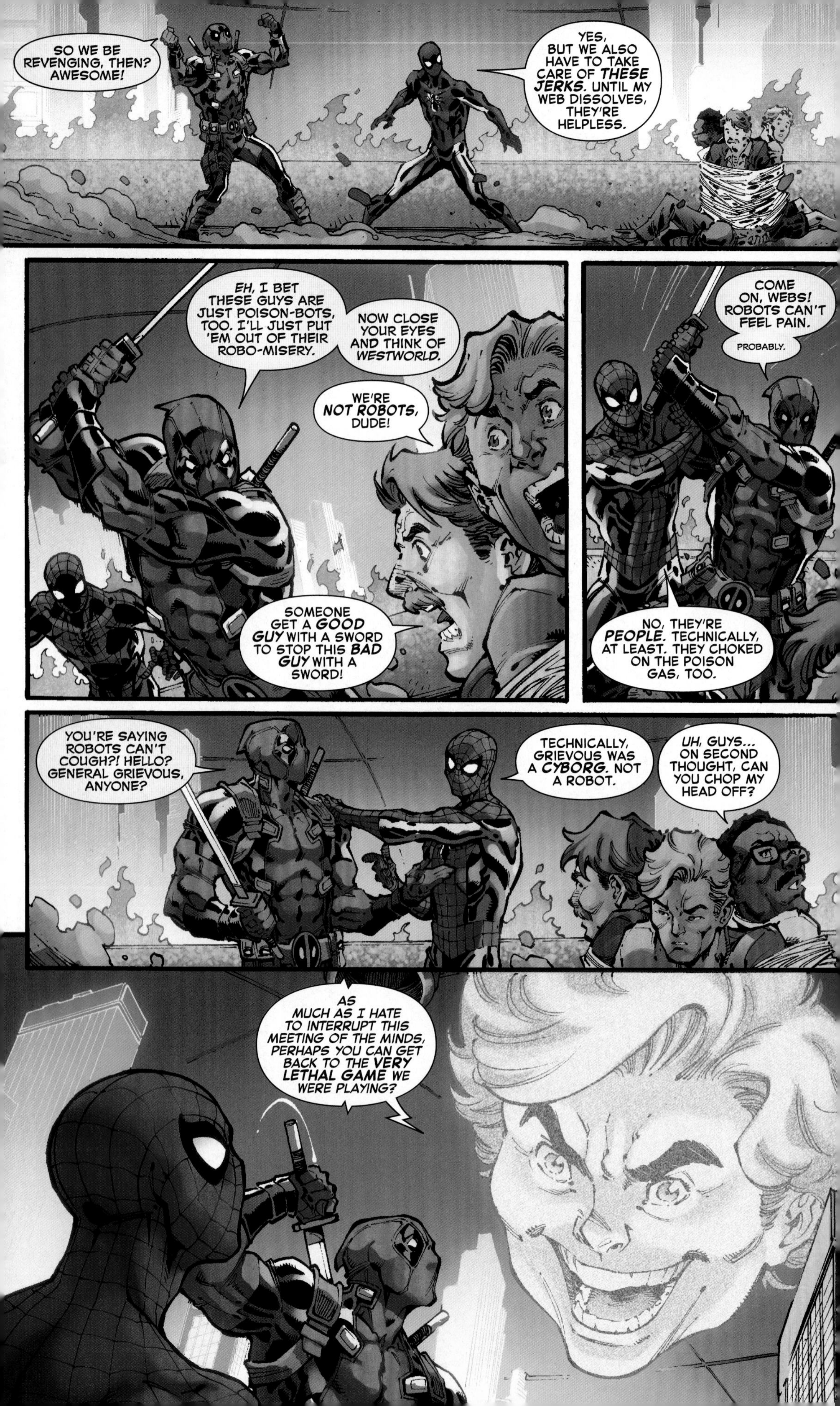

SO WE BE REVENGING, THEN? AWESOME!
YES, BUT WE ALSO HAVE TO TAKE CARE OF THESE JERKS. UNTIL MY WEB DISSOLVES, THEY'RE HELPLESS.
EH, I BET THESE GUYS ARE JUST POISON-BOTS, TOO. I'LL JUST PUT 'EM OUT OF THEIR ROBO-MISERY.
NOW CLOSE YOUR EYES AND THINK OF WESTWORLD.
WE'RE NOT ROBOTS, DUDE!
SOMEONE GET A GOOD GUY WITH A SWORD TO STOP THIS BAD GUY WITH A SWORD!
COME ON, WEBS! ROBOTS CAN'T FEEL PAIN.
PROBABLY.
NO, THEY'RE PEOPLE. TECHNICALLY, AT LEAST. THEY CHOKED ON THE POISON GAS, TOO.
YOU'RE SAYING ROBOTS CAN'T COUGH?! HELLO? GENERAL GRIEVOUS, ANYONE?
TECHNICALLY, GRIEVOUS WAS A CYBORG. NOT A ROBOT.
UH, GUYS... ON SECOND THOUGHT, CAN YOU CHOP MY HEAD OFF?
AS MUCH AS I HATE TO INTERRUPT THIS MEETING OF THE MINDS, PERHAPS YOU CAN GET BACK TO THE VERY LETHAL GAME WE WERE PLAYING?

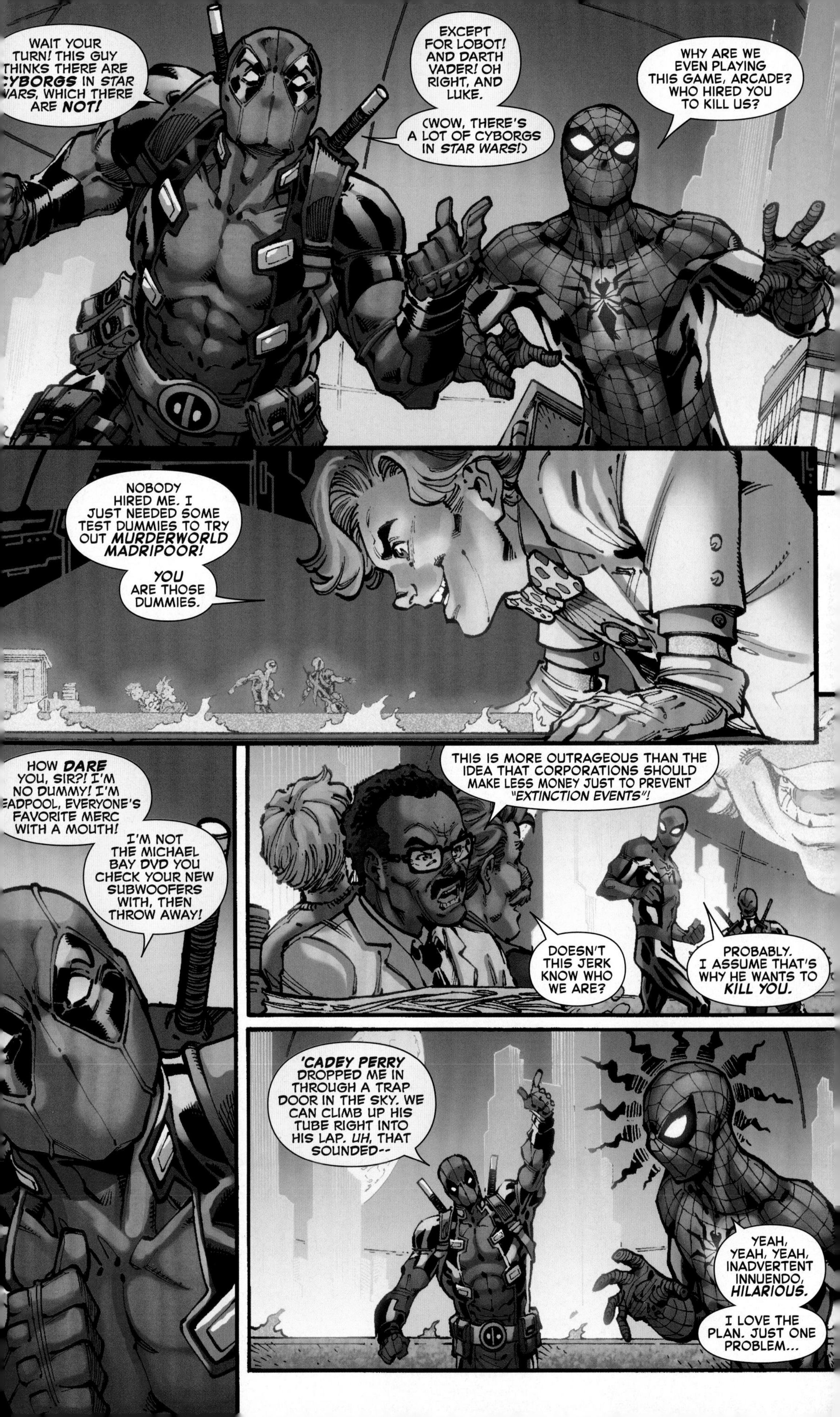
WAIT YOUR TURN! THIS GUY THINKS THERE ARE CYBORGS IN STAR WARS, WHICH THERE ARE NOT!
EXCEPT FOR LOBOT! AND DARTH VADER! OH RIGHT, AND LUKE.
(WOW, THERE'S A LOT OF CYBORGS IN STAR WARS!)
WHY ARE WE EVEN PLAYING THIS GAME, ARCADE? WHO HIRED YOU TO KILL US?
NOBODY HIRED ME. I JUST NEEDED SOME TEST DUMMIES TO TRY OUT MURDERWORLD MADRIPOOR!
YOU ARE THOSE DUMMIES.
HOW DARE YOU, SIR?! I'M NO DUMMY! I'M DEADPOOL, EVERYONE'S FAVORITE MERC WITH A MOUTH!
I'M NOT THE MICHAEL BAY DVD YOU CHECK YOUR NEW SUBWOOFERS WITH, THEN THROW AWAY!
THIS IS MORE OUTRAGEOUS THAN THE IDEA THAT CORPORATIONS SHOULD MAKE LESS MONEY JUST TO PREVENT "EXTINCTION EVENTS"!
DOESN'T THIS JERK KNOW WHO WE ARE?
PROBABLY. I ASSUME THAT'S WHY HE WANTS TO KILL YOU.
'CADEY PERRY DROPPED ME IN THROUGH A TRAP DOOR IN THE SKY. WE CAN CLIMB UP HIS TUBE RIGHT INTO HIS LAP. UH, THAT SOUNDED--
YEAH, YEAH, YEAH, INADVERTENT INNUENDO, HILARIOUS.
I LOVE THE PLAN. JUST ONE PROBLEM...

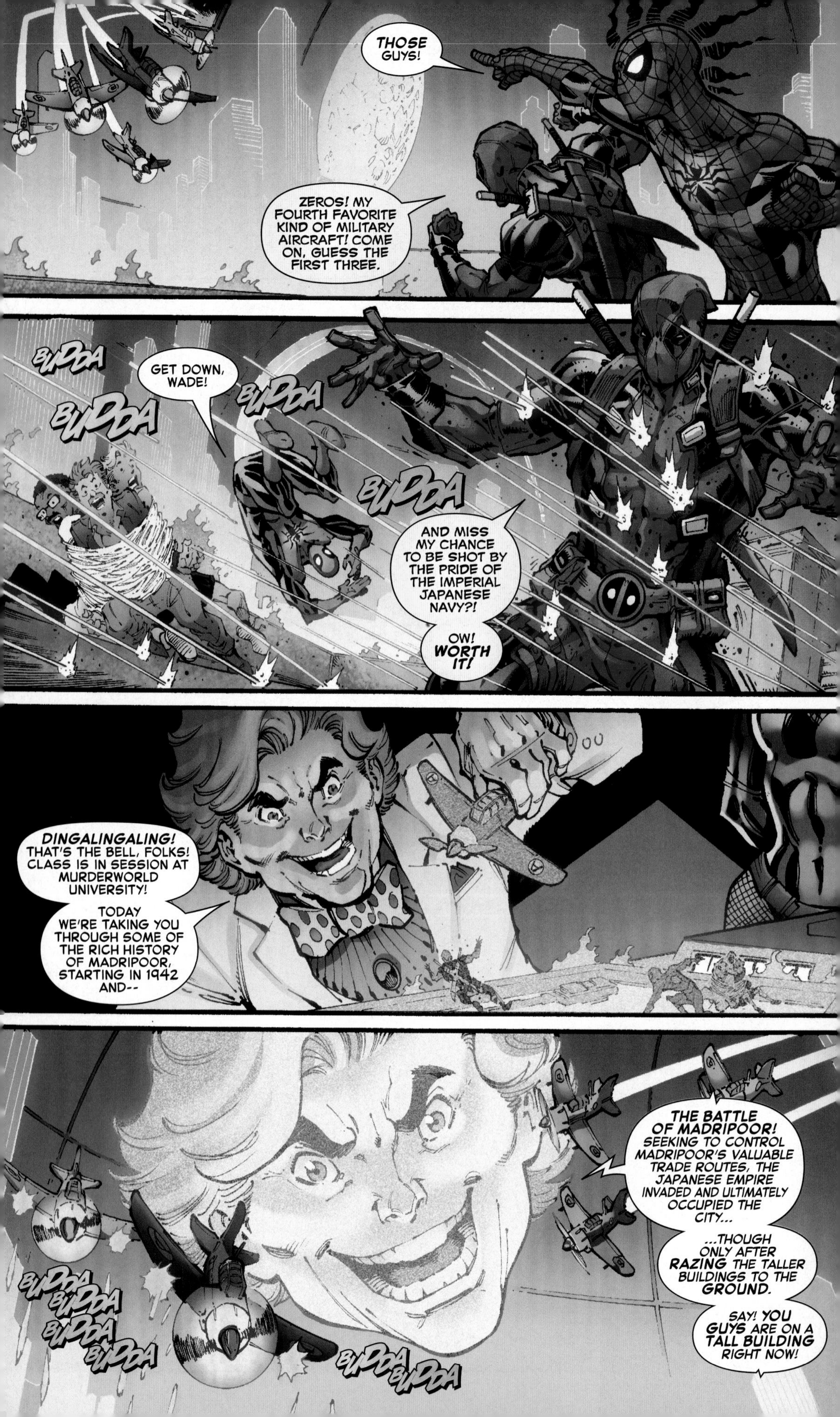

THOSE GUYS!
ZEROS! MY FOURTH FAVORITE KIND OF MILITARY AIRCRAFT! COME ON, GUESS THE FIRST THREE.
BUDDA
GET DOWN, WADE!
BUDDA
BUDDA
BUDDA
AND MISS MY CHANCE TO BE SHOT BY THE PRIDE OF THE IMPERIAL JAPANESE NAVY?!
OW! WORTH IT!
DINGALINGALING! THAT'S THE BELL, FOLKS! CLASS IS IN SESSION AT MURDERWORLD UNIVERSITY!
TODAY WE'RE TAKING YOU THROUGH SOME OF THE RICH HISTORY OF MADRIPOOR, STARTING IN 1942 AND--
THE BATTLE OF MADRIPOOR! SEEKING TO CONTROL MADRIPOOR'S VALUABLE TRADE ROUTES, THE JAPANESE EMPIRE INVADED AND ULTIMATELY OCCUPIED THE CITY...
...THOUGH ONLY AFTER RAZING THE TALLER BUILDINGS TO THE GROUND.
SAY! YOU GUYS ARE ON A TALL BUILDING RIGHT NOW!
BUDDA BUDDA BUDDA BUDDA
BUDDA BUDDA

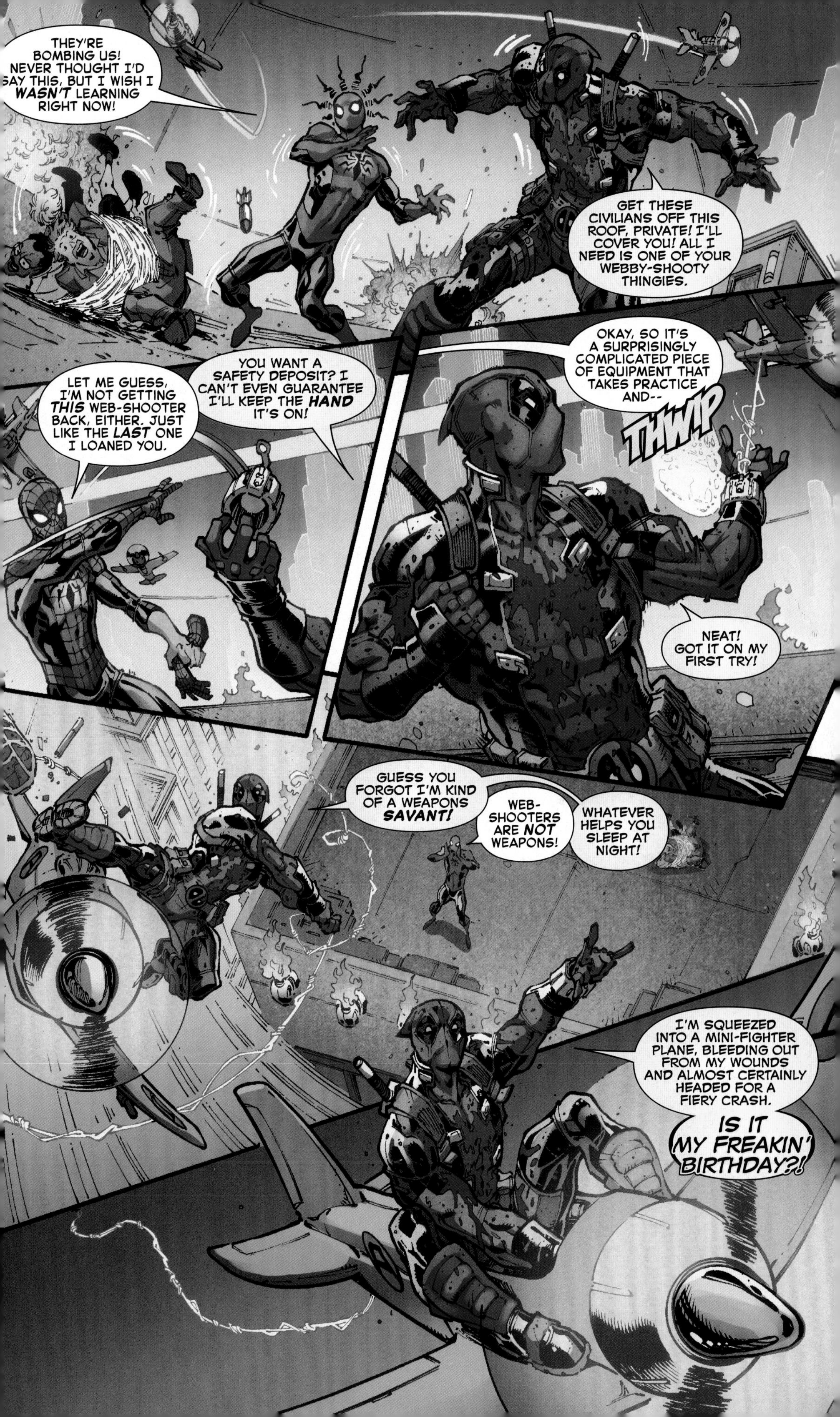
THEY'RE BOMBING US! NEVER THOUGHT I'D SAY THIS, BUT I WISH I WASN'T LEARNING RIGHT NOW!
GET THESE CIVILIANS OFF THIS ROOF, PRIVATE! I'LL COVER YOU! ALL I NEED IS ONE OF YOUR WEBBY-SHOOTY THINGIES.
LET ME GUESS, I'M NOT GETTING THIS WEB-SHOOTER BACK, EITHER. JUST LIKE THE LAST ONE I LOANED YOU.
YOU WANT A SAFETY DEPOSIT? I CAN'T EVEN GUARANTEE I'LL KEEP THE HAND IT'S ON!
OKAY, SO IT'S A SURPRISINGLY COMPLICATED PIECE OF EQUIPMENT THAT TAKES PRACTICE AND--
THWIP
NEAT! GOT IT ON MY FIRST TRY!
GUESS YOU FORGOT I'M KIND OF A WEAPONS SAVANT!
WEB-SHOOTERS ARE NOT WEAPONS!
WHATEVER HELPS YOU SLEEP AT NIGHT!
I'M SQUEEZED INTO A MINI-FIGHTER PLANE, BLEEDING OUT FROM MY WOUNDS AND ALMOST CERTAINLY HEADED FOR A FIERY CRASH.
IS IT MY FREAKIN' BIRTHDAY?!

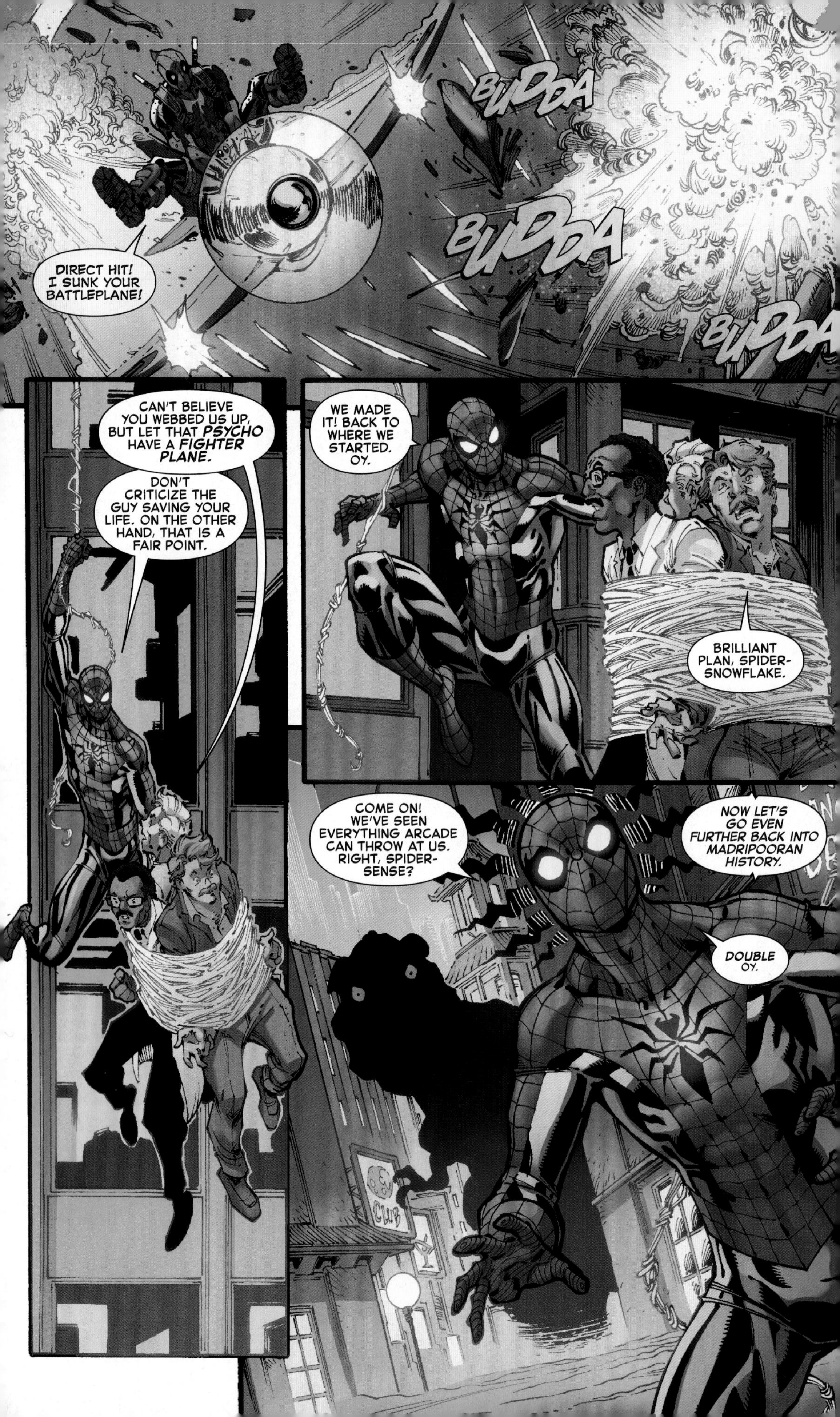
BUDDA
BUDDA
DIRECT HIT! I SUNK YOUR BATTLEPLANE!
BUDDA
CAN'T BELIEVE YOU WEBBED US UP, BUT LET THAT PSYCHO HAVE A FIGHTER PLANE.
DON'T CRITICIZE THE GUY SAVING YOUR LIFE. ON THE OTHER HAND, THAT IS A FAIR POINT.
WE MADE IT! BACK TO WHERE WE STARTED. OY.
BRILLIANT PLAN, SPIDER-SNOWFLAKE.
COME ON! WE'VE SEEN EVERYTHING ARCADE CAN THROW AT US. RIGHT, SPIDER-SENSE?
NOW LET'S GO EVEN FURTHER BACK INTO MADRIPOORAN HISTORY.
DOUBLE OY.
CLUB

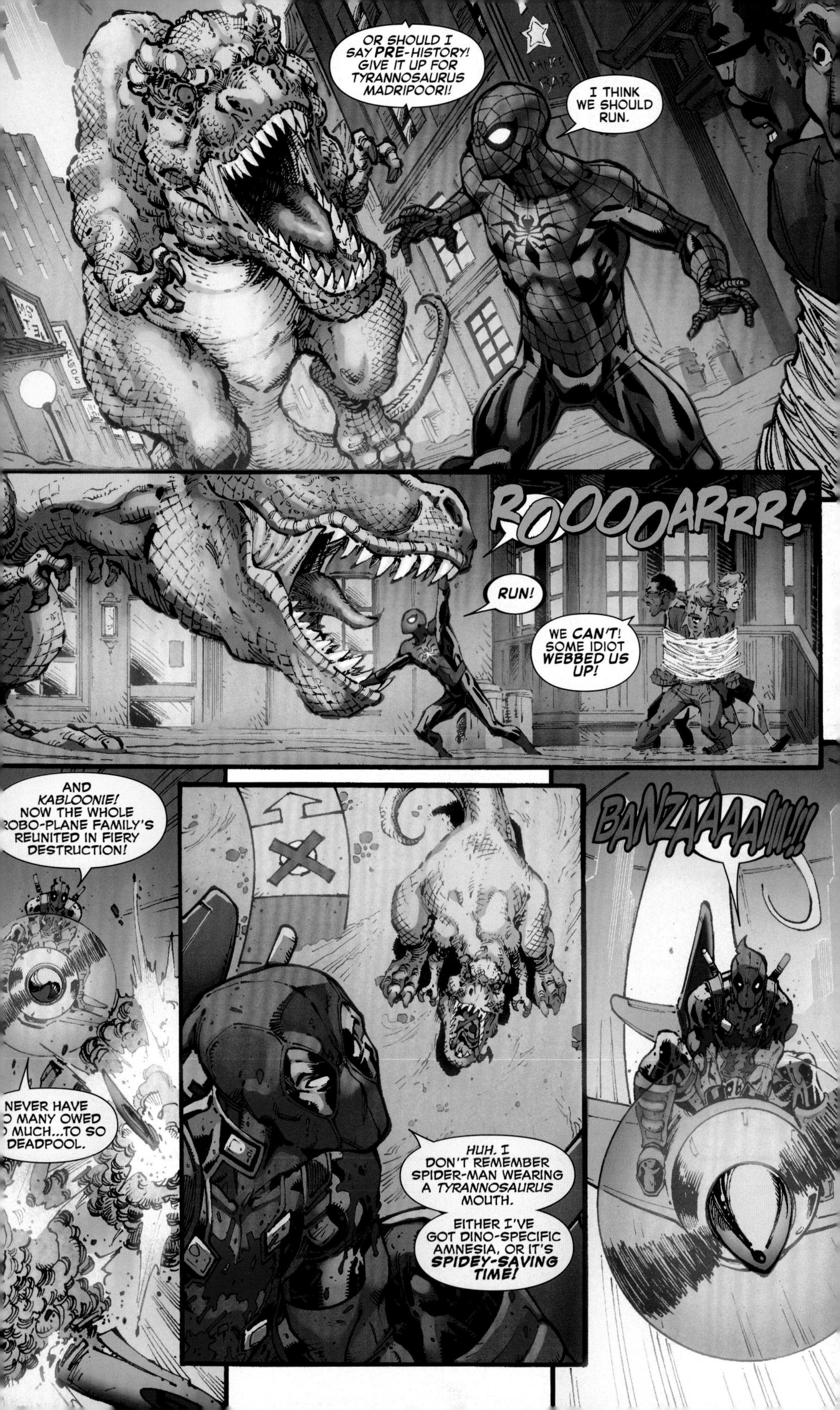
OR SHOULD I SAY PRE-HISTORY! GIVE IT UP FOR TYRANNOSAURUS MADRIPOORI!
I THINK WE SHOULD RUN.
DANCE BAR
ROOOOARRR!
RUN!
WE CAN'T! SOME IDIOT WEBBED US UP!
AND KABLOONIE! NOW THE WHOLE ROBO-PLANE FAMILY'S REUNITED IN FIERY DESTRUCTION!
NEVER HAVE O MANY OWED O MUCH...TO SO DEADPOOL.
HUH. I DON'T REMEMBER SPIDER-MAN WEARING A TYRANNOSAURUS MOUTH.
EITHER I'VE GOT DINO-SPECIFIC AMNESIA, OR IT'S SPIDEY-SAVING TIME!
BANZAAAAI!!!!!

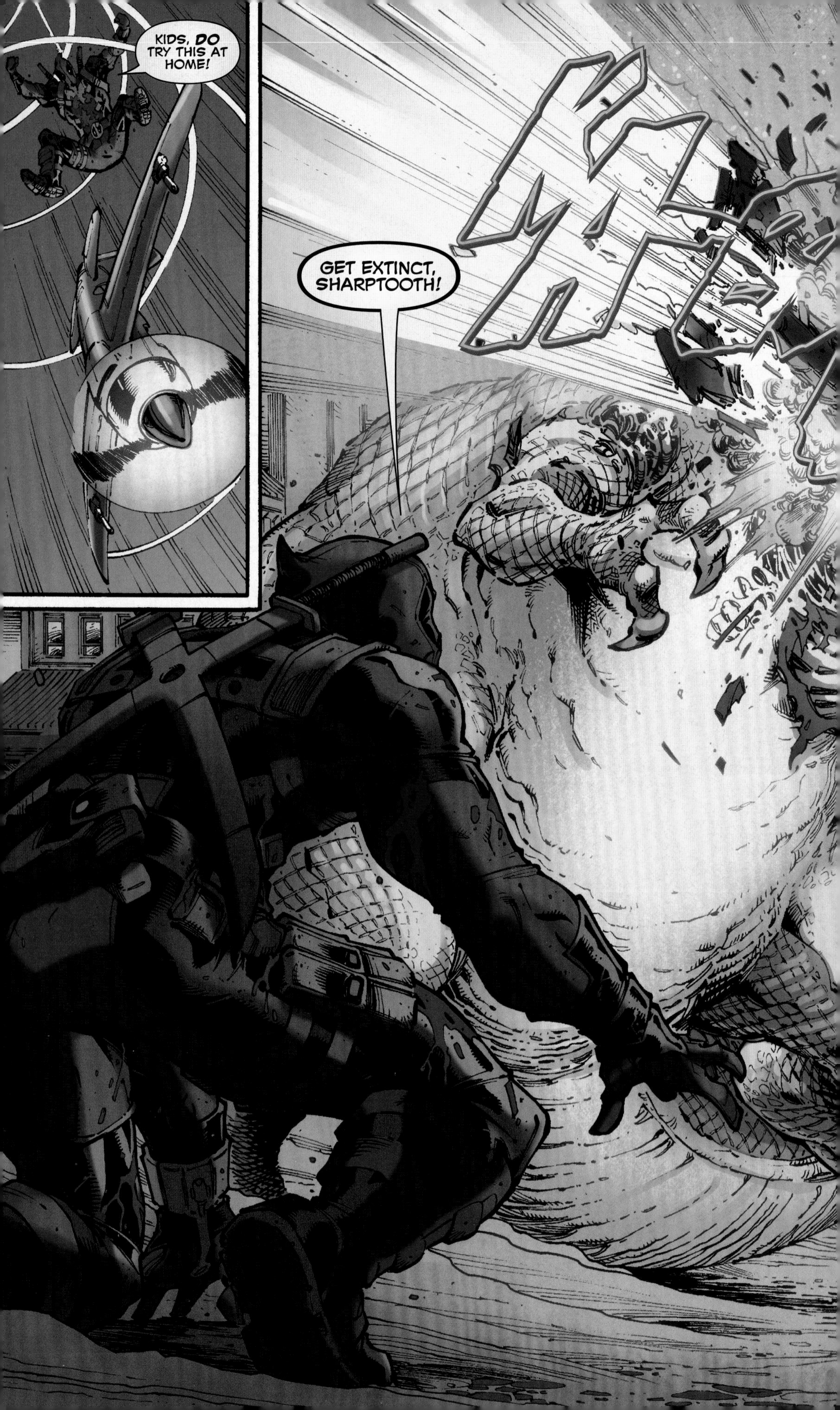
KIDS, DO TRY THIS AT HOME!
GET EXTINCT, SHARPTOOTH!

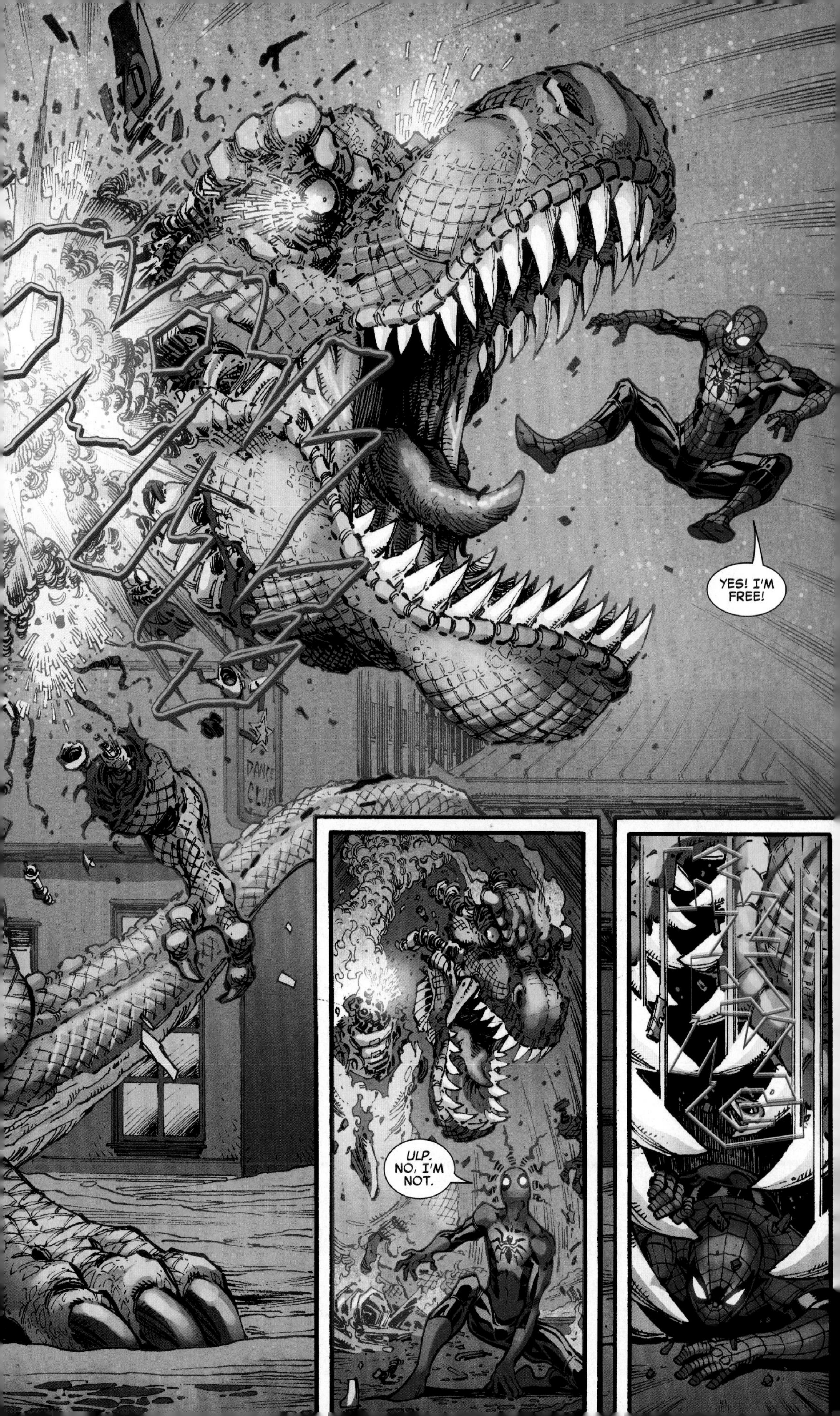
YES! I'M FREE!
ULP. NO, I'M NOT.

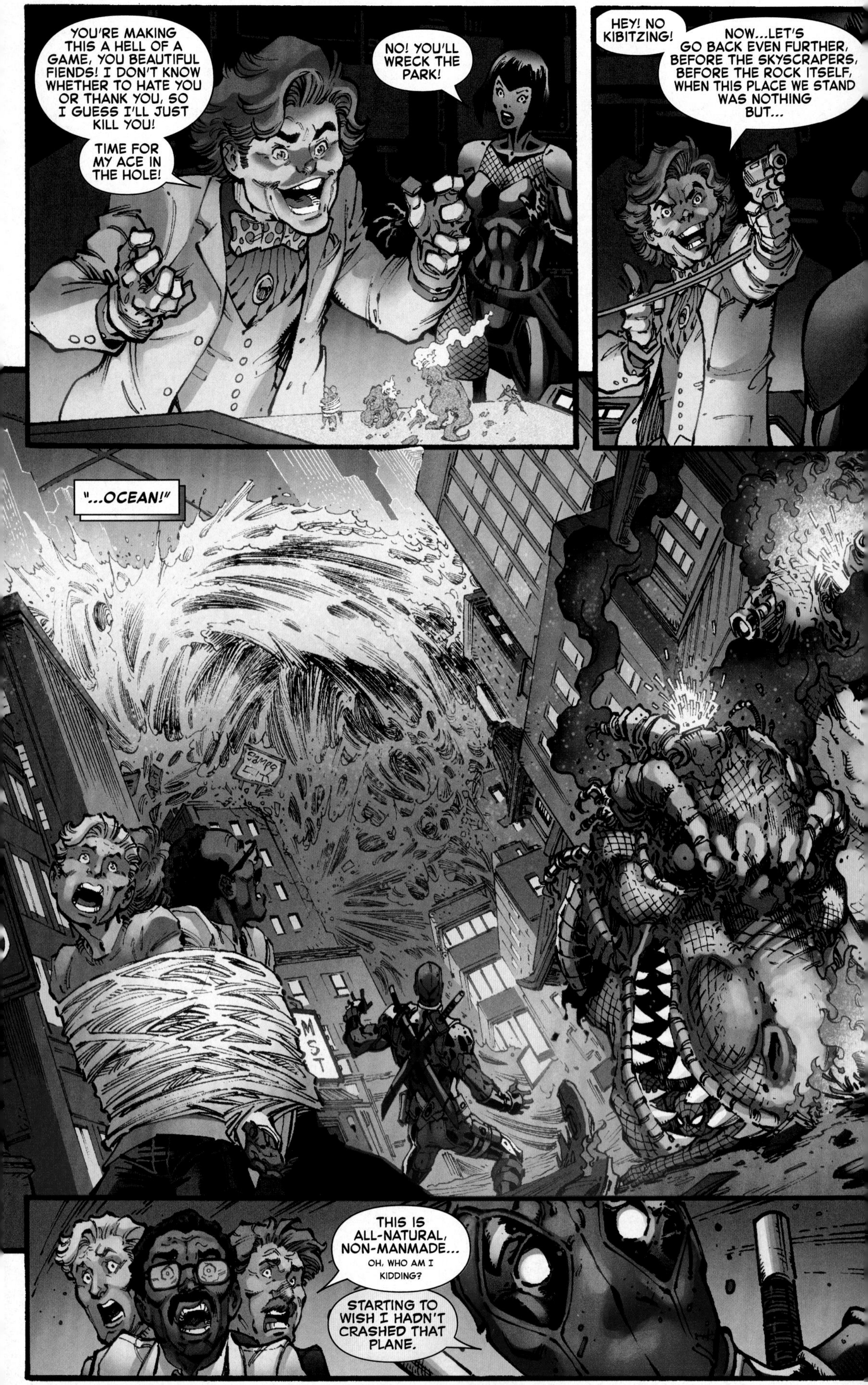
YOU'RE MAKING THIS A HELL OF A GAME, YOU BEAUTIFUL FIENDS! I DON'T KNOW WHETHER TO HATE YOU OR THANK YOU, SO I GUESS I'LL JUST KILL YOU!
TIME FOR MY ACE IN THE HOLE!
NO! YOU'LL WRECK THE PARK!
HEY! NO KIBITZING!
NOW...LET'S GO BACK EVEN FURTHER, BEFORE THE SKYSCRAPERS, BEFORE THE ROCK ITSELF, WHEN THIS PLACE WE STAND WAS NOTHING BUT...
"...OCEAN!"
MST
THIS IS ALL-NATURAL, NON-MANMADE... OH, WHO AM I KIDDING?
STARTING TO WISH I HADN'T CRASHED THAT PLANE.

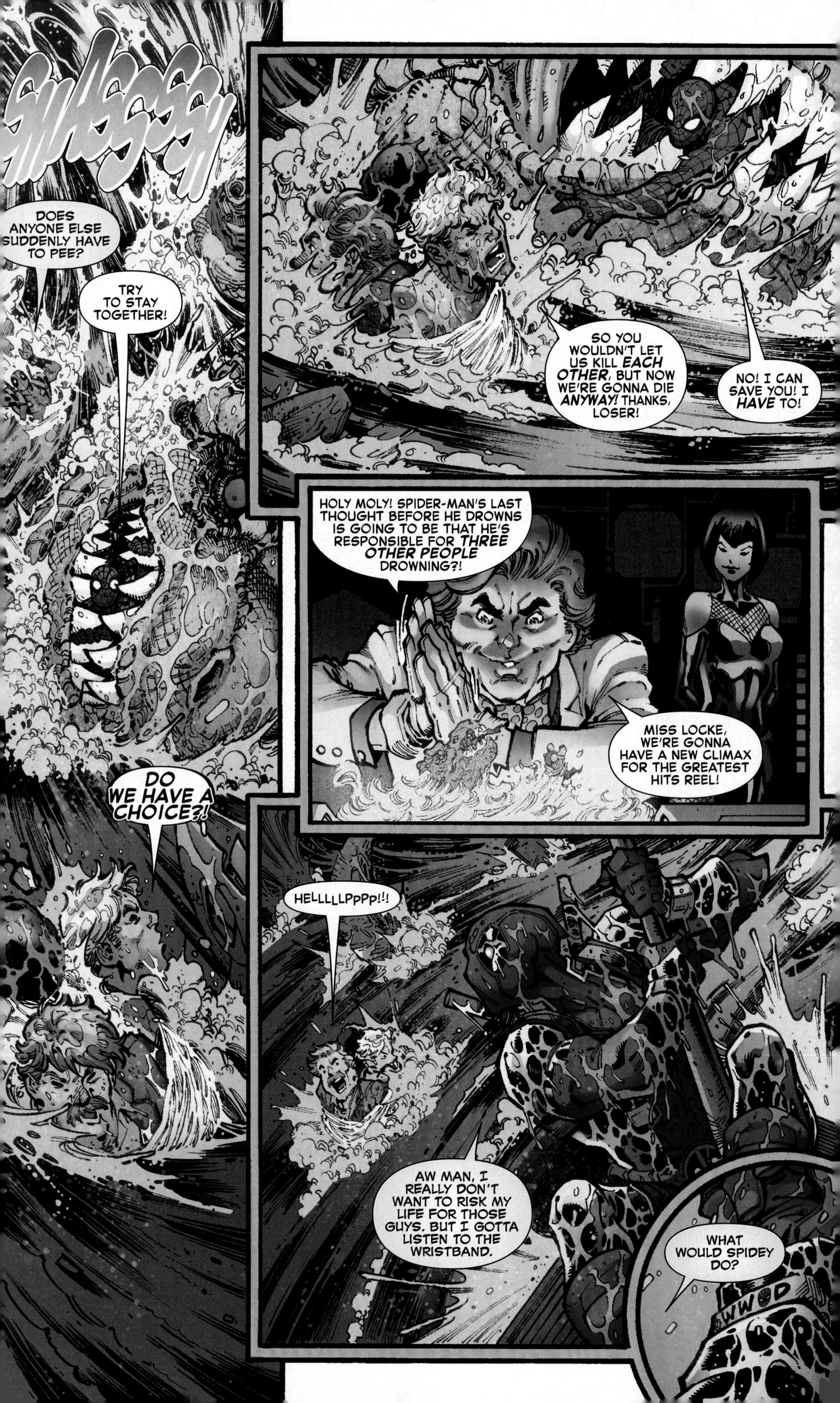
SWASSSSH
DOES ANYONE ELSE SUDDENLY HAVE TO PEE?
TRY TO STAY TOGETHER!
SO YOU WOULDN'T LET US KILL EACH OTHER, BUT NOW WE'RE GONNA DIE ANYWAY! THANKS, LOSER!
NO! I CAN SAVE YOU! I HAVE TO!
HOLY MOLY! SPIDER-MAN'S LAST THOUGHT BEFORE HE DROWNS IS GOING TO BE THAT HE'S RESPONSIBLE FOR THREE OTHER PEOPLE DROWNING?!
MISS LOCKE, WE'RE GONNA HAVE A NEW CLIMAX FOR THE GREATEST HITS REEL!
DO WE HAVE A CHOICE?!
HELLLLLPPPP!!!
AW MAN, I REALLY DON'T WANT TO RISK MY LIFE FOR THOSE GUYS. BUT I GOTTA LISTEN TO THE WRISTBAND.
WHAT WOULD SPIDEY DO?
WWSD

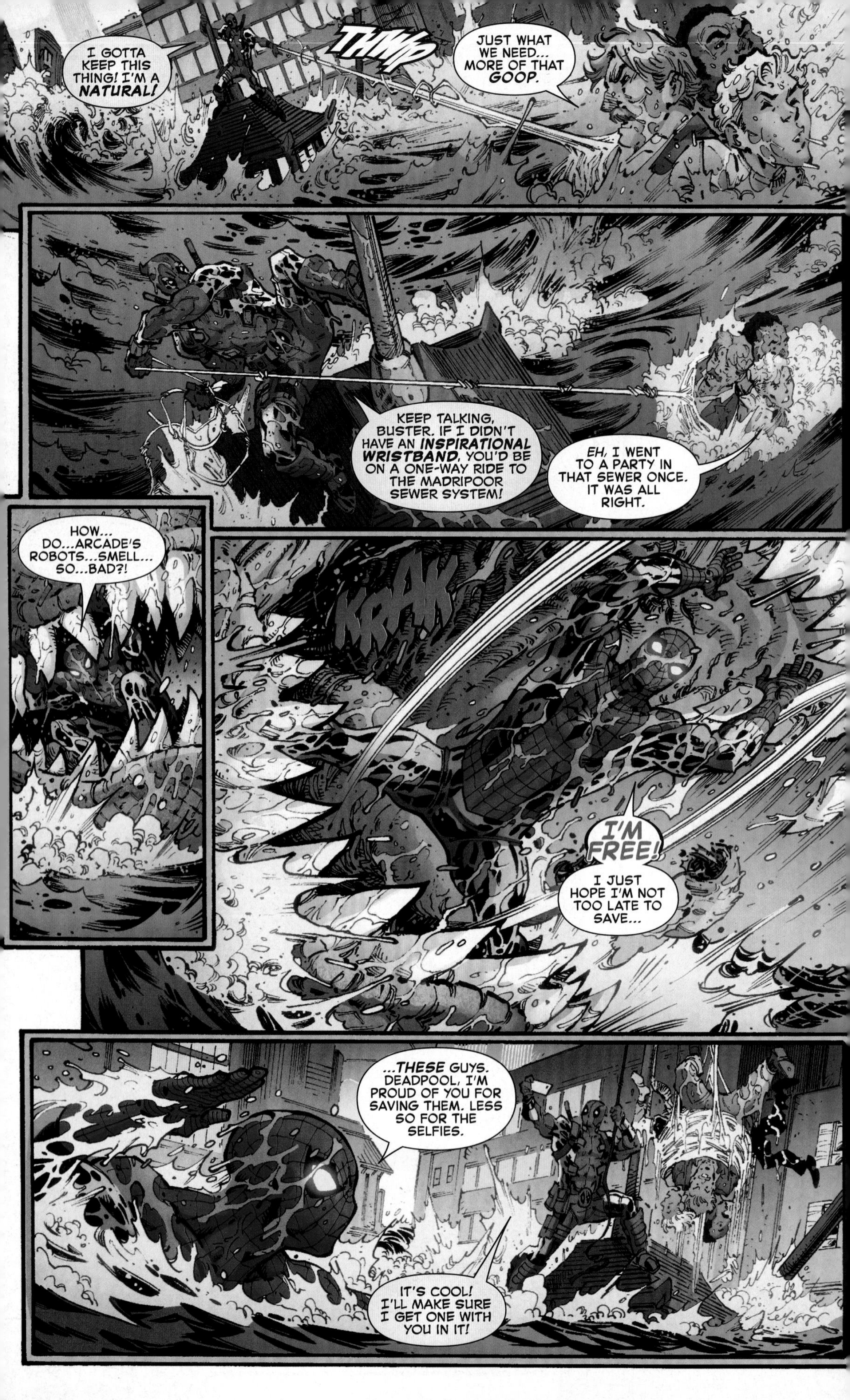
I GOTTA KEEP THIS THING! I'M A *NATURAL!*
THWIP
JUST WHAT WE NEED... MORE OF THAT *GOOP.*
KEEP TALKING, BUSTER. IF I DIDN'T HAVE AN ***INSPIRATIONAL WRISTBAND,*** YOU'D BE ON A ONE-WAY RIDE TO THE MADRIPOOR SEWER SYSTEM!
EH, I WENT TO A PARTY IN THAT SEWER ONCE. IT WAS ALL RIGHT.
HOW... DO...ARCADE'S ROBOTS...SMELL... SO...BAD?!
KRAK
I'M FREE!
I JUST HOPE I'M NOT TOO LATE TO SAVE...
...*THESE* GUYS. DEADPOOL, I'M PROUD OF YOU FOR SAVING THEM. LESS SO FOR THE SELFIES.
IT'S COOL! I'LL MAKE SURE I GET ONE WITH YOU IN IT!

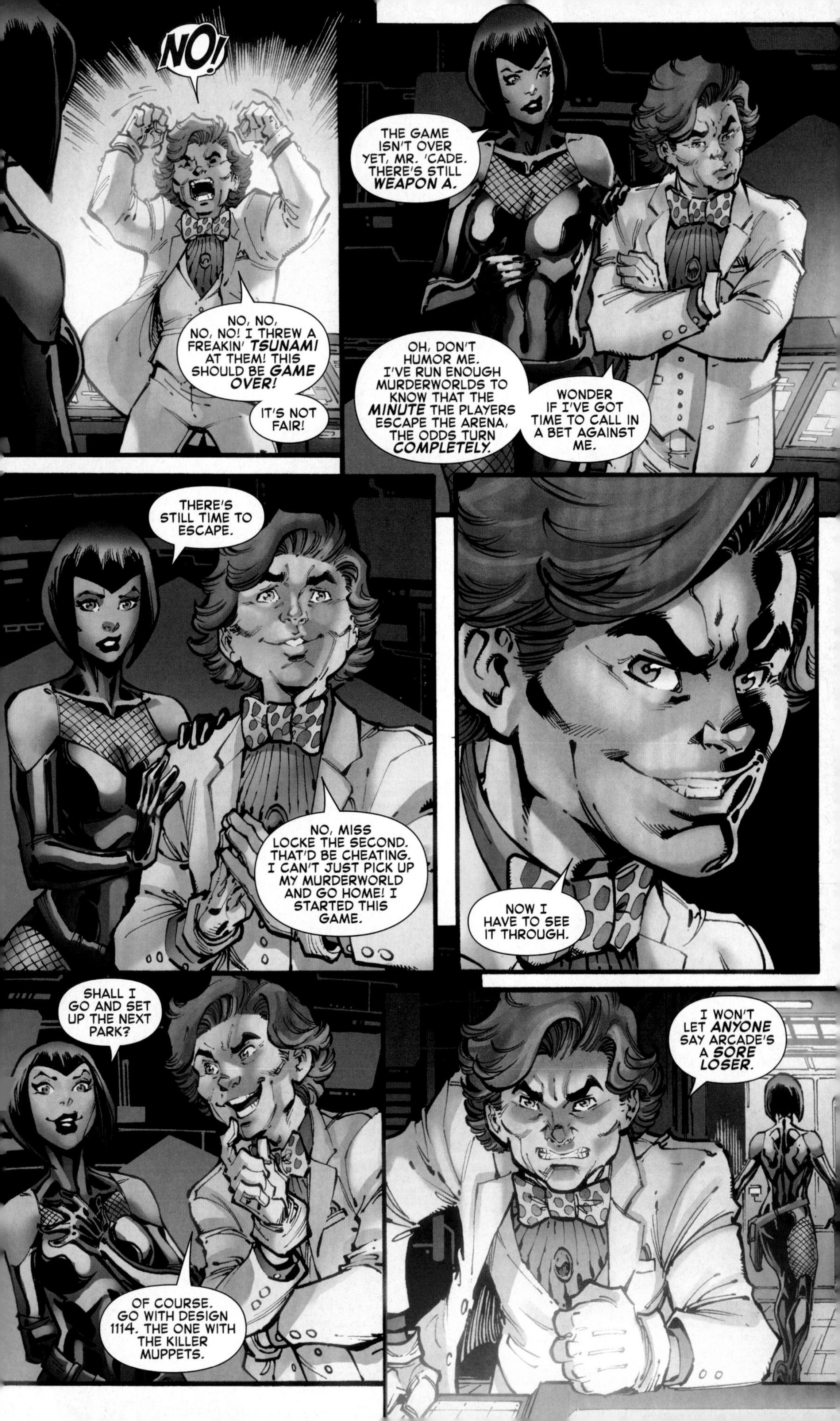
NO!
NO, NO, NO, NO! I THREW A FREAKIN' TSUNAMI AT THEM! THIS SHOULD BE GAME OVER!
IT'S NOT FAIR!
THE GAME ISN'T OVER YET, MR. 'CADE. THERE'S STILL WEAPON A.
OH, DON'T HUMOR ME. I'VE RUN ENOUGH MURDERWORLDS TO KNOW THAT THE MINUTE THE PLAYERS ESCAPE THE ARENA, THE ODDS TURN COMPLETELY.
WONDER IF I'VE GOT TIME TO CALL IN A BET AGAINST ME.
THERE'S STILL TIME TO ESCAPE.
NO, MISS LOCKE THE SECOND. THAT'D BE CHEATING. I CAN'T JUST PICK UP MY MURDERWORLD AND GO HOME! I STARTED THIS GAME.
NOW I HAVE TO SEE IT THROUGH.
SHALL I GO AND SET UP THE NEXT PARK?
OF COURSE. GO WITH DESIGN 1114. THE ONE WITH THE KILLER MUPPETS.
I WON'T LET ANYONE SAY ARCADE'S A SORE LOSER.

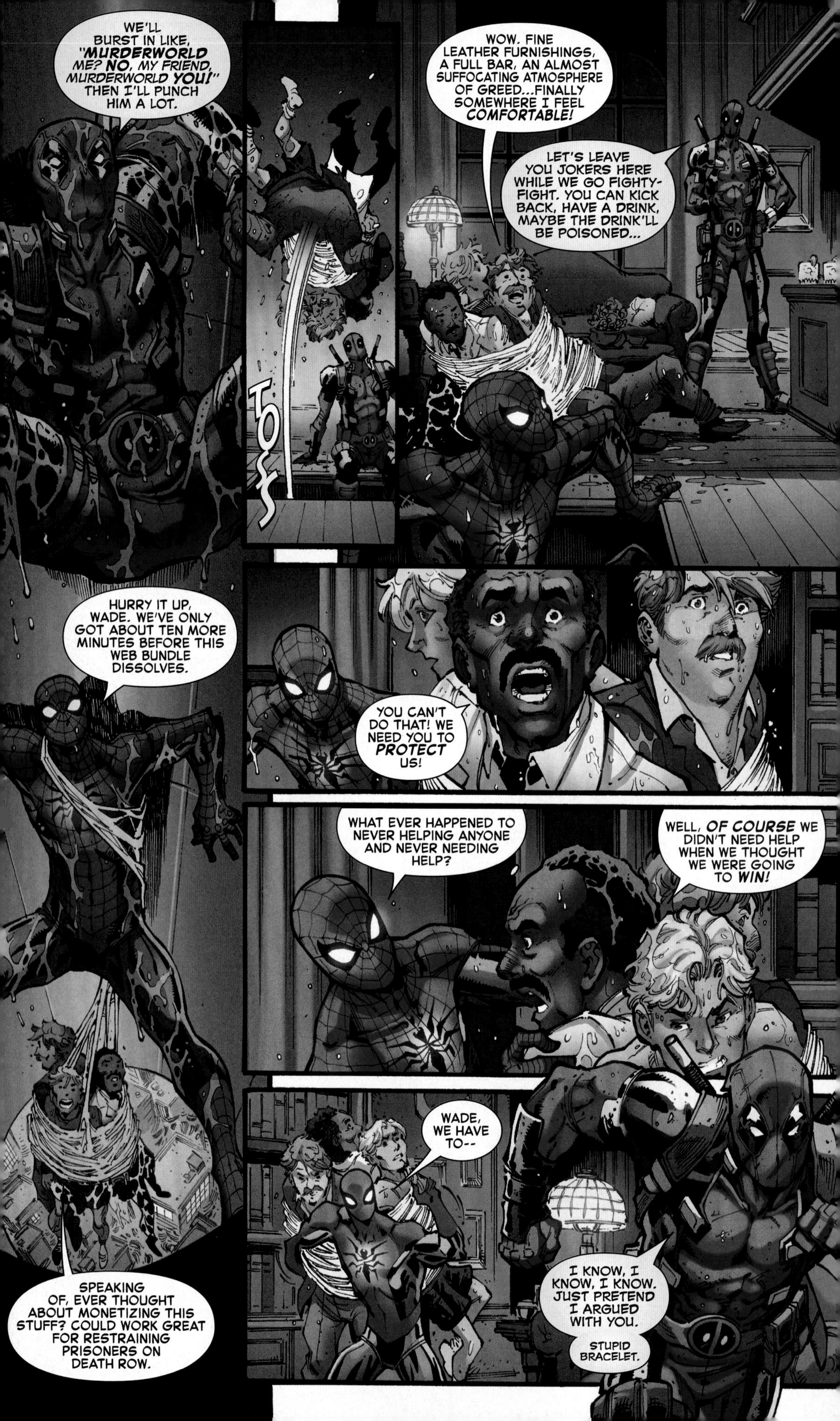
WE'LL BURST IN LIKE, "MURDERWORLD ME? NO, MY FRIEND, MURDERWORLD YOU!" THEN I'LL PUNCH HIM A LOT.
TOSS
WOW. FINE LEATHER FURNISHINGS, A FULL BAR, AN ALMOST SUFFOCATING ATMOSPHERE OF GREED...FINALLY SOMEWHERE I FEEL COMFORTABLE!
LET'S LEAVE YOU JOKERS HERE WHILE WE GO FIGHTY-FIGHT. YOU CAN KICK BACK, HAVE A DRINK, MAYBE THE DRINK'LL BE POISONED...
HURRY IT UP, WADE. WE'VE ONLY GOT ABOUT TEN MORE MINUTES BEFORE THIS WEB BUNDLE DISSOLVES.
SPEAKING OF, EVER THOUGHT ABOUT MONETIZING THIS STUFF? COULD WORK GREAT FOR RESTRAINING PRISONERS ON DEATH ROW.
YOU CAN'T DO THAT! WE NEED YOU TO PROTECT US!
WHAT EVER HAPPENED TO NEVER HELPING ANYONE AND NEVER NEEDING HELP?
WELL, OF COURSE WE DIDN'T NEED HELP WHEN WE THOUGHT WE WERE GOING TO WIN!
WADE, WE HAVE TO--
I KNOW, I KNOW, I KNOW. JUST PRETEND I ARGUED WITH YOU.
STUPID BRACELET.

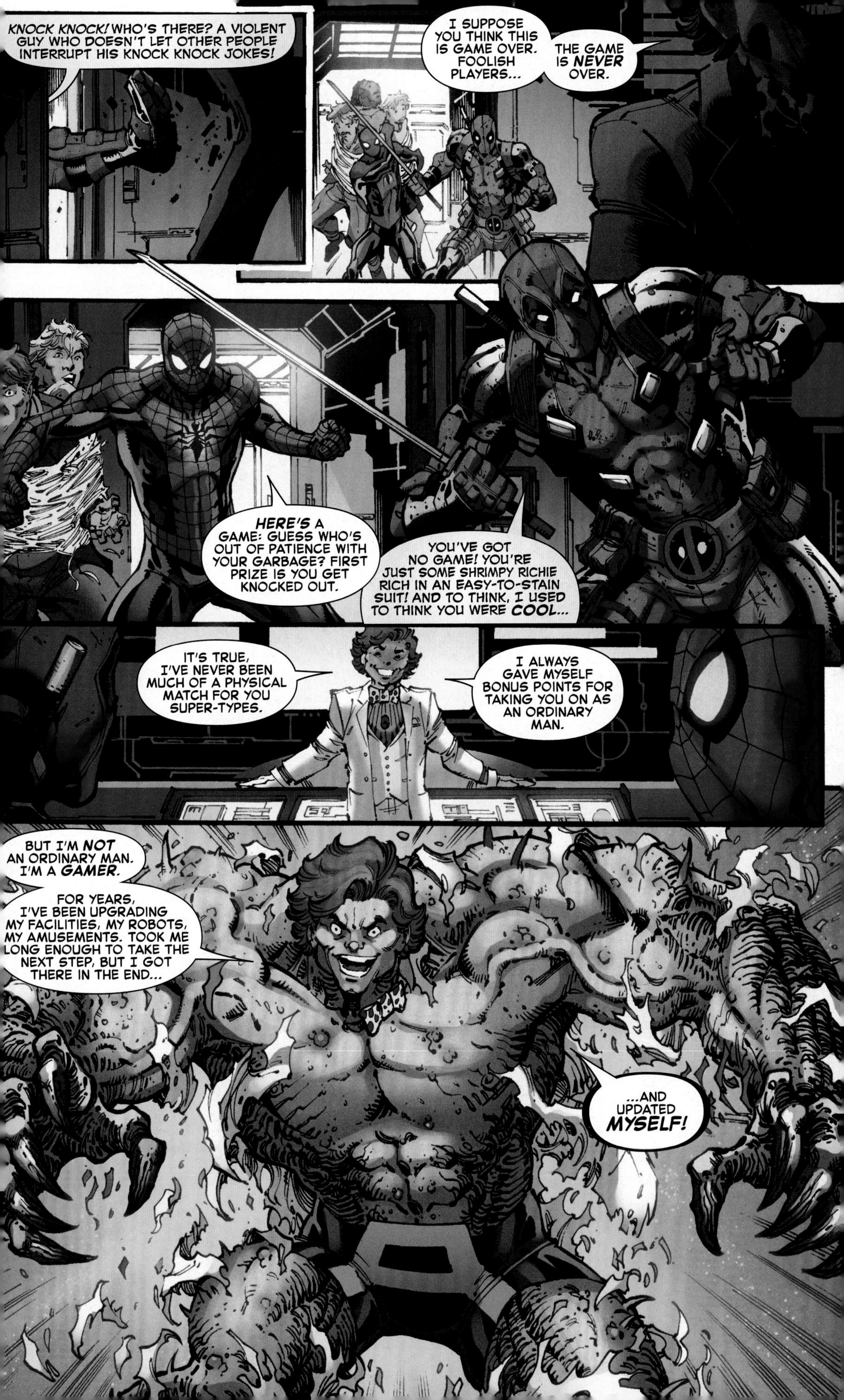

KNOCK KNOCK! WHO'S THERE? A VIOLENT GUY WHO DOESN'T LET OTHER PEOPLE INTERRUPT HIS KNOCK KNOCK JOKES!
I SUPPOSE YOU THINK THIS IS GAME OVER. FOOLISH PLAYERS...
THE GAME IS NEVER OVER.
HERE'S A GAME: GUESS WHO'S OUT OF PATIENCE WITH YOUR GARBAGE? FIRST PRIZE IS YOU GET KNOCKED OUT.
YOU'VE GOT NO GAME! YOU'RE JUST SOME SHRIMPY RICHIE RICH IN AN EASY-TO-STAIN SUIT! AND TO THINK, I USED TO THINK YOU WERE COOL...
IT'S TRUE, I'VE NEVER BEEN MUCH OF A PHYSICAL MATCH FOR YOU SUPER-TYPES.
I ALWAYS GAVE MYSELF BONUS POINTS FOR TAKING YOU ON AS AN ORDINARY MAN.
BUT I'M NOT AN ORDINARY MAN. I'M A GAMER.
FOR YEARS, I'VE BEEN UPGRADING MY FACILITIES, MY ROBOTS, MY AMUSEMENTS. TOOK ME LONG ENOUGH TO TAKE THE NEXT STEP, BUT I GOT THERE IN THE END...
...AND UPDATED MYSELF!

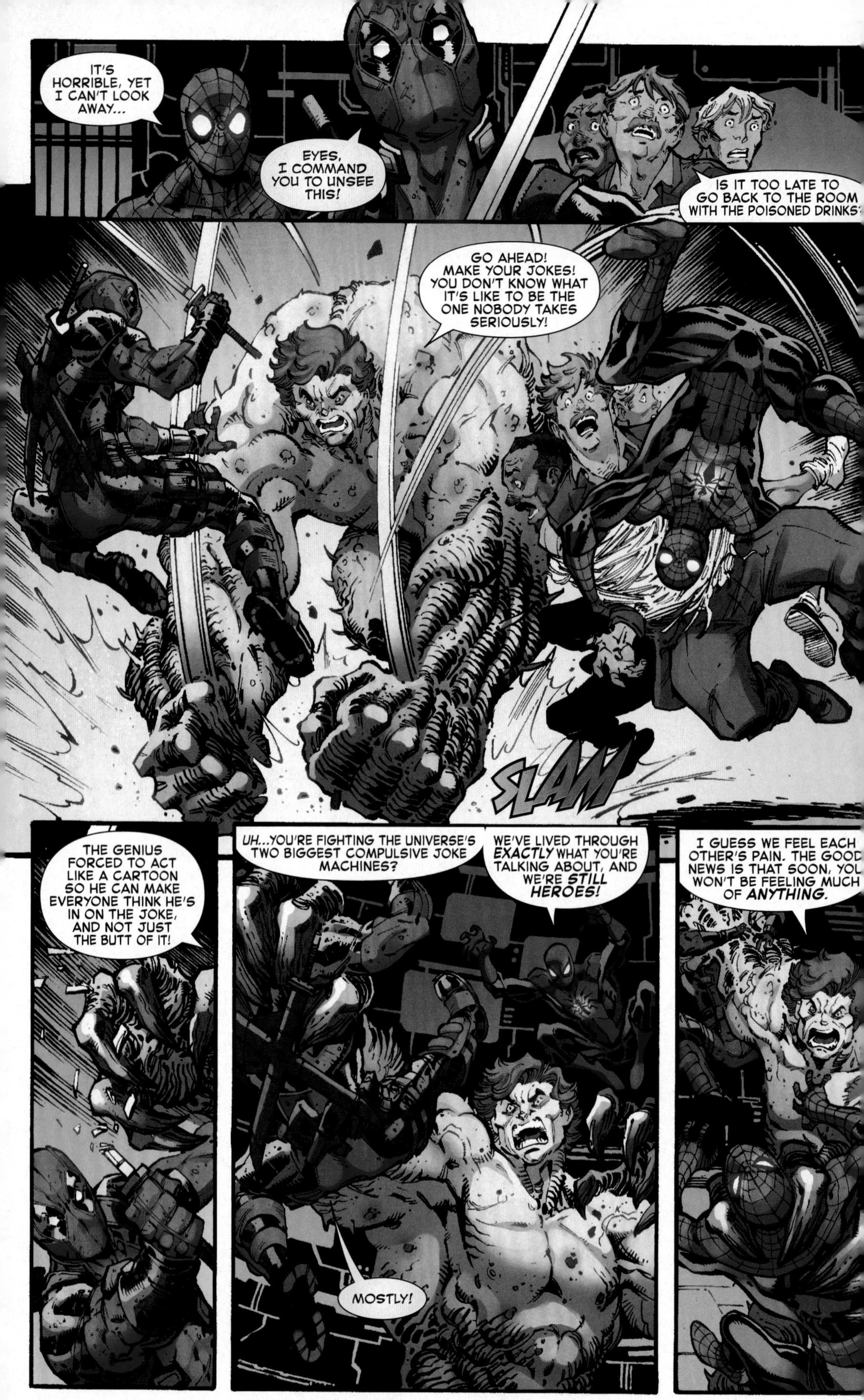
IT'S HORRIBLE, YET I CAN'T LOOK AWAY...
EYES, I COMMAND YOU TO UNSEE THIS!
IS IT TOO LATE TO GO BACK TO THE ROOM WITH THE POISONED DRINKS?
GO AHEAD! MAKE YOUR JOKES! YOU DON'T KNOW WHAT IT'S LIKE TO BE THE ONE NOBODY TAKES SERIOUSLY!
SLAM
THE GENIUS FORCED TO ACT LIKE A CARTOON SO HE CAN MAKE EVERYONE THINK HE'S IN ON THE JOKE, AND NOT JUST THE BUTT OF IT!
UH...YOU'RE FIGHTING THE UNIVERSE'S TWO BIGGEST COMPULSIVE JOKE MACHINES?
WE'VE LIVED THROUGH EXACTLY WHAT YOU'RE TALKING ABOUT, AND WE'RE STILL HEROES!
MOSTLY!
I GUESS WE FEEL EACH OTHER'S PAIN. THE GOOD NEWS IS THAT SOON, YOU WON'T BE FEELING MUCH OF ANYTHING.

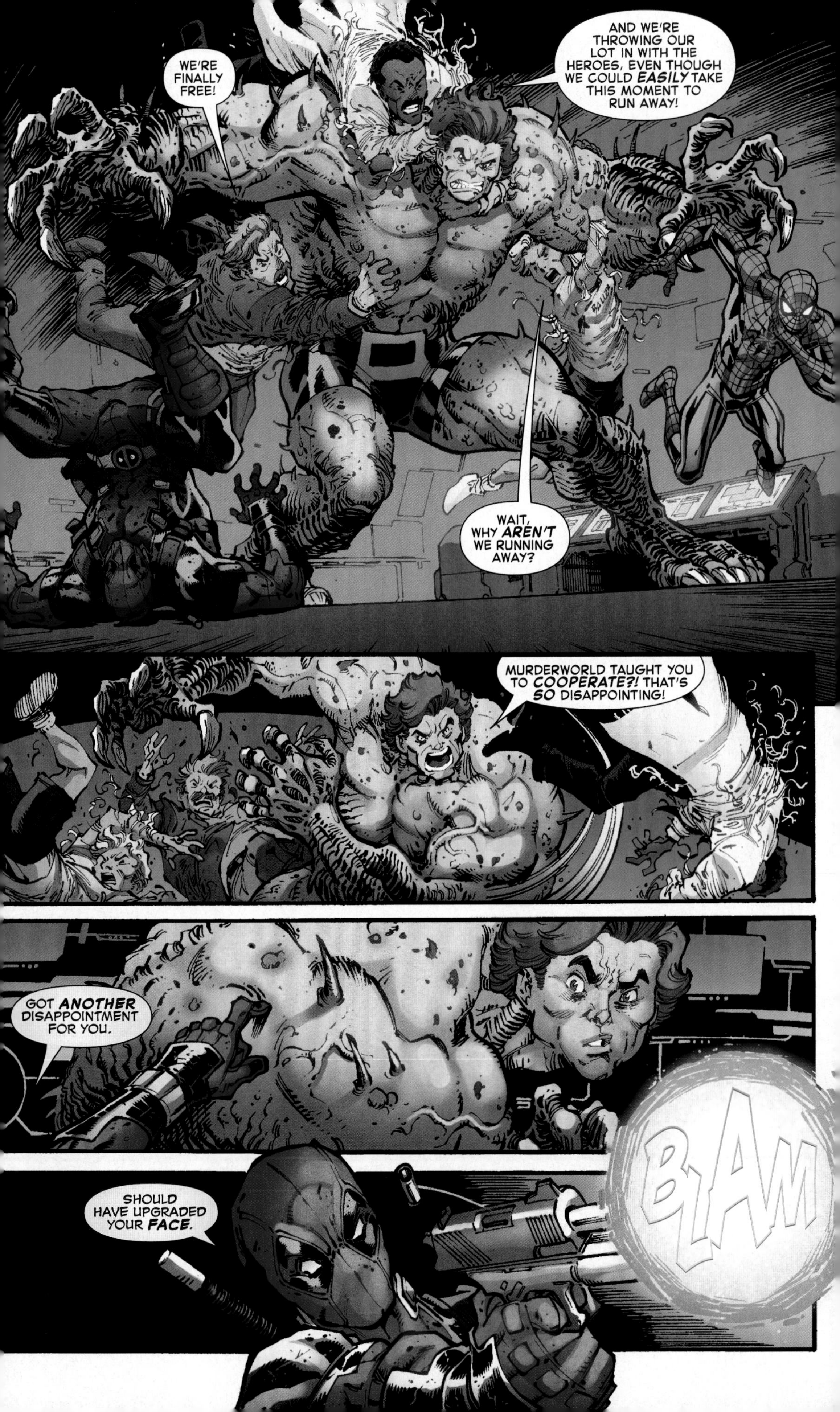

WE'RE FINALLY FREE!
AND WE'RE THROWING OUR LOT IN WITH THE HEROES, EVEN THOUGH WE COULD EASILY TAKE THIS MOMENT TO RUN AWAY!
WAIT, WHY AREN'T WE RUNNING AWAY?
MURDERWORLD TAUGHT YOU TO COOPERATE?! THAT'S SO DISAPPOINTING!
GOT ANOTHER DISAPPOINTMENT FOR YOU.
SHOULD HAVE UPGRADED YOUR FACE.
BLAM

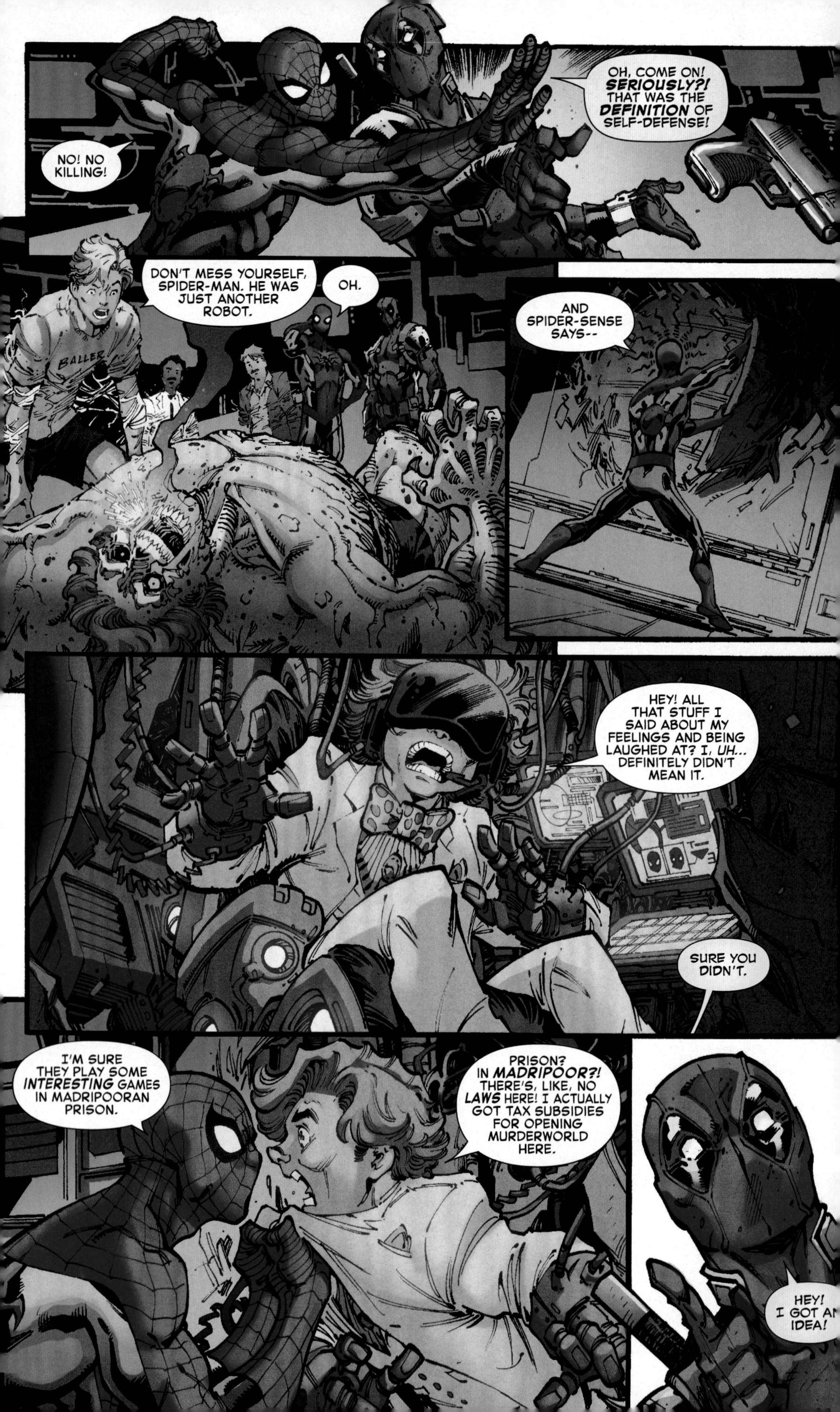
OH, COME ON! SERIOUSLY?! THAT WAS THE DEFINITION OF SELF-DEFENSE!
NO! NO KILLING!
DON'T MESS YOURSELF, SPIDER-MAN. HE WAS JUST ANOTHER ROBOT.
OH.
BALLER
AND SPIDER-SENSE SAYS--
HEY! ALL THAT STUFF I SAID ABOUT MY FEELINGS AND BEING LAUGHED AT? I, UH... DEFINITELY DIDN'T MEAN IT.
SURE YOU DIDN'T.
I'M SURE THEY PLAY SOME INTERESTING GAMES IN MADRIPOORAN PRISON.
PRISON? IN MADRIPOOR?! THERE'S, LIKE, NO LAWS HERE! I ACTUALLY GOT TAX SUBSIDIES FOR OPENING MURDERWORLD HERE.
HEY! I GOT AN IDEA!

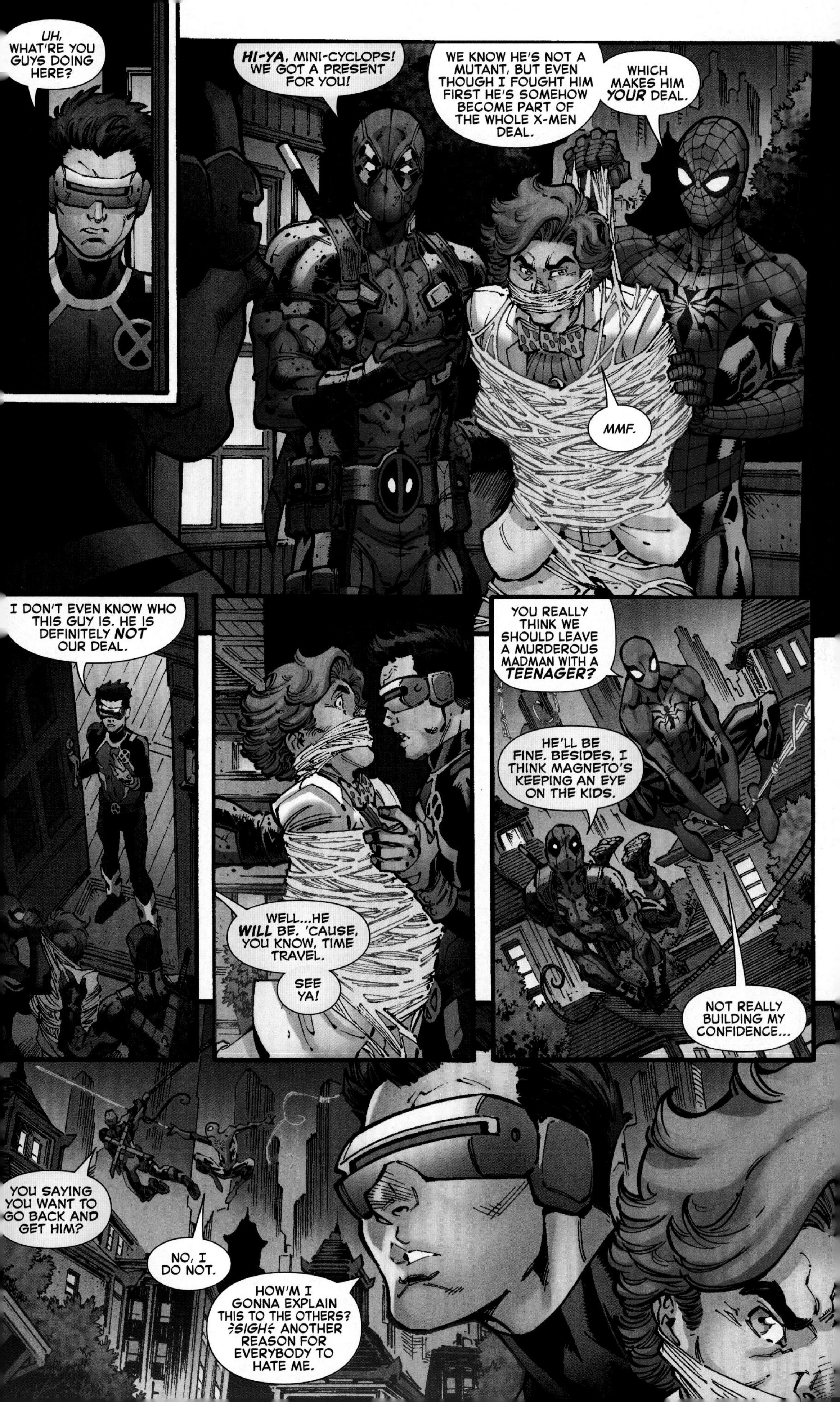

UH, WHAT'RE YOU GUYS DOING HERE?
HI-YA, MINI-CYCLOPS! WE GOT A PRESENT FOR YOU!
WE KNOW HE'S NOT A MUTANT, BUT EVEN THOUGH I FOUGHT HIM FIRST HE'S SOMEHOW BECOME PART OF THE WHOLE X-MEN DEAL.
WHICH MAKES HIM YOUR DEAL.
MMF.
I DON'T EVEN KNOW WHO THIS GUY IS. HE IS DEFINITELY NOT OUR DEAL.
WELL...HE WILL BE. 'CAUSE, YOU KNOW, TIME TRAVEL.
SEE YA!
YOU REALLY THINK WE SHOULD LEAVE A MURDEROUS MADMAN WITH A TEENAGER?
HE'LL BE FINE. BESIDES, I THINK MAGNETO'S KEEPING AN EYE ON THE KIDS.
NOT REALLY BUILDING MY CONFIDENCE...
YOU SAYING YOU WANT TO GO BACK AND GET HIM?
NO, I DO NOT.
HOW'M I GONNA EXPLAIN THIS TO THE OTHERS? ≠SIGH≠ ANOTHER REASON FOR EVERYBODY TO HATE ME.

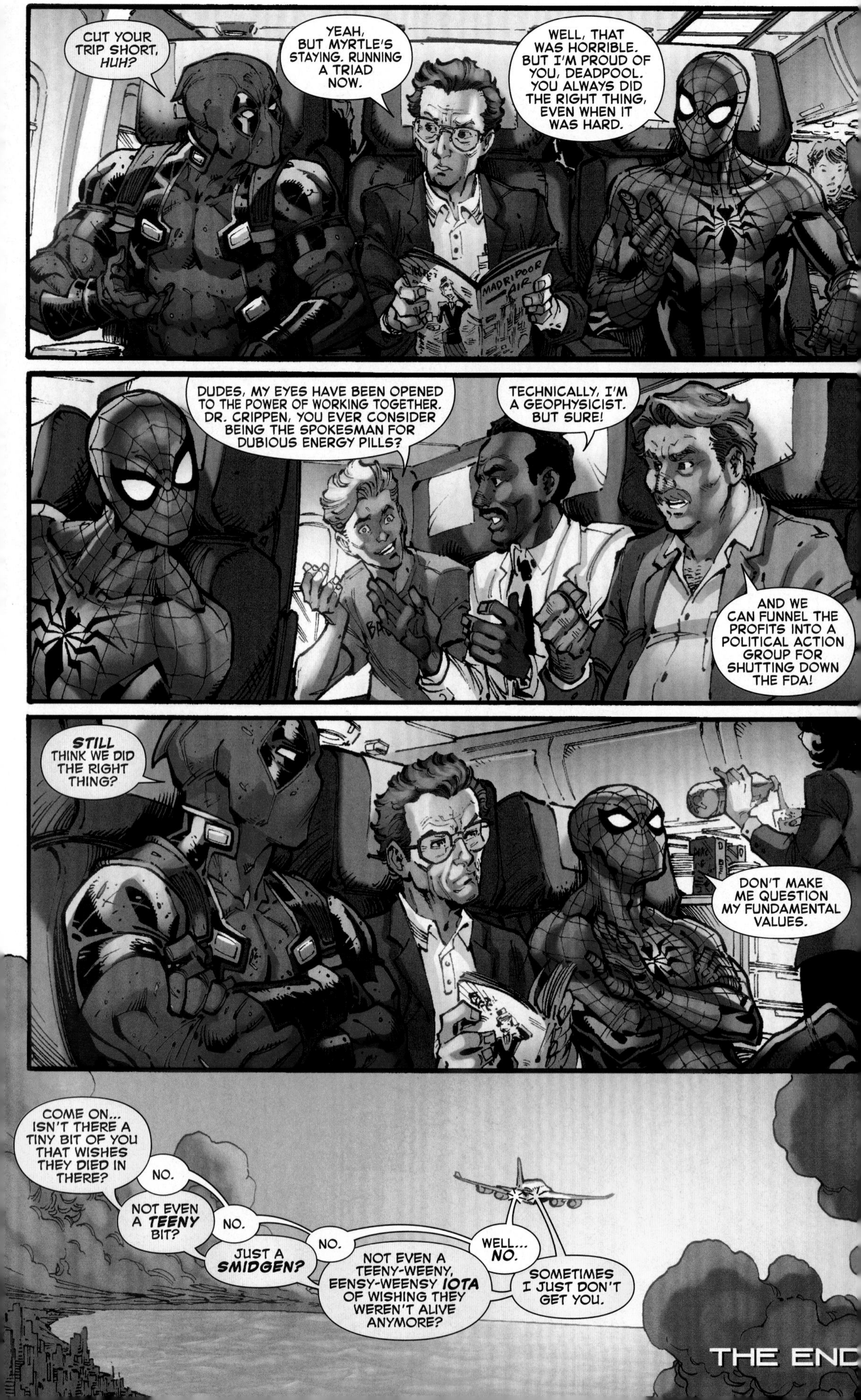

CUT YOUR TRIP SHORT, HUH?
YEAH, BUT MYRTLE'S STAYING. RUNNING A TRIAD NOW.
WELL, THAT WAS HORRIBLE. BUT I'M PROUD OF YOU, DEADPOOL. YOU ALWAYS DID THE RIGHT THING, EVEN WHEN IT WAS HARD.
MADRIPOOR AIR
DUDES, MY EYES HAVE BEEN OPENED TO THE POWER OF WORKING TOGETHER. DR. CRIPPEN, YOU EVER CONSIDER BEING THE SPOKESMAN FOR DUBIOUS ENERGY PILLS?
TECHNICALLY, I'M A GEOPHYSICIST. BUT SURE!
AND WE CAN FUNNEL THE PROFITS INTO A POLITICAL ACTION GROUP FOR SHUTTING DOWN THE FDA!
STILL THINK WE DID THE RIGHT THING?
DON'T MAKE ME QUESTION MY FUNDAMENTAL VALUES.
COME ON... ISN'T THERE A TINY BIT OF YOU THAT WISHES THEY DIED IN THERE?
NO.
NOT EVEN A TEENY BIT?
NO.
JUST A SMIDGEN?
NO.
NOT EVEN A TEENY-WEENY, EENSY-WEENSY IOTA OF WISHING THEY WEREN'T ALIVE ANYMORE?
WELL... NO.
SOMETIMES I JUST DON'T GET YOU.
THE END

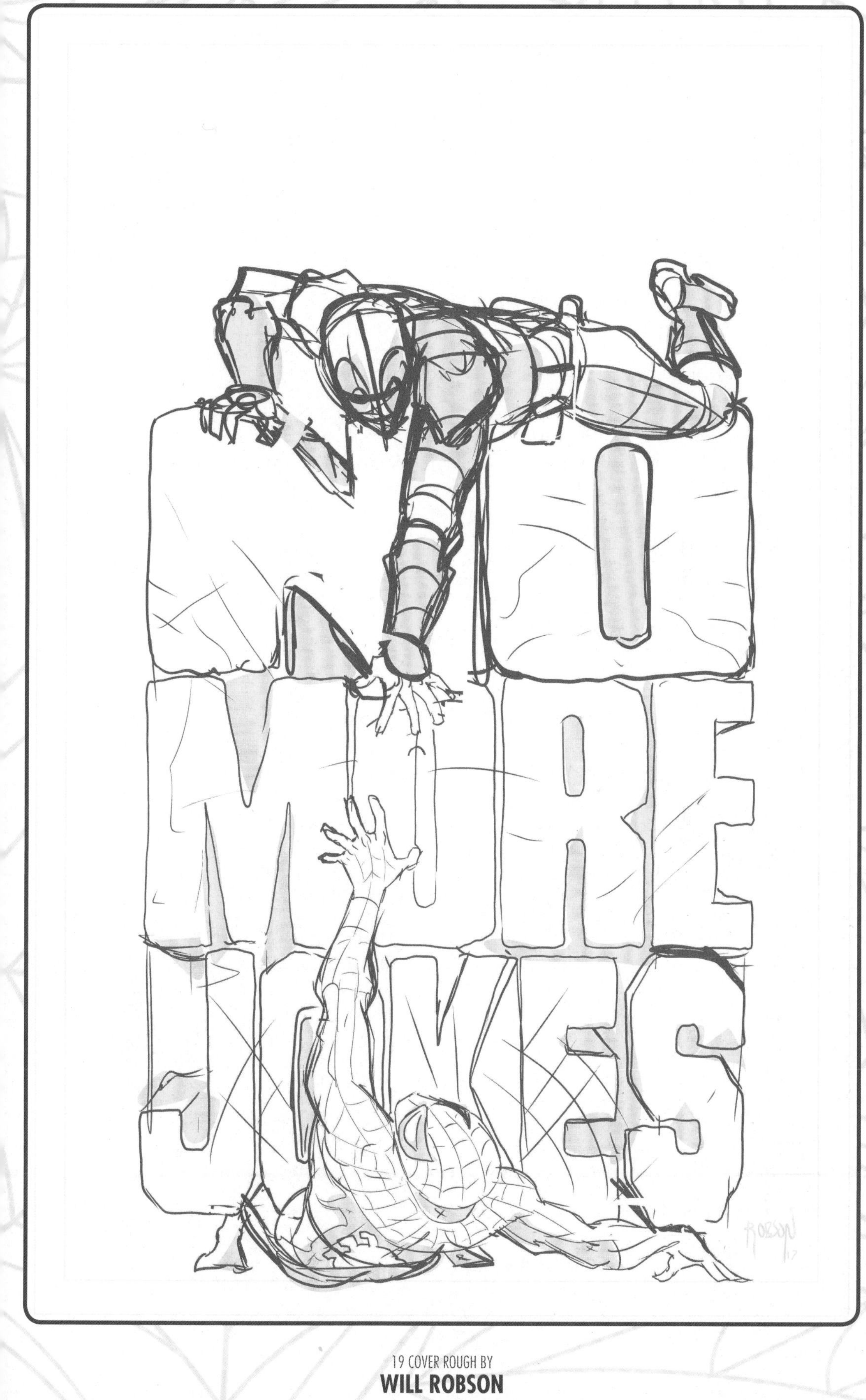
NO
MORE
JOKES
ROBSON '17

19 COVER ROUGH BY
WILL ROBSON

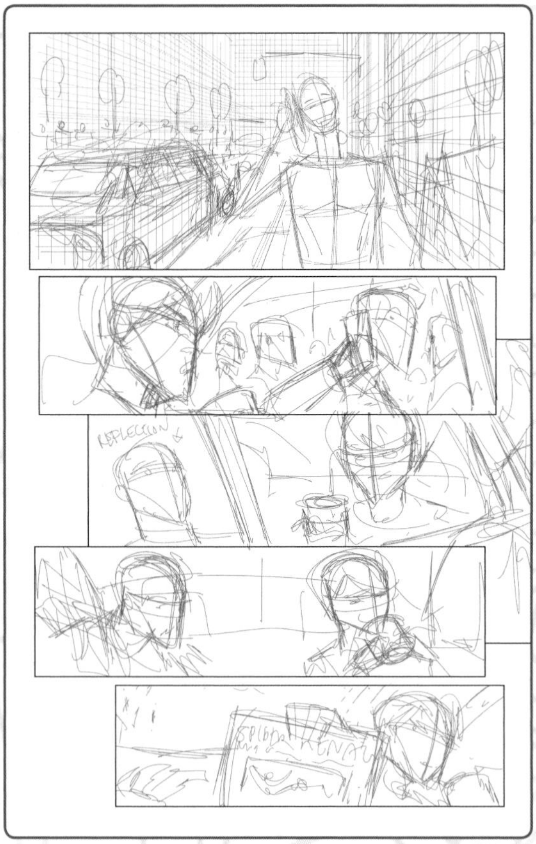

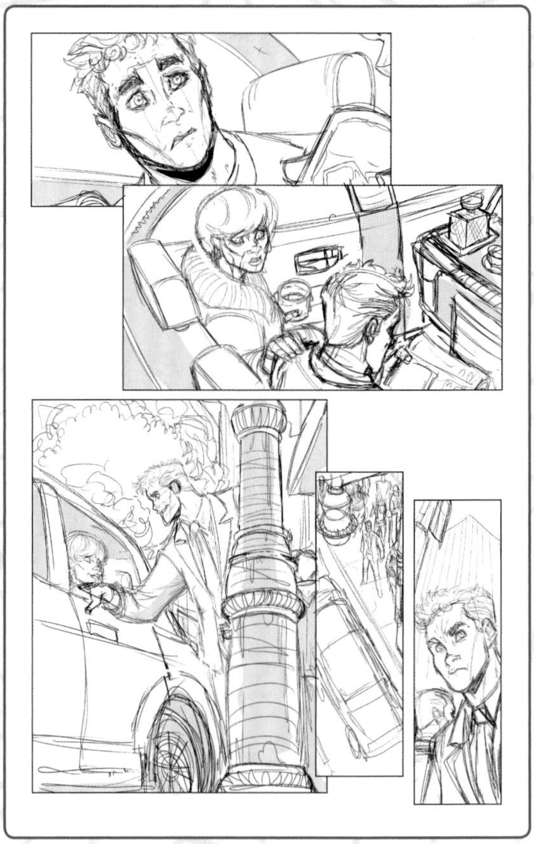

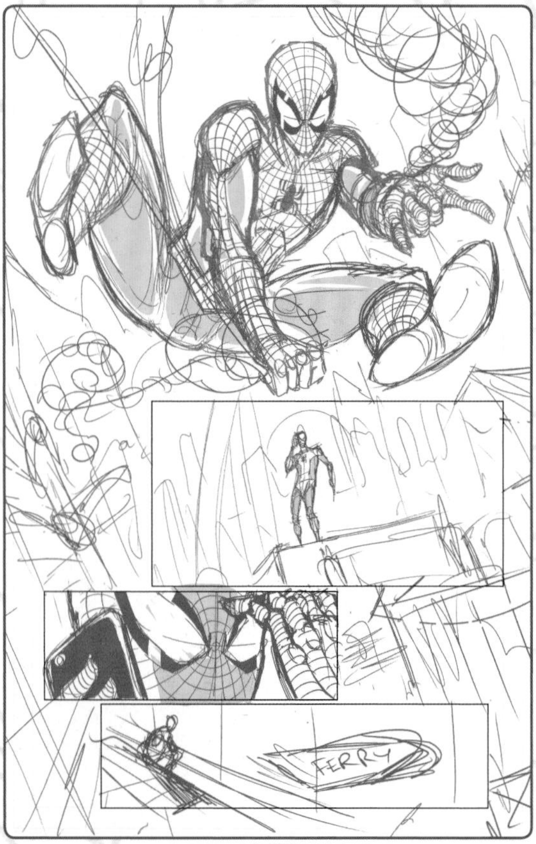
FERRY

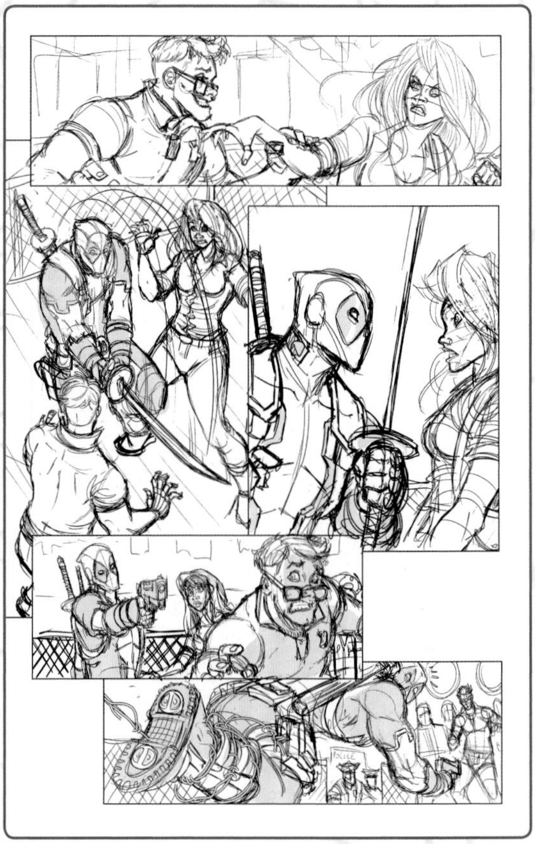

19, PAGES 1-4 LAYOUTS BY
WILL ROBSON

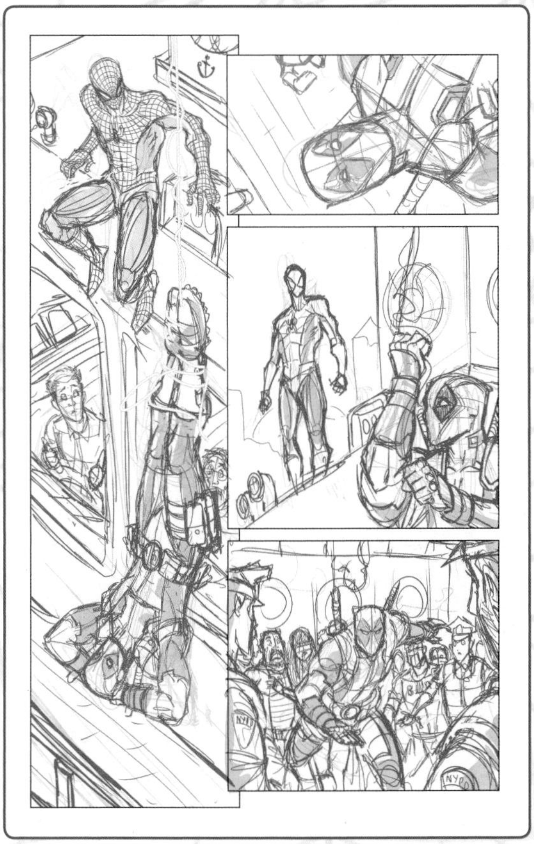

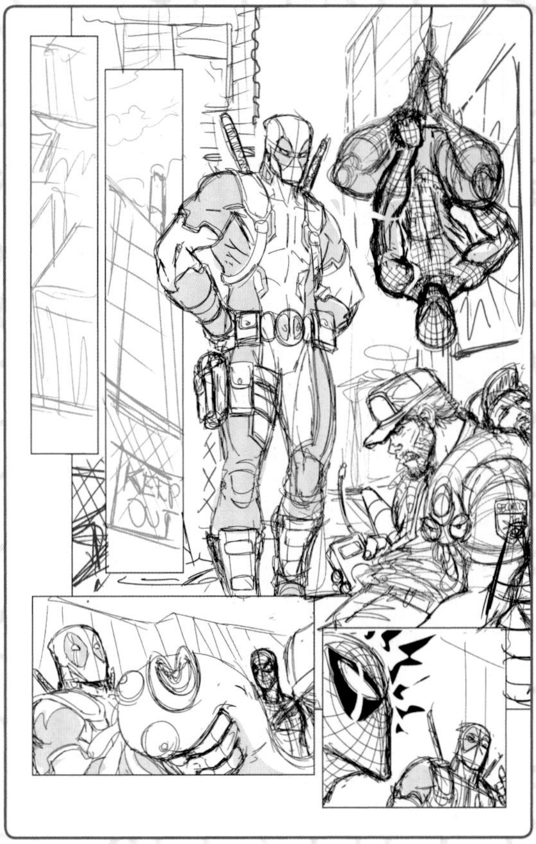
KEEP OUT

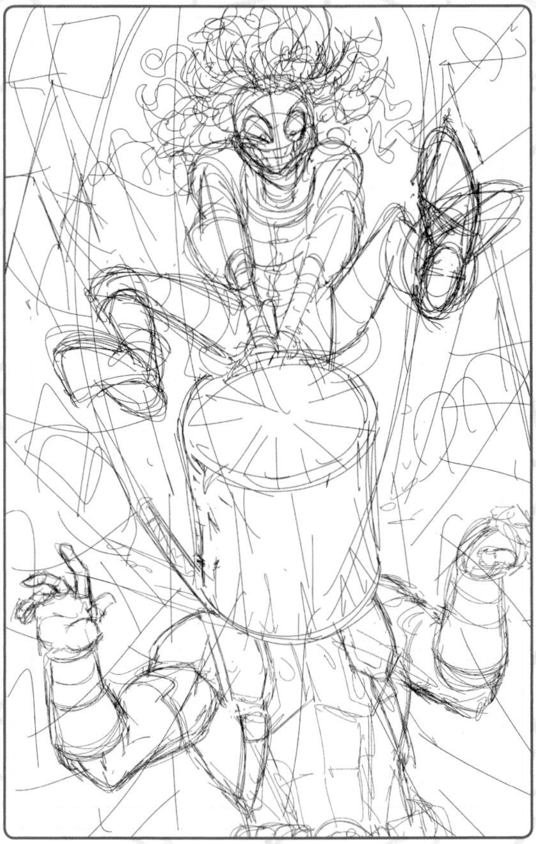

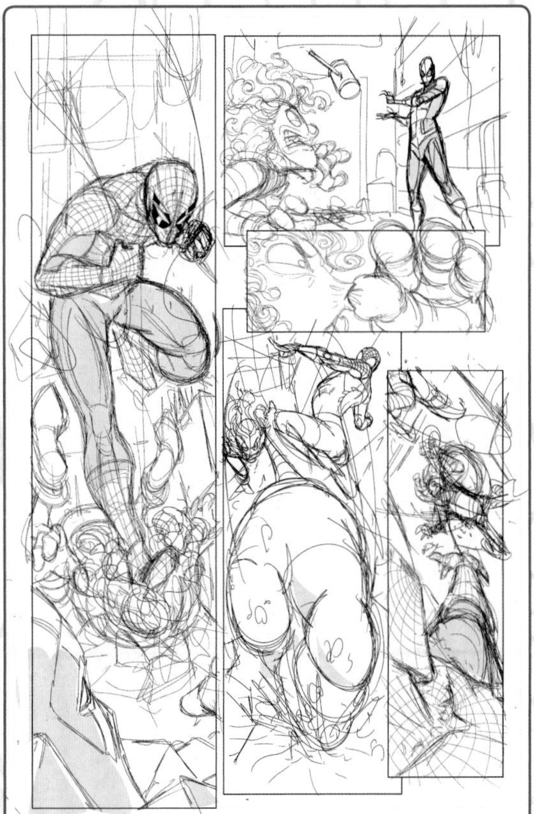

19, PAGES 5, 6, 8 & 10 LAYOUTS BY
WILL ROBSON

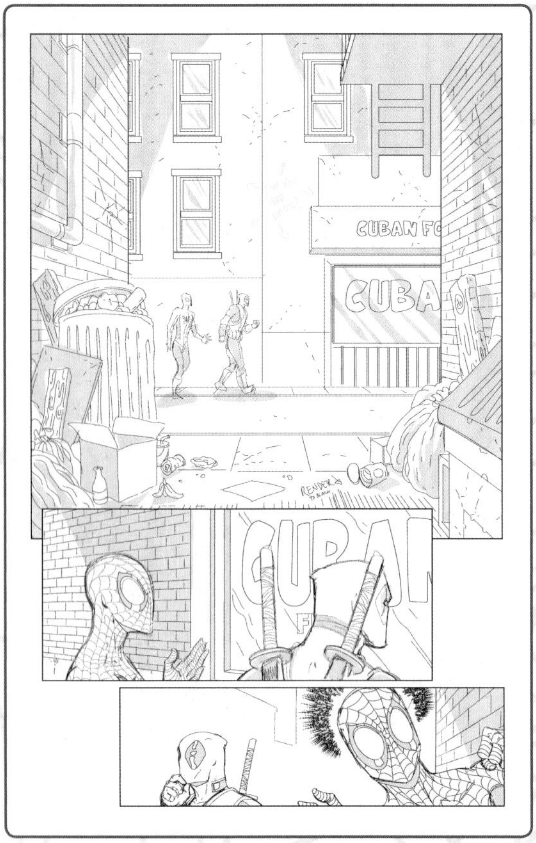
CUBAN FO
CUBA

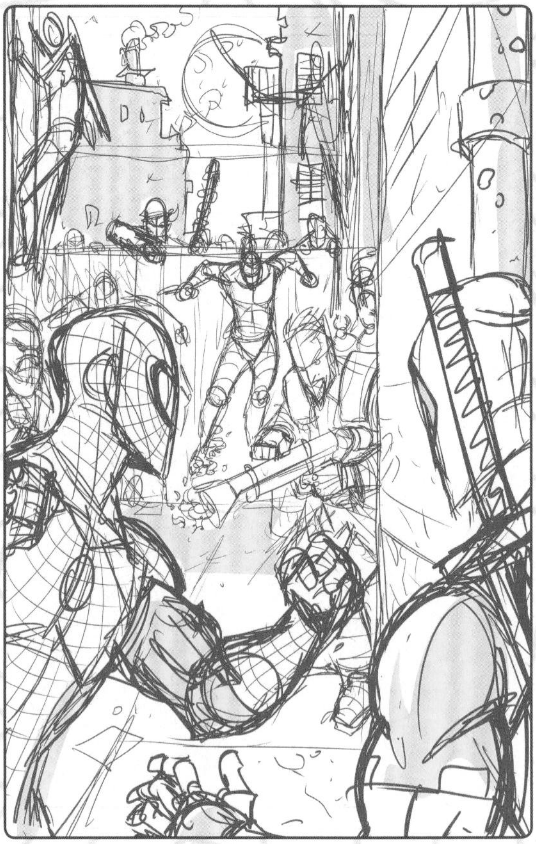

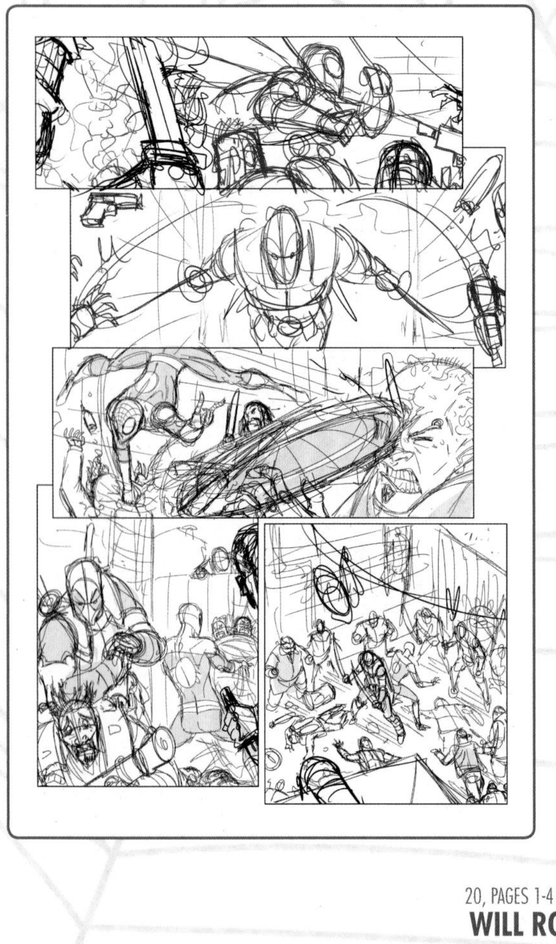

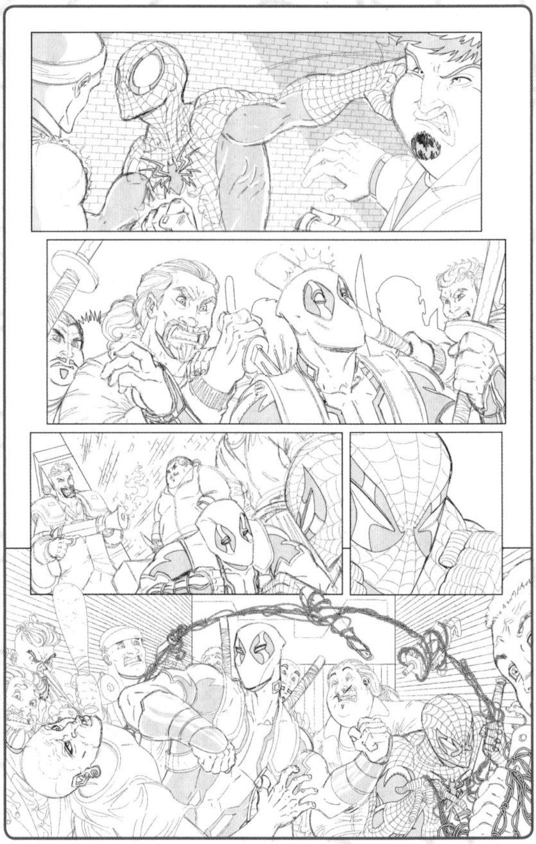

20, PAGES 1-4 LAYOUTS BY
WILL ROBSON

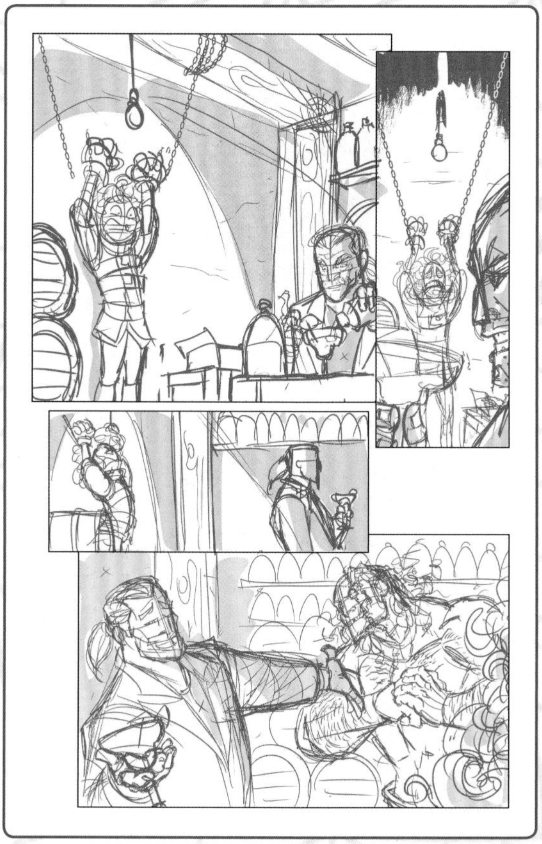

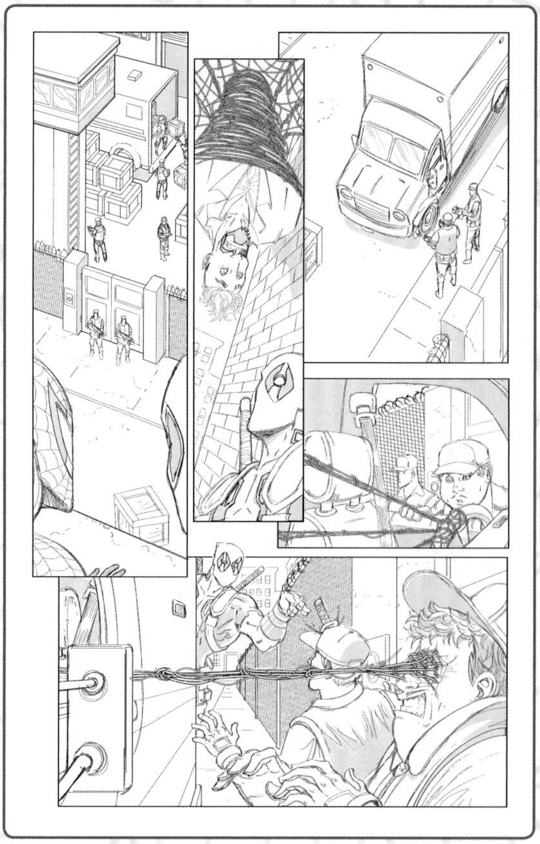

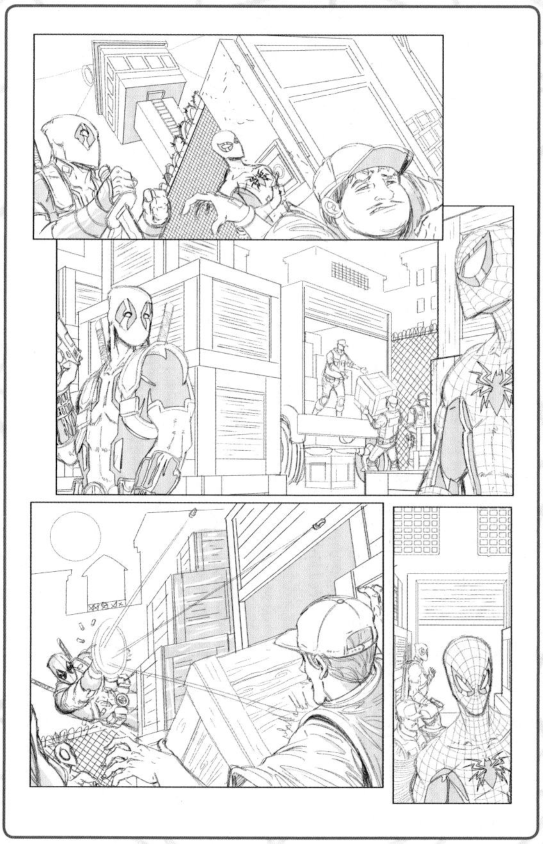

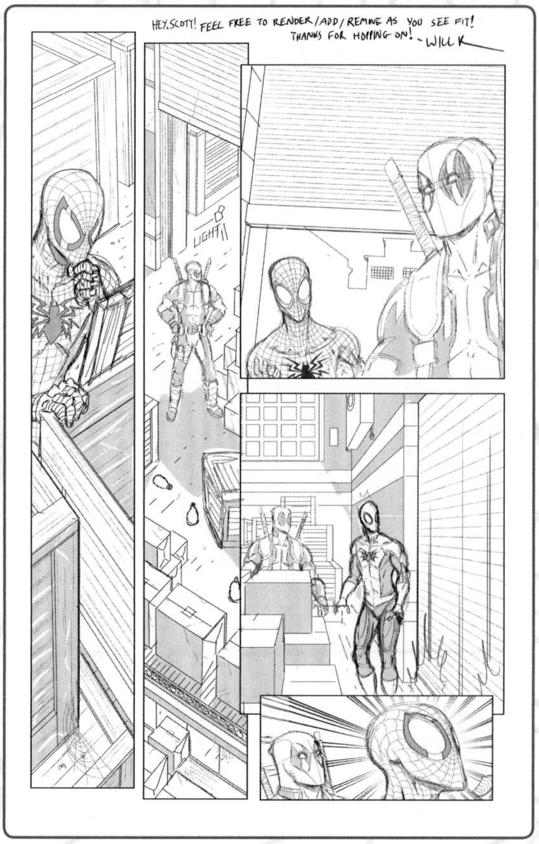
HEY, SCOTT! FEEL FREE TO RENDER/ADD/REMOVE AS YOU SEE FIT!
THANKS FOR HOPPING ON! -WILL R

20, PAGES 5-8 LAYOUTS BY

WILL ROBSON

A. SPIDEY SWINGING, DEADPOOL RUNNING, SLAPSTICK RIDING ON ROCKET OR SOMETHING ELSE FUNNY. PIDGEONS ABOUT.

B. SPIDEY AND DEADPOOL IN BG. SLAPSTICK TAKING A SELFIE WITH THEM.

C. AS SPIDEY AND DEADPOOL LOOK AT A MONITOR FULL OF VILLAINS, SLAPSTICK PLAYS NINTENDO AND IS SURROUNDED BY SODA AND PIZZA BOXES.

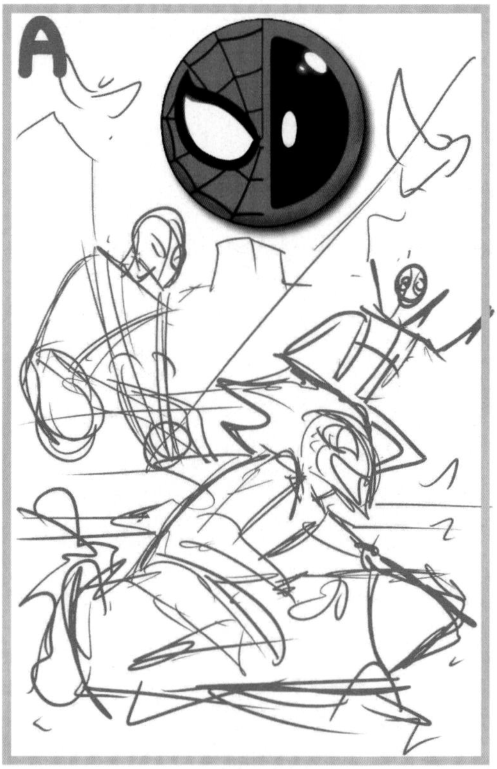
A

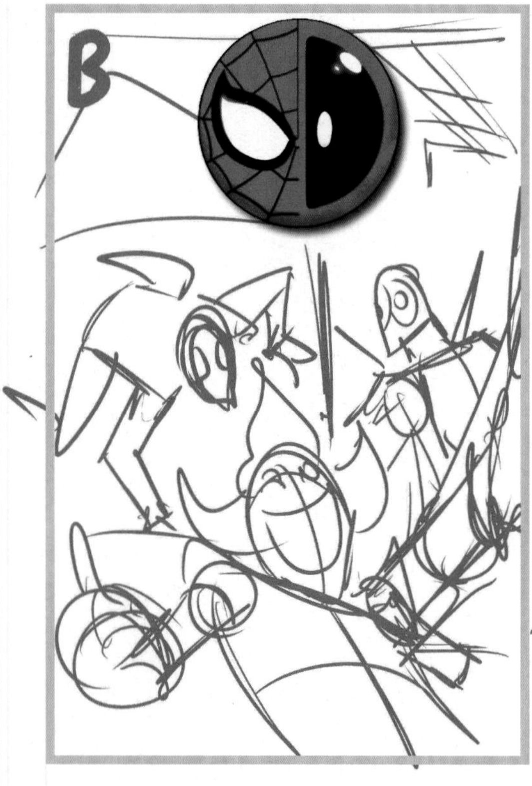
B

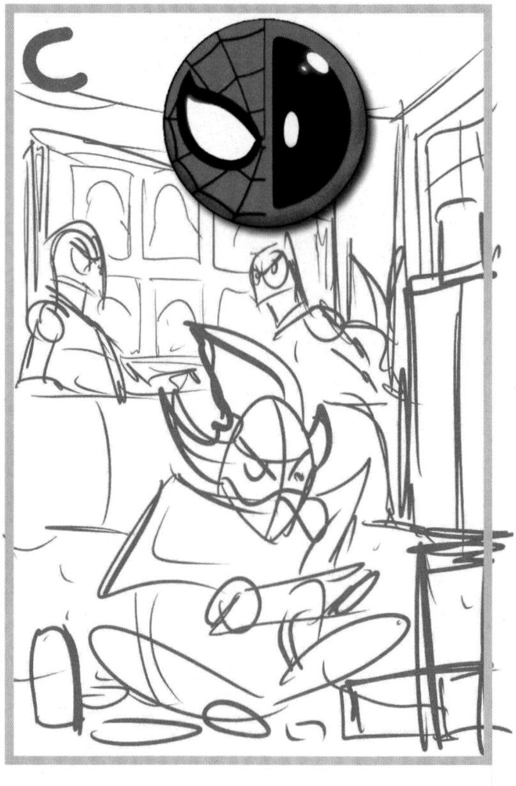
C

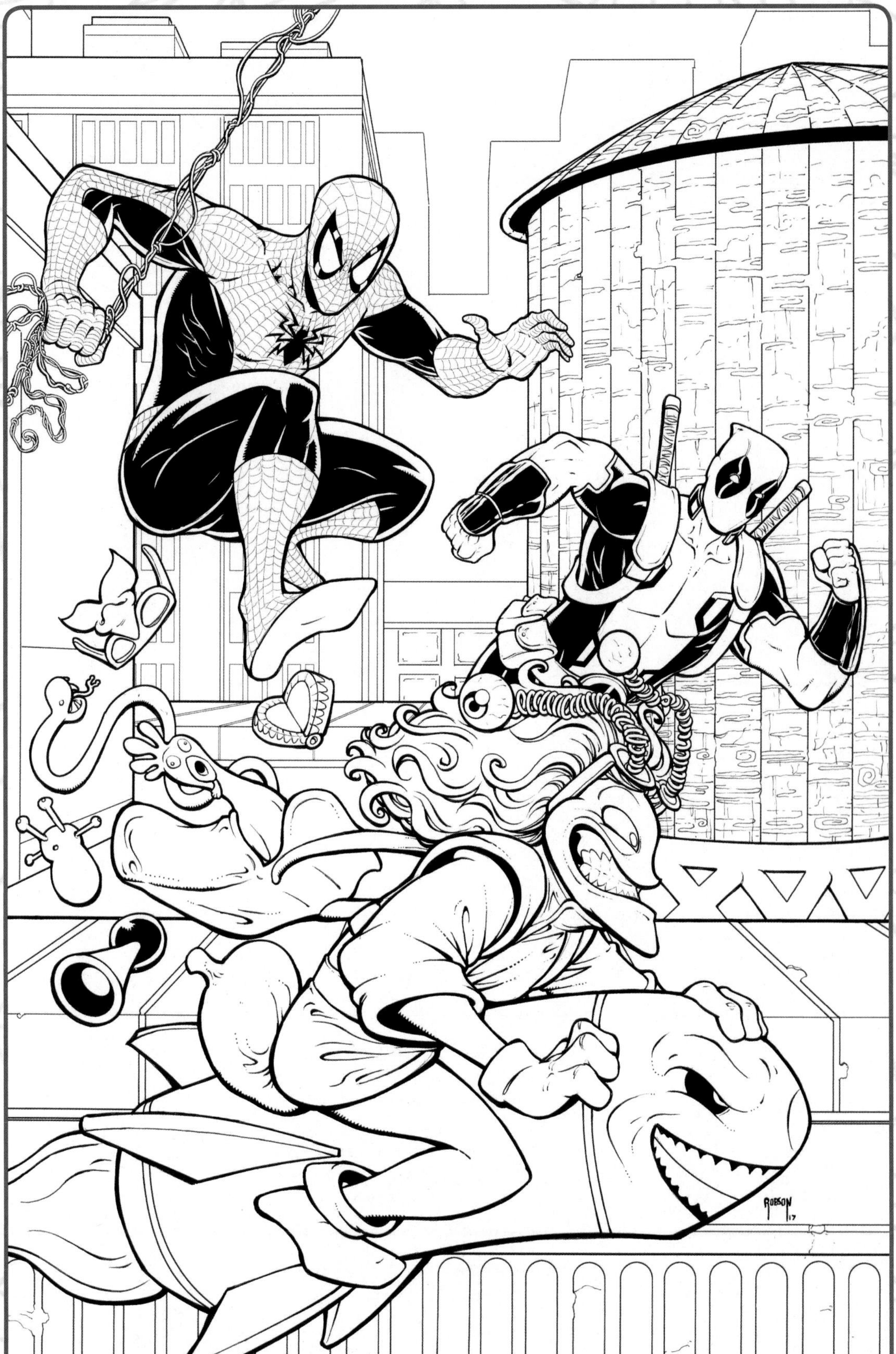
ROBSON '17

20 COVER ART BY
WILL ROBSON

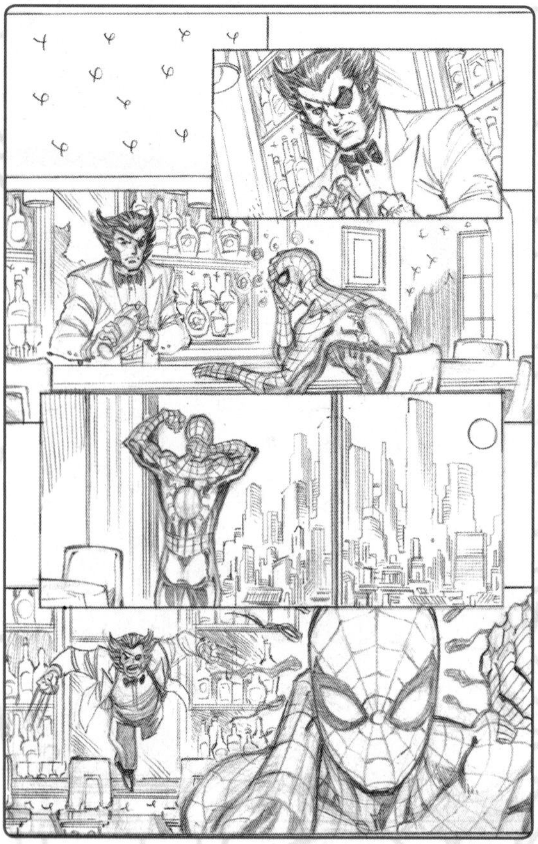

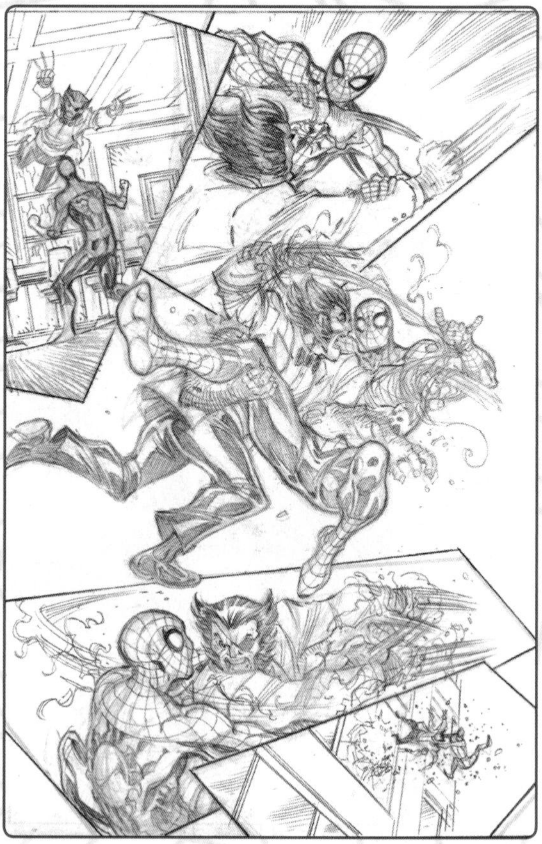

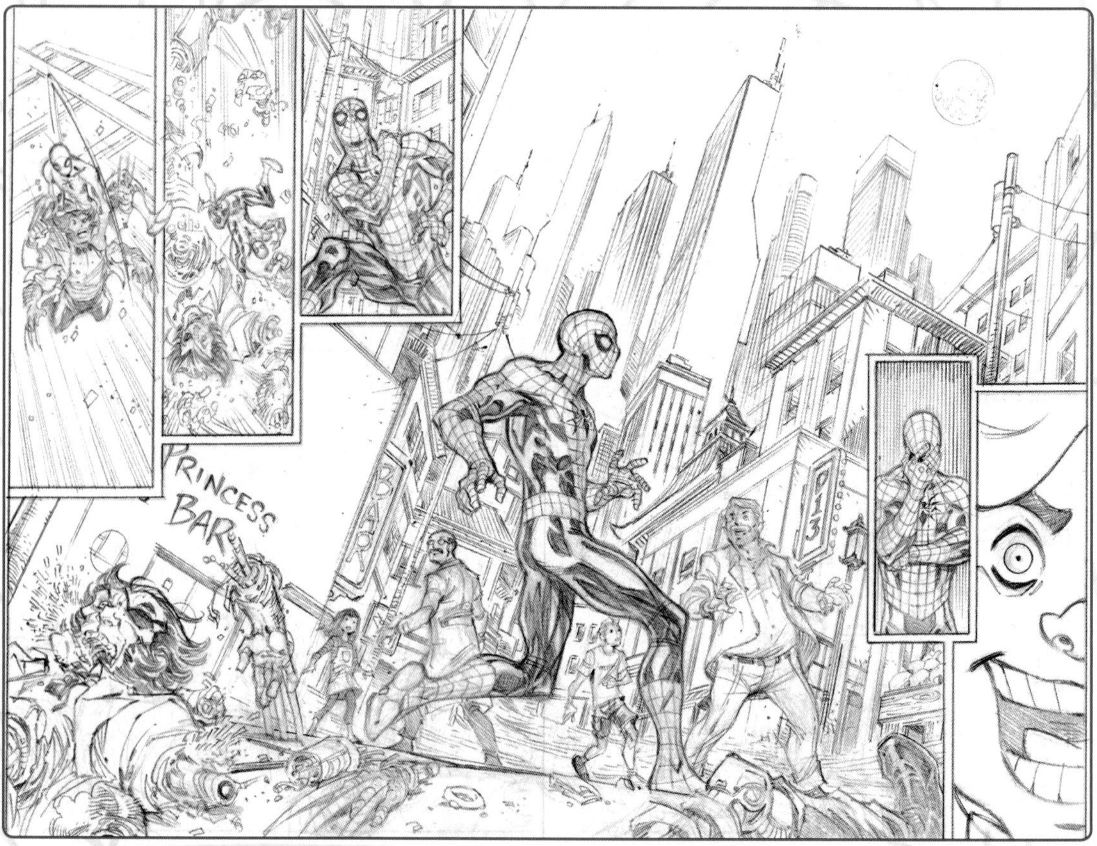
PRINCESS BAR

21, PAGES 1-4 PENCILS BY
TODD NAUCK

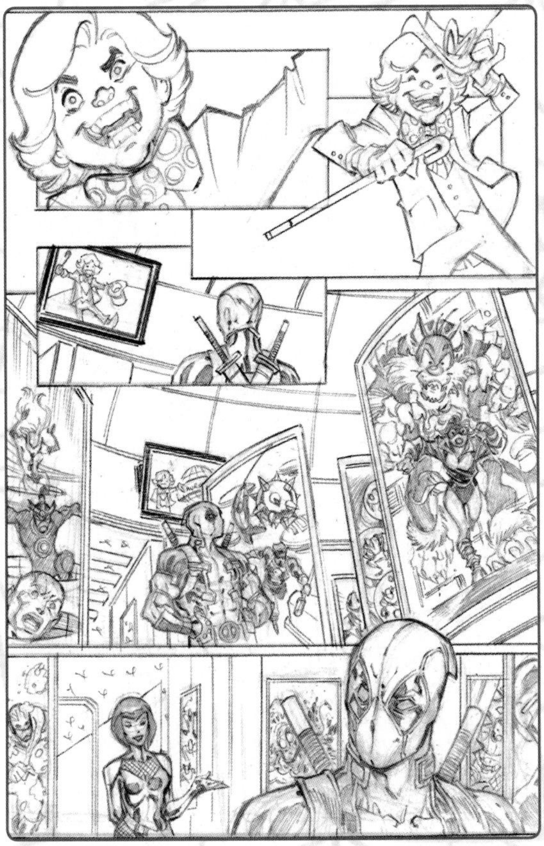

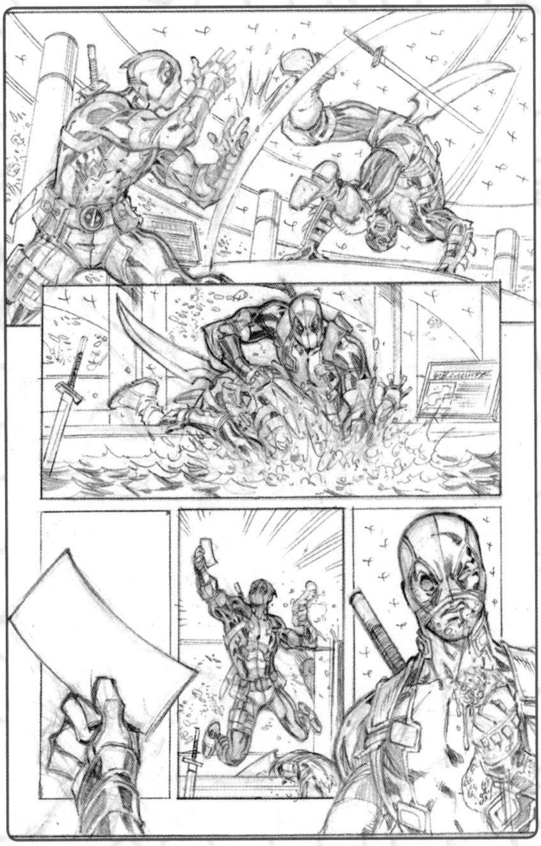

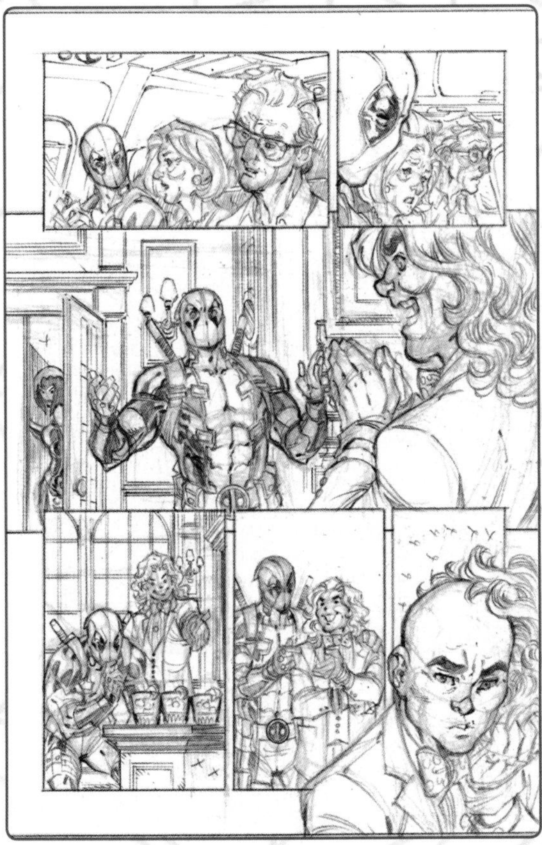

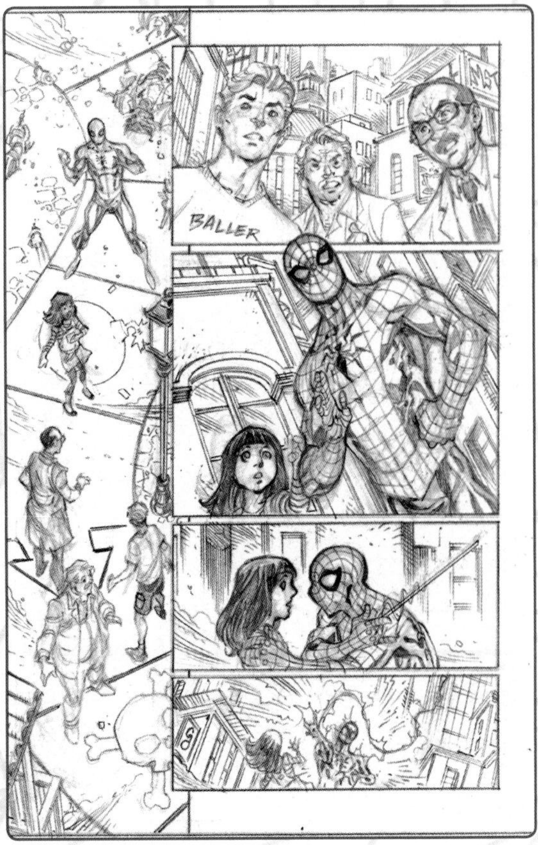
BALLER

21, PAGES 5-8 PENCILS BY
TODD NAUCK

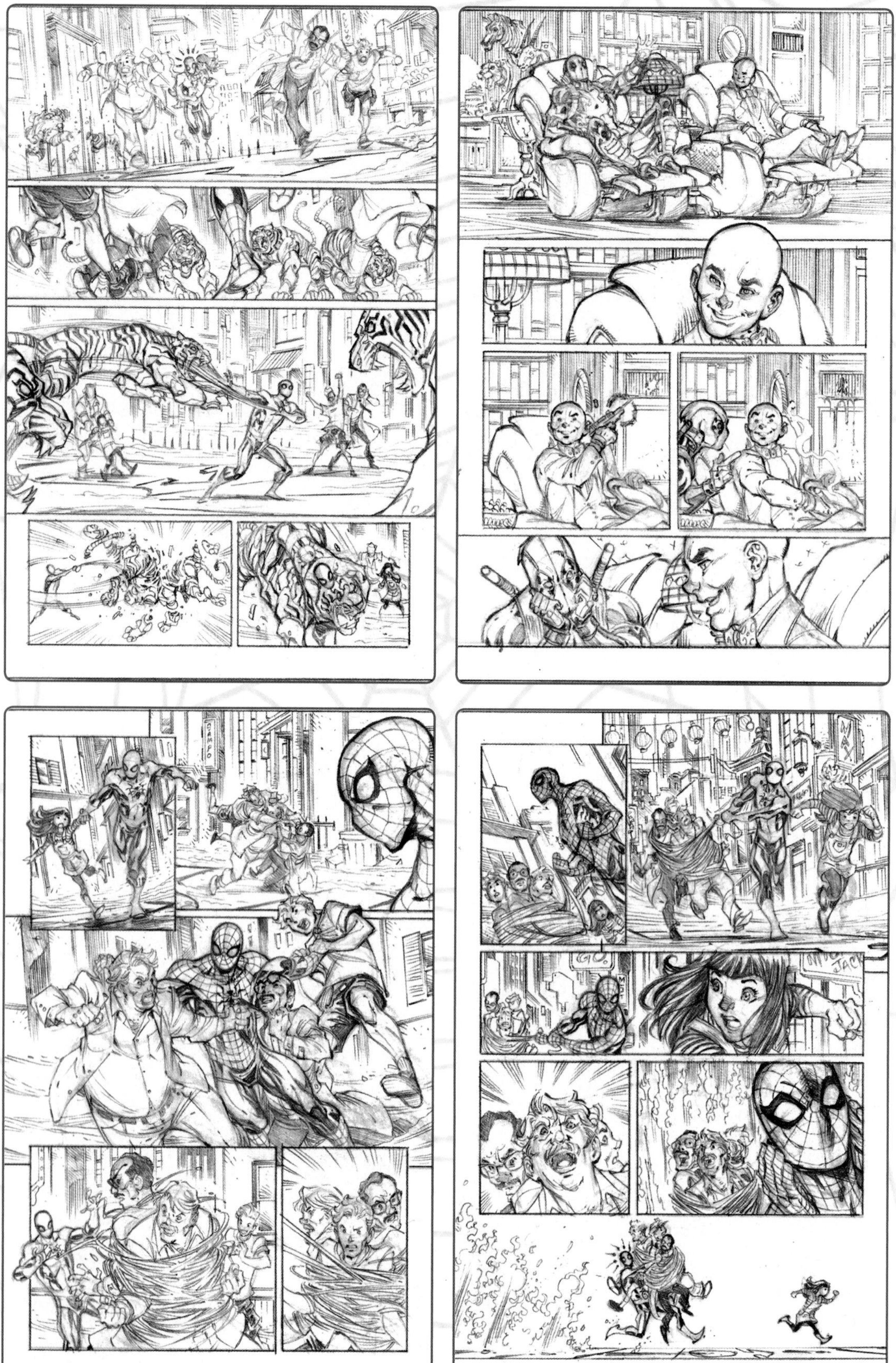

21, PAGES 9-12 PENCILS BY
TODD NAUCK

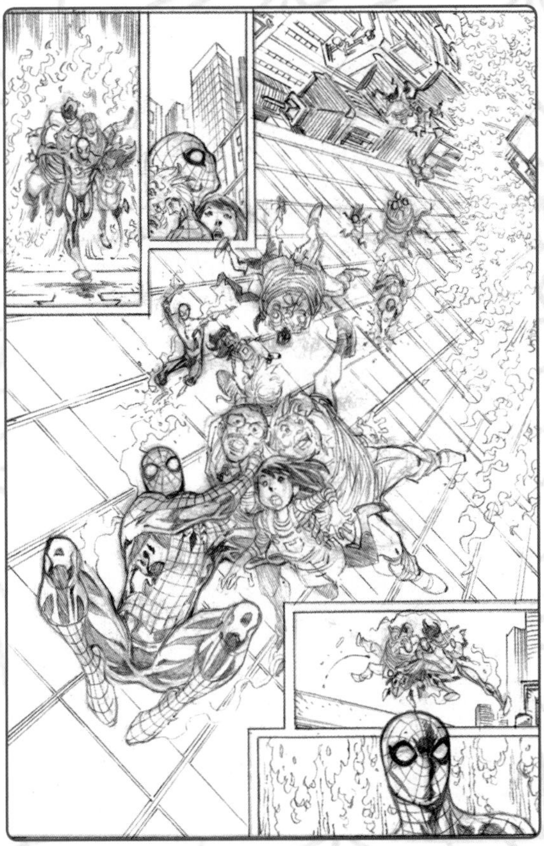
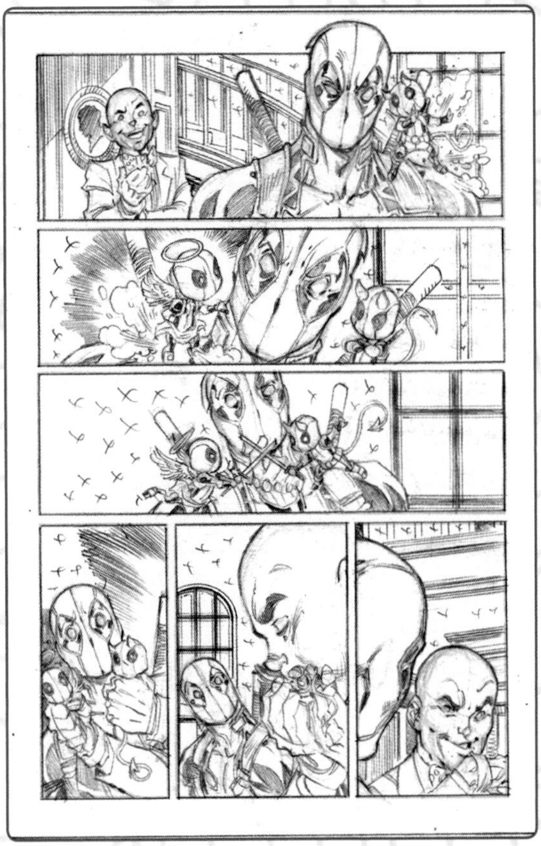
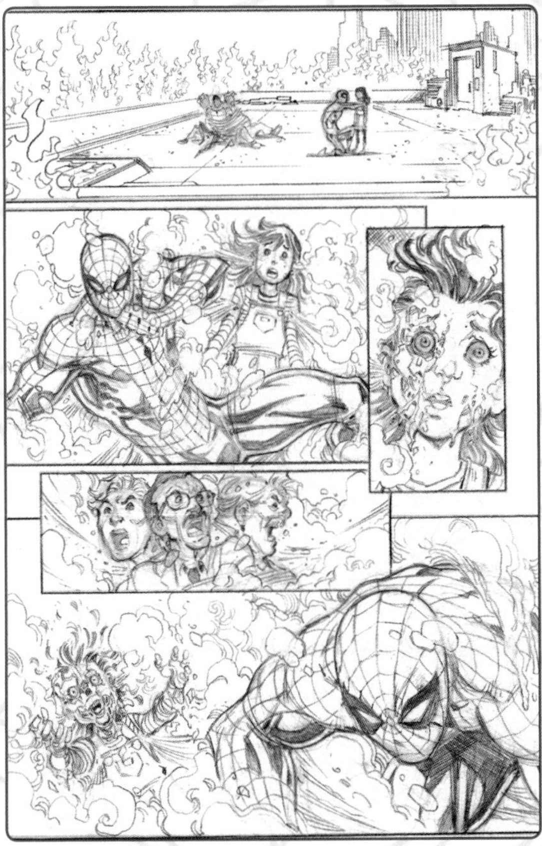
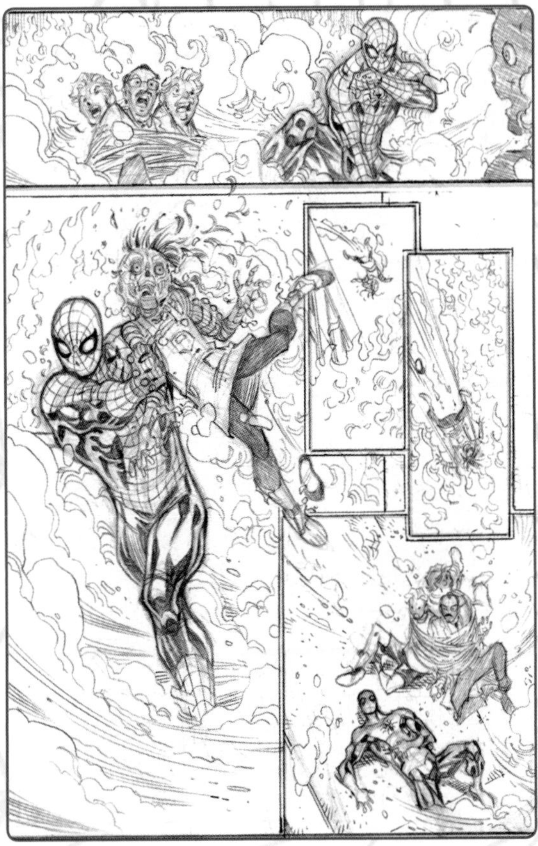

21, PAGES 13-16 PENCILS BY
TODD NAUCK

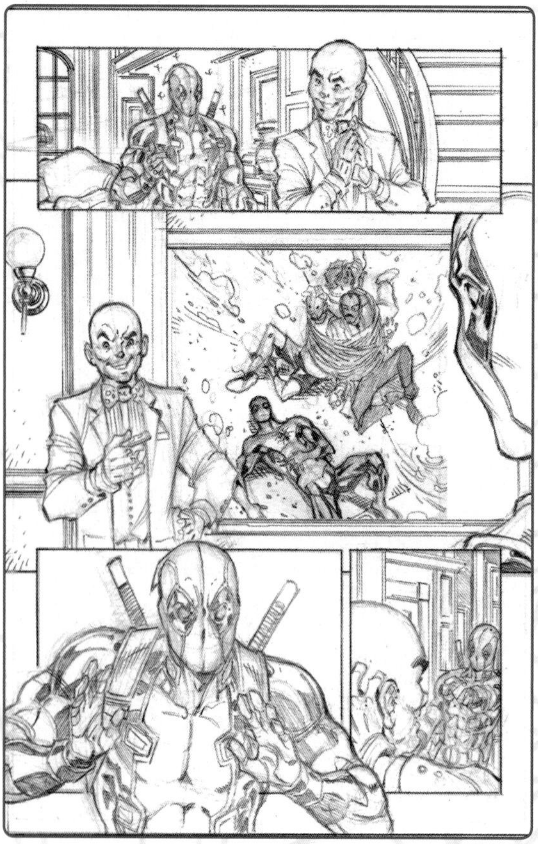
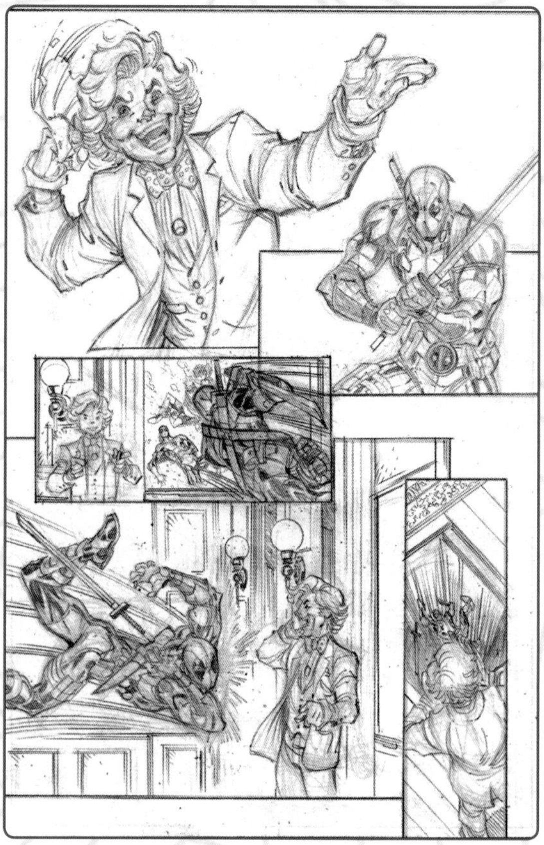
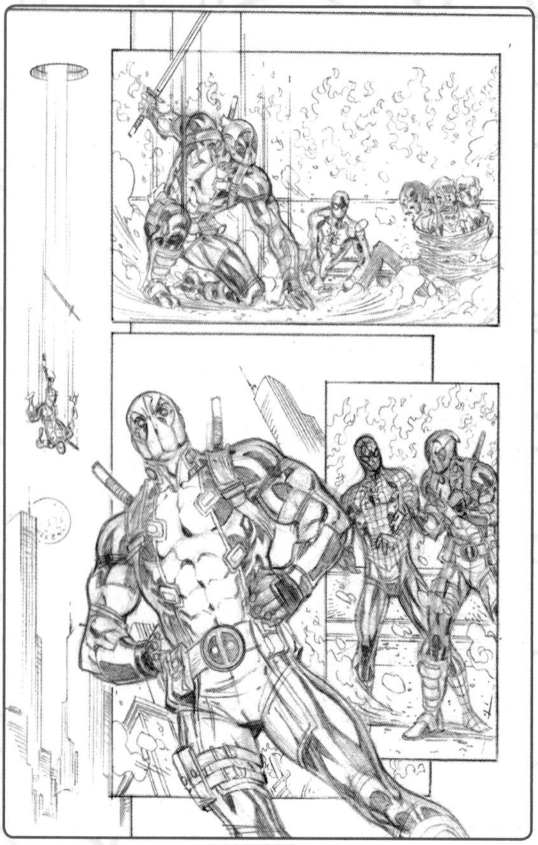
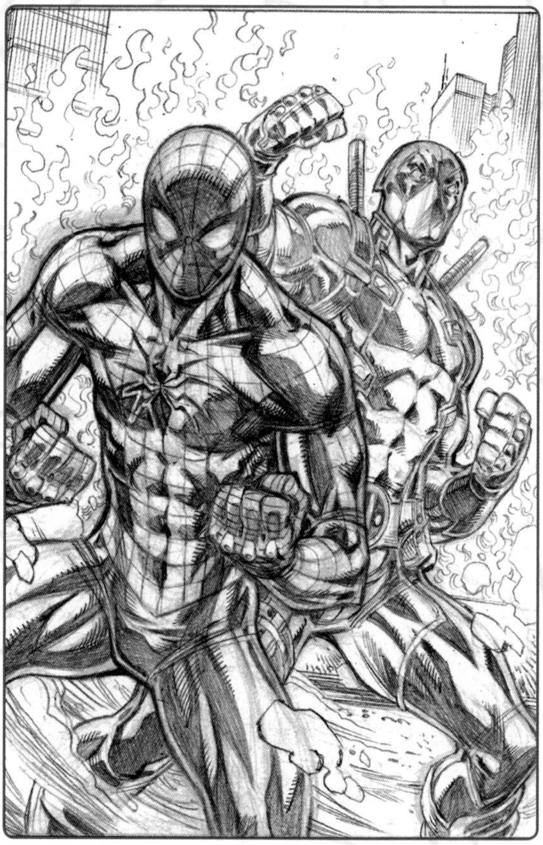

21, PAGES 17-20 PENCILS BY
TODD NAUCK

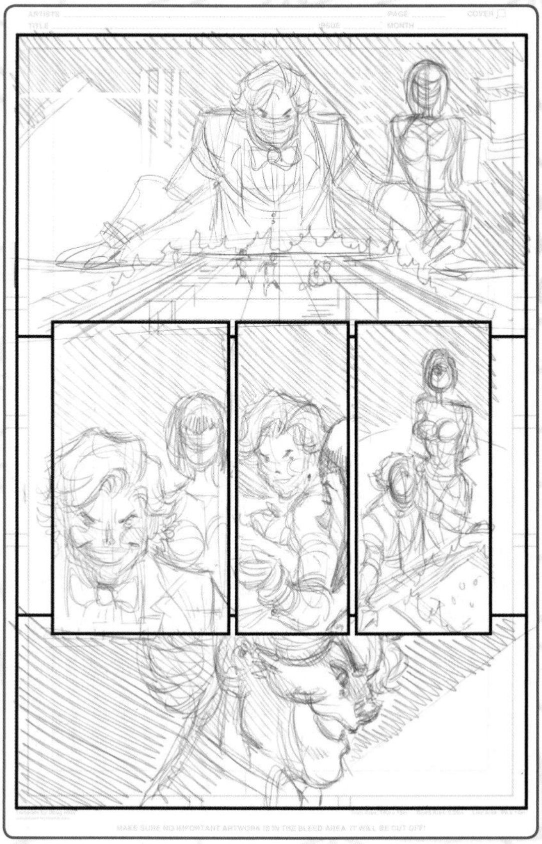

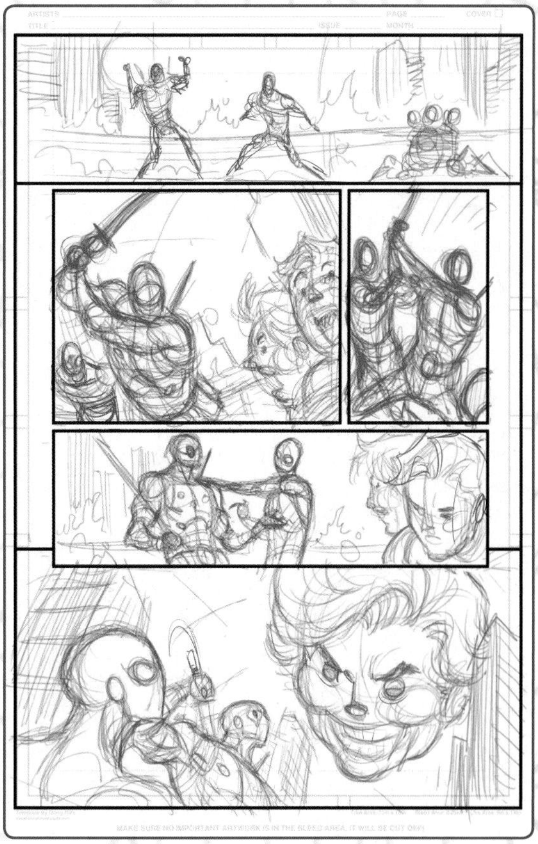

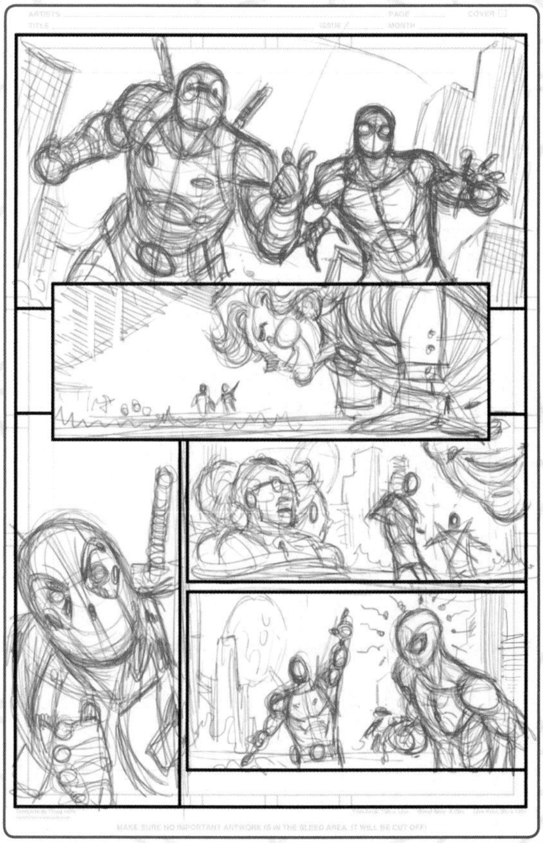

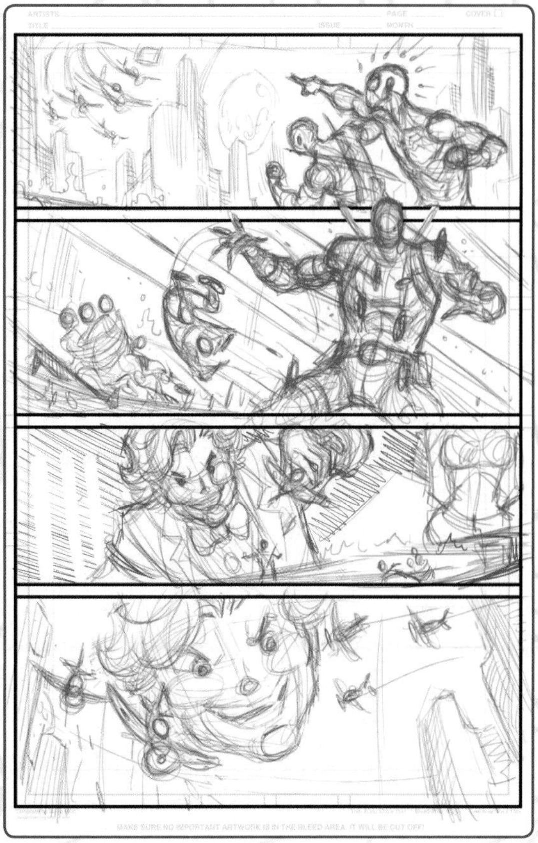

22, PAGES 1-4 LAYOUTS BY
TODD NAUCK

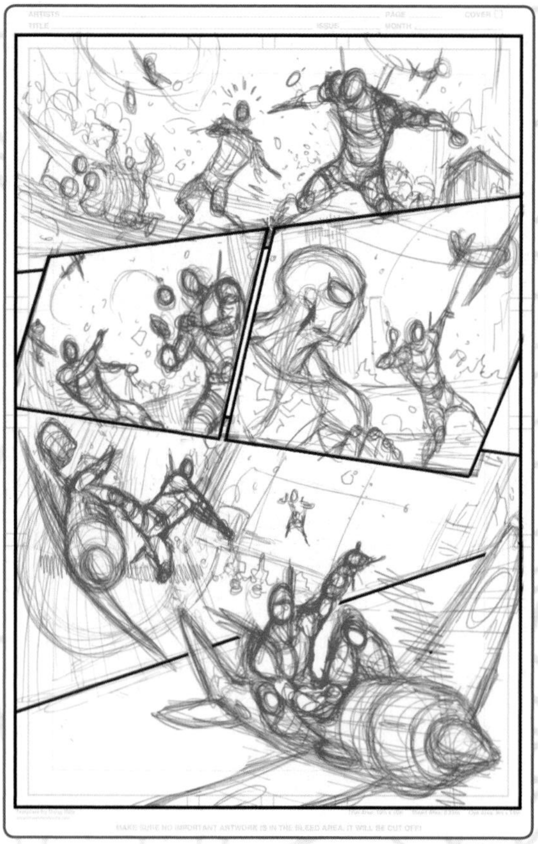

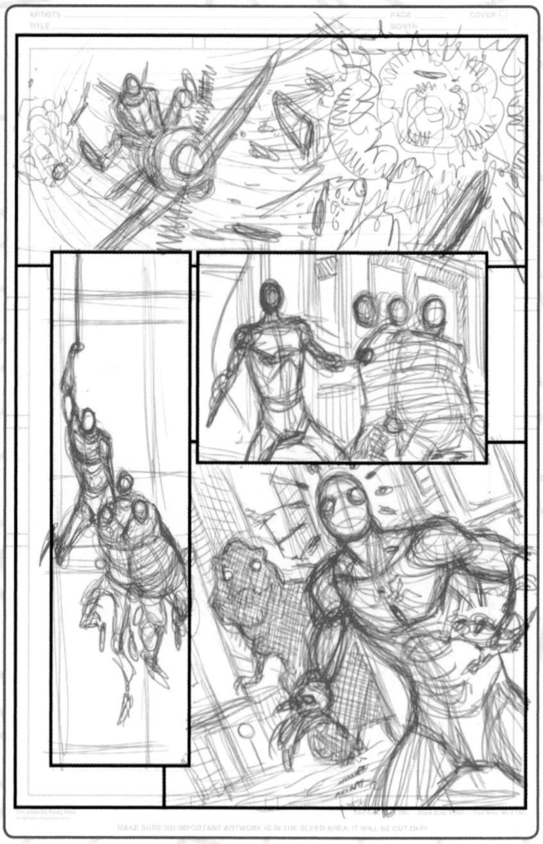

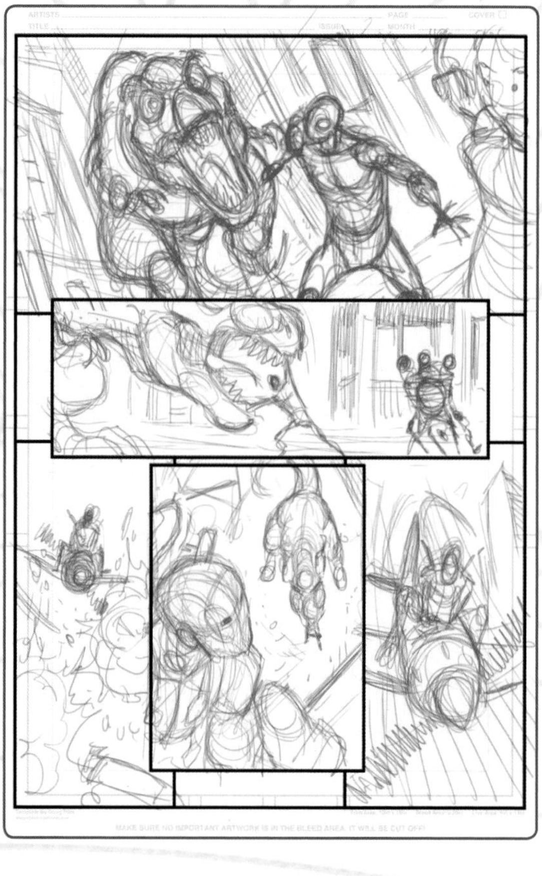

22, PAGES 5-7 PENCILS BY
TODD NAUCK

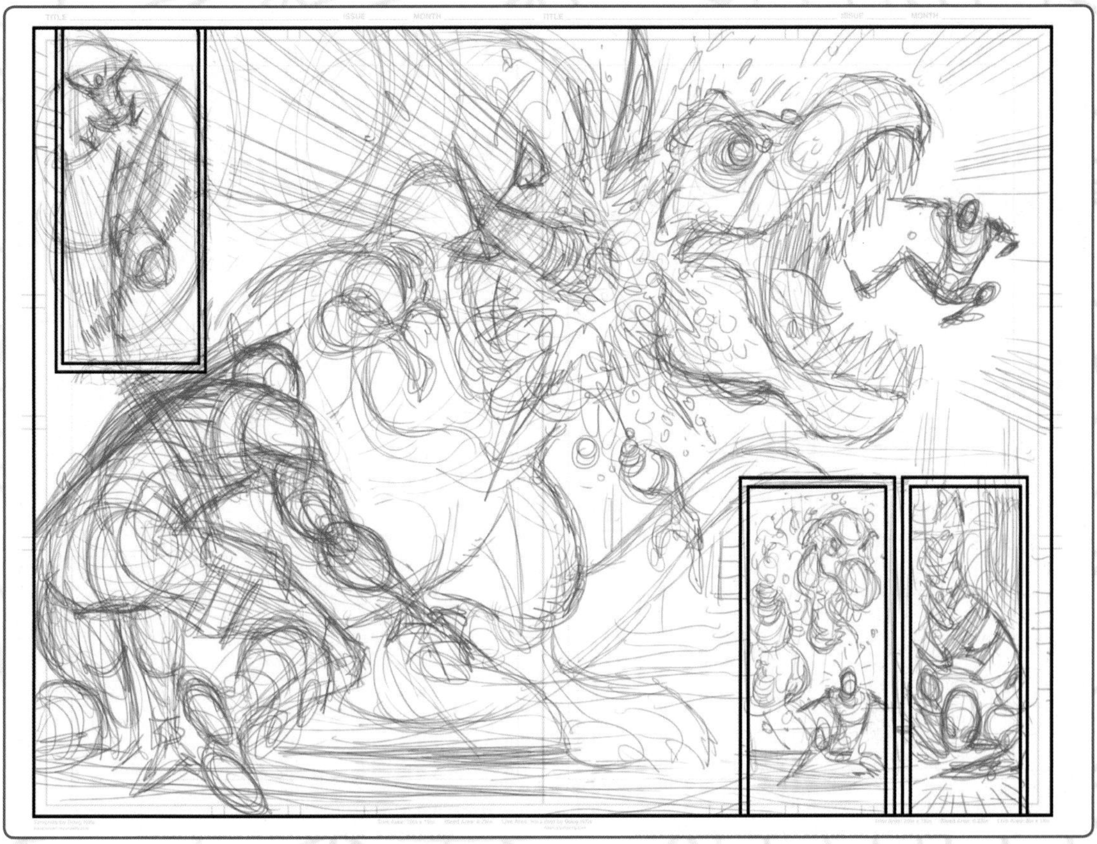

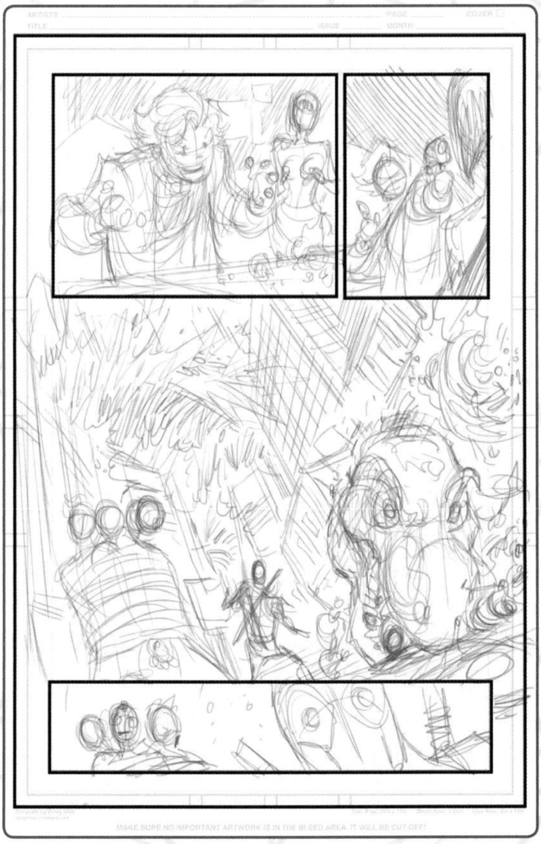

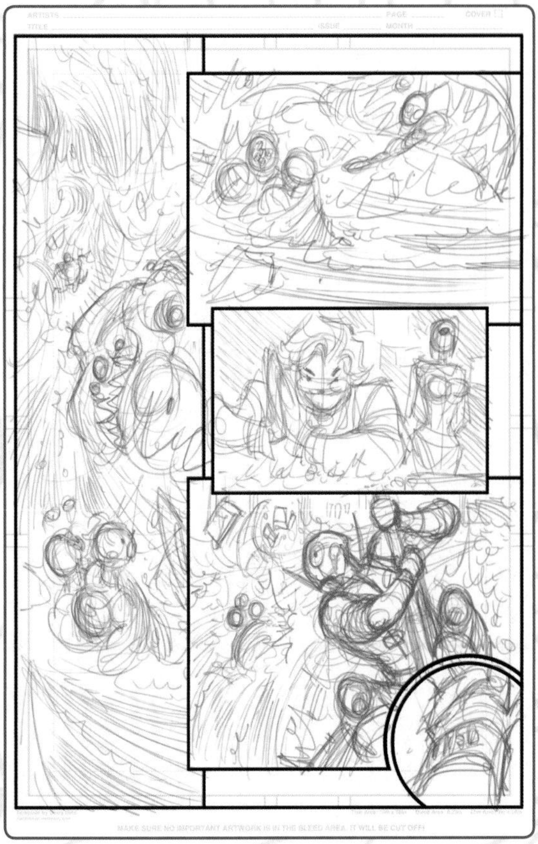

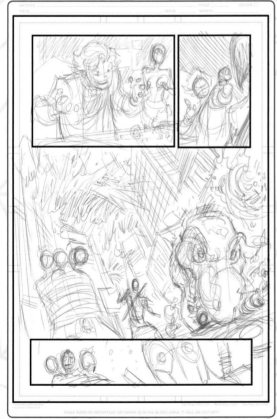

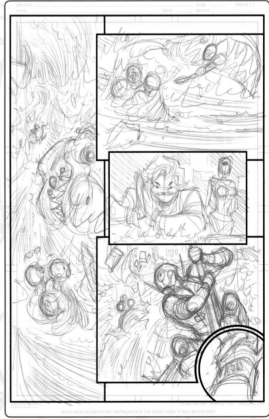

22, PAGES 8-11 LAYOUTS BY
TODD NAUCK

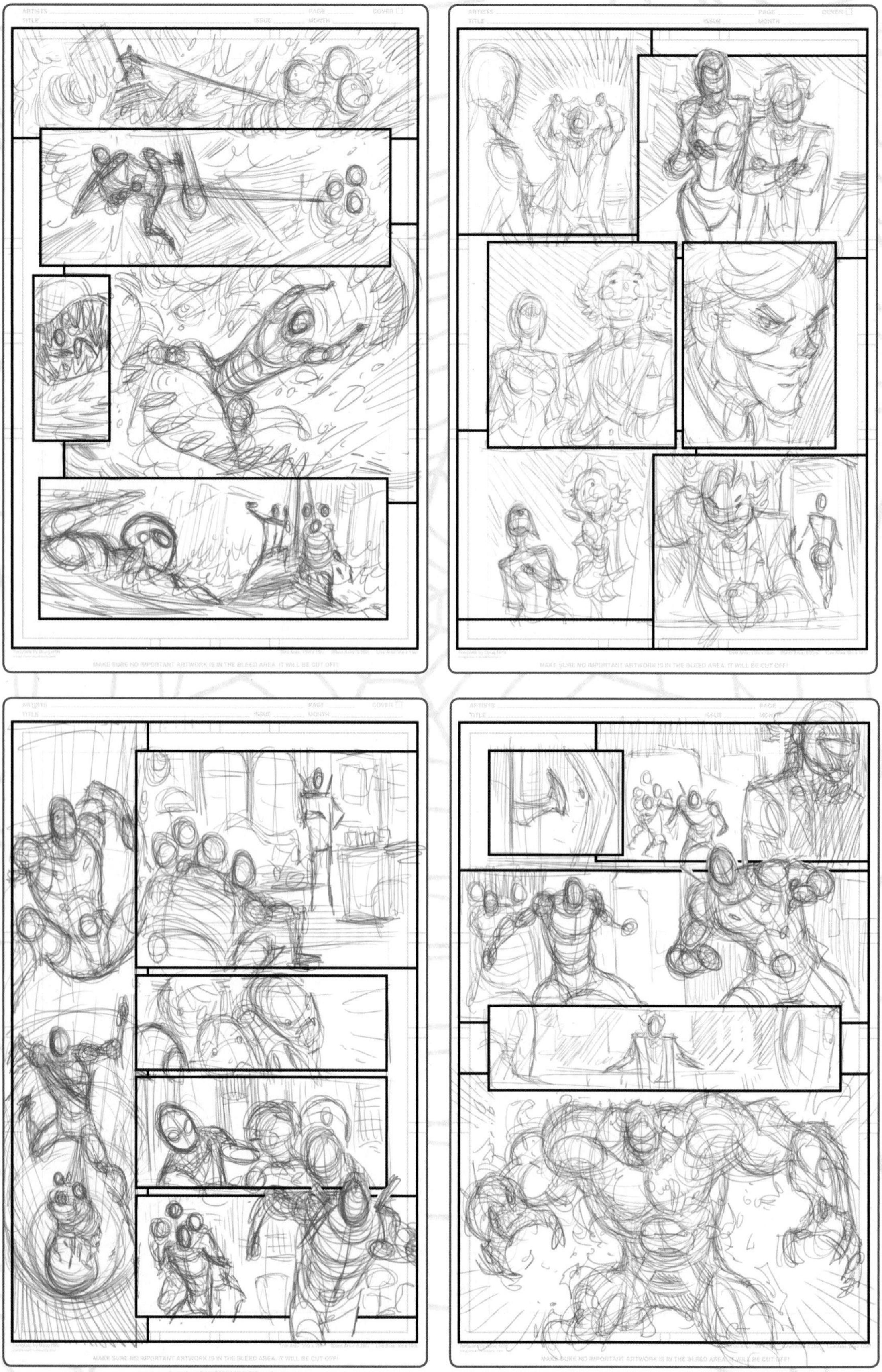

22, PAGES 12-15 PENCILS BY
TODD NAUCK

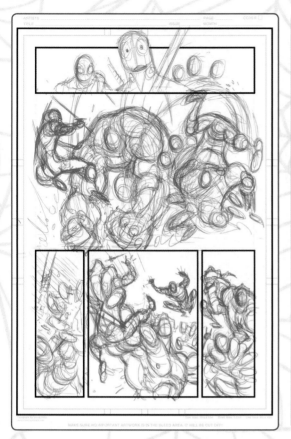

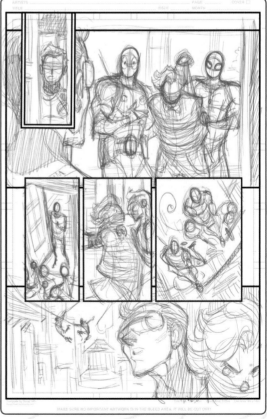

22, PAGES 16-19 LAYOUTS BY
TODD NAUCK

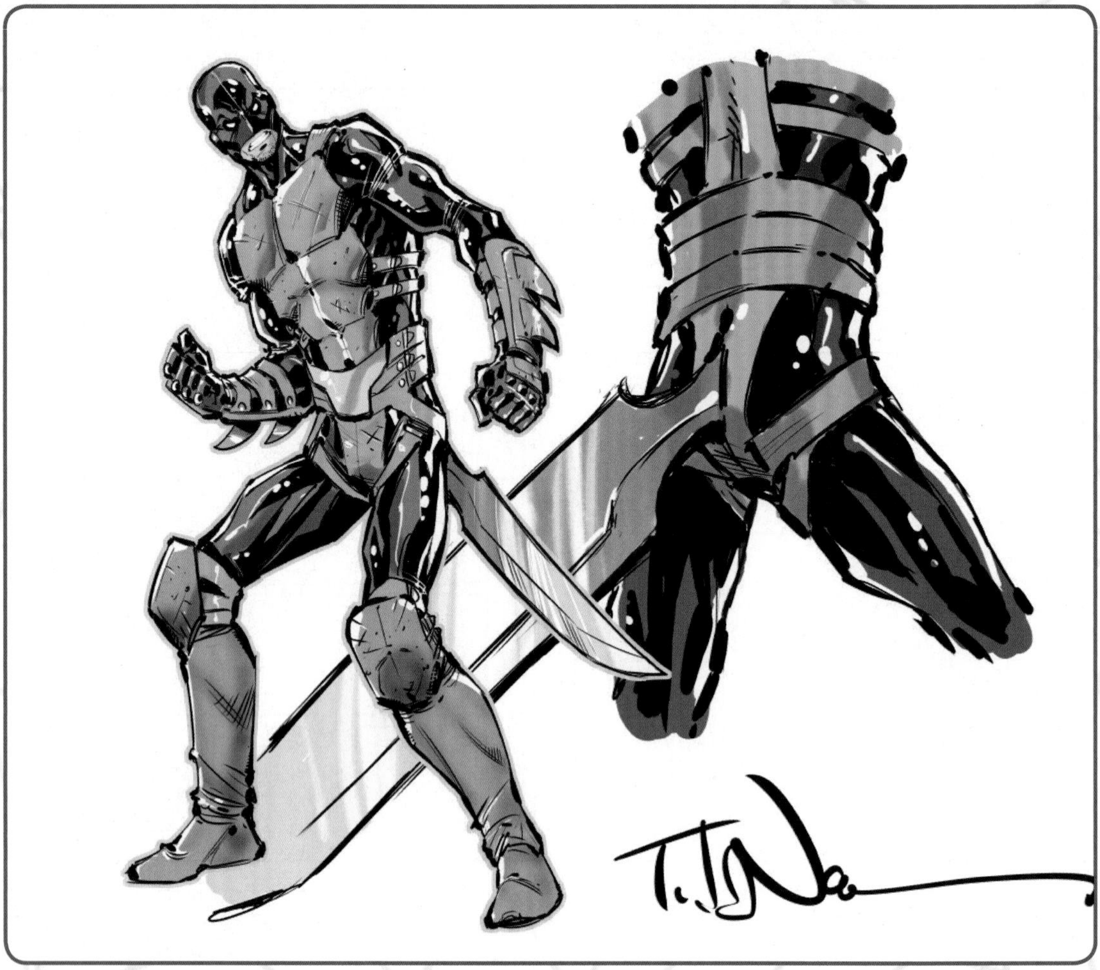

STINGER CHARACTER DESIGN BY
TODD NAUCK

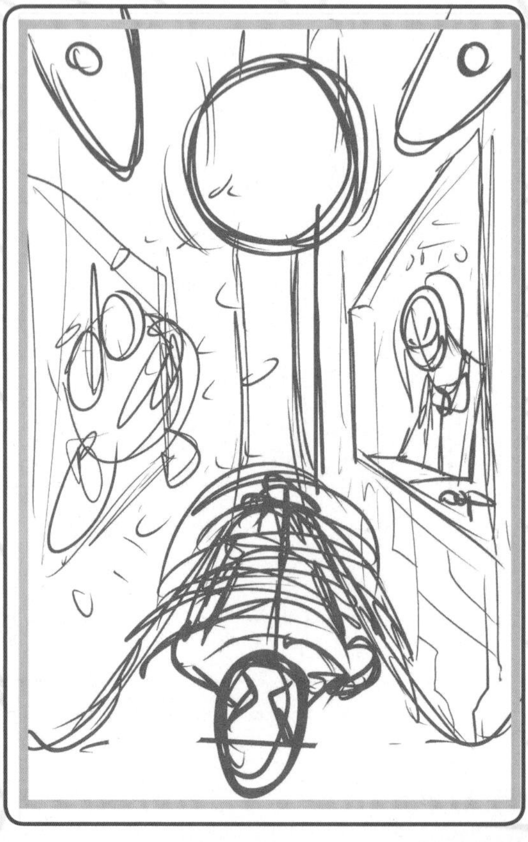

22 COVER SKETCH BY
WILL ROBSON

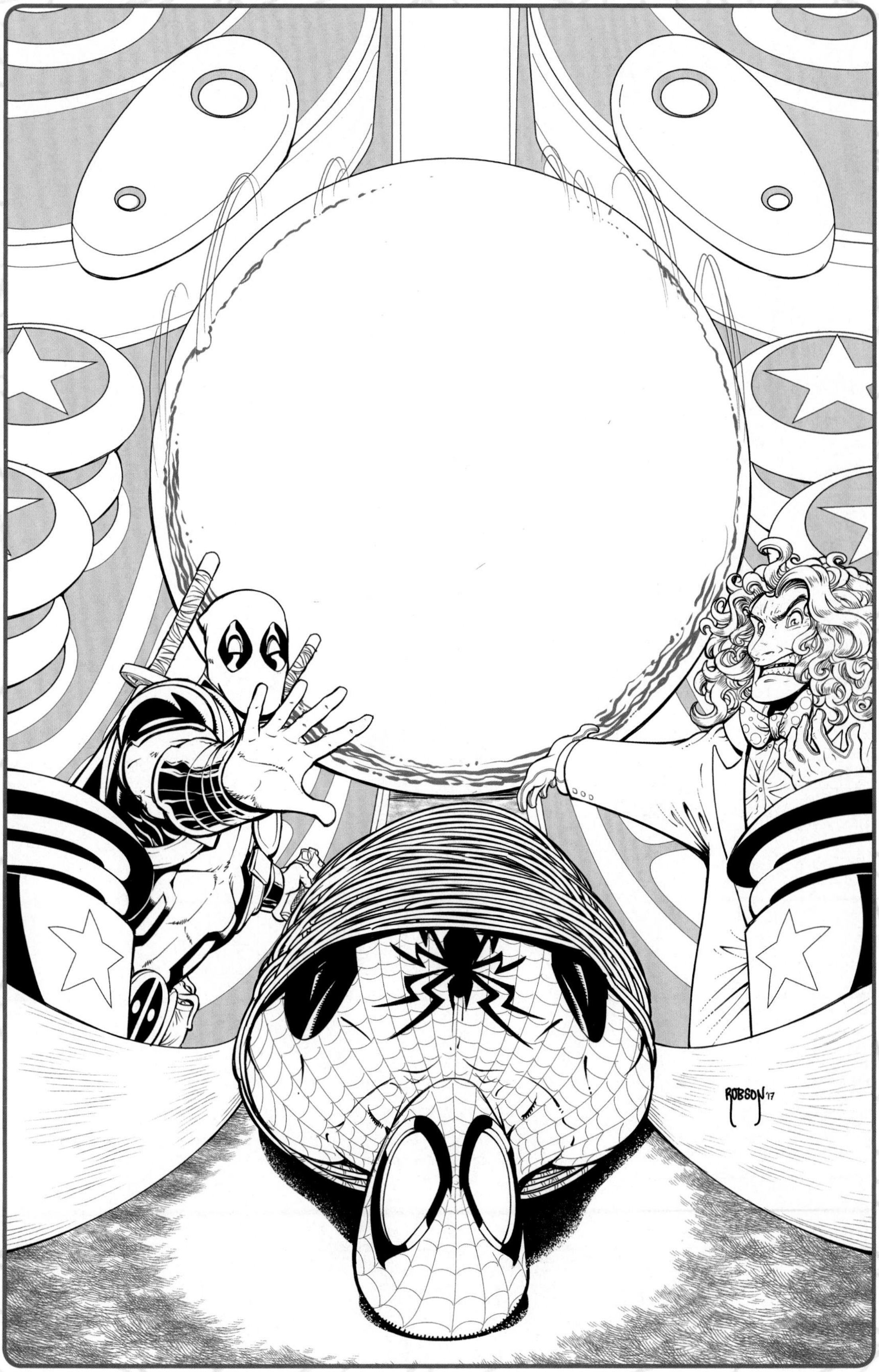
ROBSON '17

22 COVER ART BY
WILL ROBSON

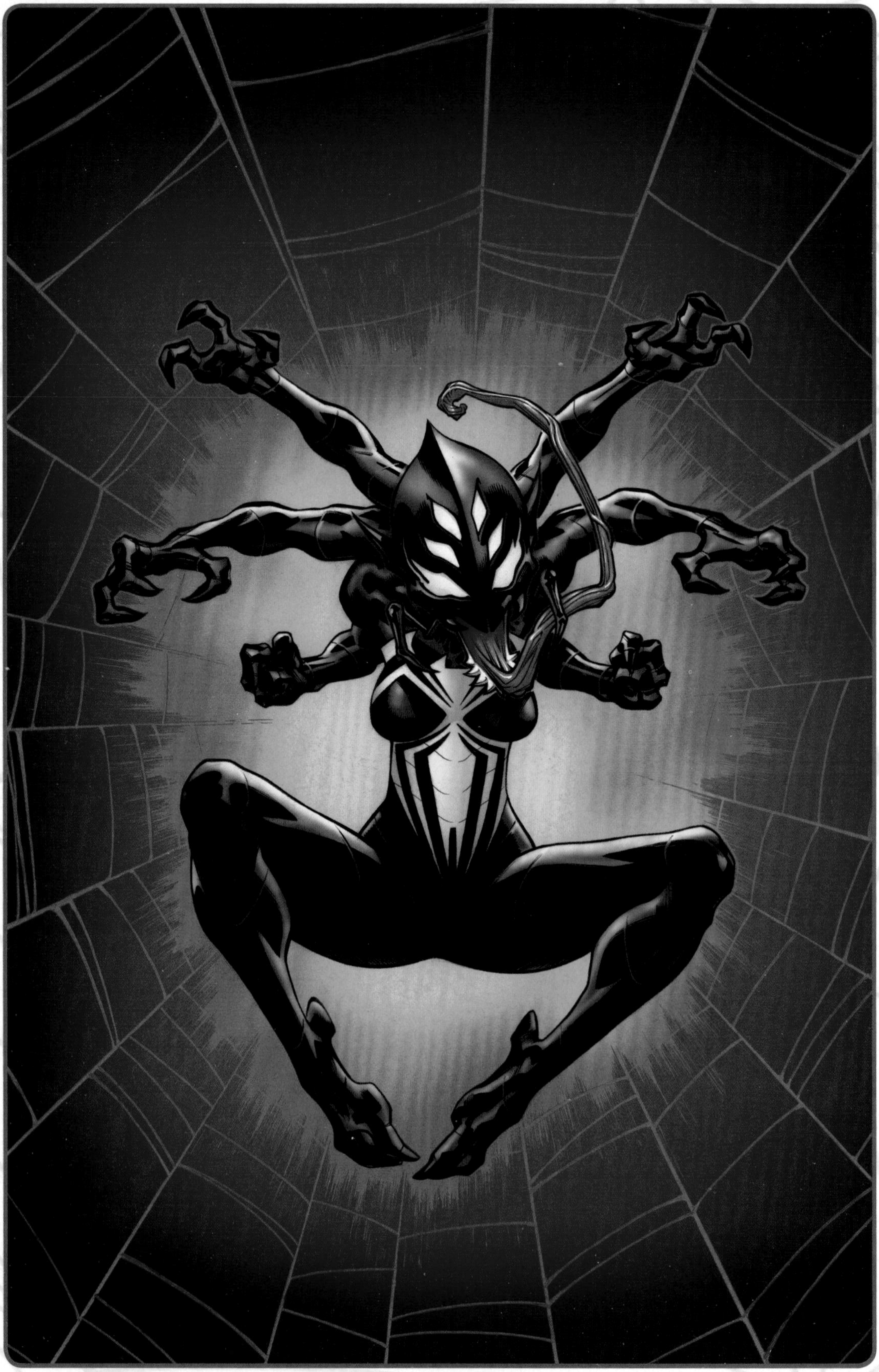

21 VENOMIZED VARIANT BY
ED McGUINNESS & EDGAR DELGADO